The European Challenge

THE
EUROPEAN
CHALLENGE

LOUIS ARMAND
AND
MICHEL DRANCOURT

*Translated from the French
by Patrick Evans*

NEW YORK   ATHENEUM   *1970*

CONTENTS

INTRODUCTION

Eight years ago Michel Drancourt suggested that I gather certain ideas together into a book; ideas which gravitated round the imperatives of the twentieth century like planets round the sun, and which had been reflected in some of my writings and lectures.

We decided to collaborate. The result was *Plaidoyer pour l'avenir* ('The Case for the Future'): a volume whose purpose was to exorcize the wariness felt by many Frenchmen towards the growth and implication of modern techniques and technologies, and to show how futile it was to oppose certain inevitable aspects of progress by fighting rearguard actions in defence of outdated forms of social organization. We said it was essential, in this period of *mouvance* or fluidity – 'the acceleration of history', as it has been called – to bring about a harmony between three things: the means and methods resulting from modern technical advance; the minds on which these new results directly or indirectly impinge, notably the minds of the young; and the structures of society, structures whose obsolete character, in the contemporary context of widespread mutation,[1]

---

[1] Mutation: a fundamental and decisive change. The term is borrowed from the language of genetics. It occurs frequently in the original text and, though less familiar as a handy metaphor in English than in French, has been retained here to avoid tiresome circumlocutions. (*Tr.*)

is the cause of most of the social disturbances of the present day.

We laid much stress on the need to remodel education, and various people have been kind enough to tell us in conversation or by letter, following the events of May 1968, that many of our thoughts had been abundantly prophetic. In fact the recent brutal reactions of the young have given unhappy confirmation to those thoughts, and have amply demonstrated that the university was quite as obstructive and out-of-date in both its teaching and its privileges as was the Church when it behaved similarly in the time of Galileo.

In 1967, when Jean-Jacques Servan-Schreiber decided to assemble certain home truths under the subsequently famous title of *Le Défi américain* ('The American Challenge'), he kindly invited me to express my views on the problems with which he was concerned, knowing how close my own ideas were to some of those destined for his book. I complied with pleasure.

A number of the readers of *Le Défi américain* considered that my own small share in it included a number of thoughts meriting development in greater detail. *Plaidoyer pour l'avenir* had proved itself to be, if I may say so, a valid approach to the position of the United States and Europe respectively in the present-day world. So it was natural that I should resume with Michel Drancourt a collaboration which had left me with pleasant memories.

This time there was no need to plead for the future. Mutations and the need for making-over social structures are in the air; everyone is talking about them, including those most reluctant to accept the findings in our first book. Everyone concedes that, in our century, education terminates only with life, that for-mation and information are a continuing process; no one doubts the harmful character of certain fixed attitudes, based on a superstitious love of the past.

So the present book is aimed at a different objective: the question of eliminating, in France and in Europe generally, the time-lag between ideas on European construction and the imperatives of our century. Those ideas have been hampered and retarded by a lack of understanding, a deficiency whose manifestations are many and various; consequently they have become out of date before they could be put into action and have fallen into premature old age; their impetus has dwindled, the faith they once commanded is fading. This decline is all the more serious in that the urgent grounds for action have been increasing meanwhile, in a context which has changed greatly since the early constructive creations of the Europe of the Six – those first embodiments of the conceptions of three great Europeans, de Gasperi, Robert Schuman and Adenauer, whose thinking had been catalysed by Jean Monnet. Technical advances – quicker transport and communications, in particular – have caused a change of scale: the plane of action is no longer continental but planetary.

Whether the subject be trade, or travel, or nuclear attack, the whole planet is now the frame of reference.

Starting from this addition to life's data, and striving to ignore the epiphenomenal and contingent and stick to the implications arising from the established applications of technical progress – implications whose origin makes them irreversible, part of the facts of life – we have made it our task to define the guide-lines which ought to shape the policies of Europeans. Our cogitations convinced us more than ever that an open, flexible association of the countries of which Europe is constituted is the next stage on the road for this 'semi-continent'.

If it rejects such an association, which would be in line with the closer connections arising between men through technology, a stagnant Europe will remain fixed within its own divisions and antagonisms and even slide down a one-way slope of regression; it will start to be eroded, like a peninsula under attack by the sea. Its energies, and the driving impulses which raise thought to a higher level and widen mental horizons, would then find no point of application and would decline into provincialism and the renewal of tribal rivalries, characterized by a built-in desire not to communicate.

Like ancient Greece, Europe would become an illustration of Paul Valéry's arresting dictum, 'Civilizations are mortal too.'

We are at a juncture when the intellectual disciplines are becoming more and more interdependent, and industry, commerce and administration more and more complicated; hence the need to relax tension by seeking wider dimensions of operation. To abandon Europe's efforts towards integration would produce the opposite effect, cramping those efforts inside a framework which has become too narrow: to put it another way, institutions would get overheated.

Changing the metaphor, a cluster of states which isolated themselves from one another instead of forming an association while retaining their individual independence, would not thereby become so many Gardens of Eden or happy little principalities of Monaco. On the contrary, their insistence on thinking small would land them in far greater difficulties than would the adventure of accommodating themselves to new structures.

The extension of collectivities, in the sense we have in mind, is a modern form of the spirit of conquest, and would enlarge frontiers by very different means from those of the past.

A Frenchman, Dutchman or German can feel at home in Florence today without having to cross the Alps with an army before finding lodgings; he can arrive in a perfectly peaceful manner as a student, a tourist or an insurance agent. But merely doing without weapons is not enough. Europe must not content itself with being a customs union and possessing a few joint organizations for administrative and economic purposes.

What this amounts to is that the political aspect is the one to which the architects of Europe's future must now give priority – 'political' in the sense which commands respect because it implies big responsibilities. Among the considerations which dictated our subject-matter, we felt it necessary to give high priority to a certain essential task: that of initiating on the political plane the processes of development for which every alert European is waiting. In addition, we felt it possible to point out that these processes have everything to gain, and nothing to lose, from a study of the experience of certain very large firms, particularly in the United States, Scandinavia and Holland.

Goals of the kind we are indicating here are what every dynamic political movement ought to pursue. This has been well understood by MM. Robert Lattès and G. Mathé, the proponents of 'society orientated towards development' (*la Société pour le Développement*), the movement they founded as a result of the French crisis of May 1968, which they say will eventually prove to have had a salutary side to it:

... This crisis will have served a purpose if it makes all serious-minded, responsible people aware of the necessity for advancing from the idea of a consumer society to that of a society for development.

Producing goods in increasing quantity and rising quality is an aim which can be fundamentally opposed only by romantics, and romantics have always been reactionaries. And 'Revolution or a car for everyone' is an antithesis which simply will not do, because the true revolution consists of building a society in which having a car really does make people happier.

The duty of the men of our time – men with a scientific background which includes the science of management, men who have mastered the techniques necessary for the material progress which is an essential condition for Man's happiness – is to be generous and imaginative enough to create, publicize and implement the measures required to place those material benefits at the service of human beings, and in the first place of those who produce them.

The development society we wish to see is a society which implies economic development, but also the free development of the individual. The individual's dignity must be respected, and his participation, initiative and imagination must be sought, so that he may lose his fear of technological progress and regard it as a friendly force.

We have included this quotation in our Introduction because what the authors say about their movement's motives and aims is completely in tune with the contents of our book; but we might equally well have quoted from many other works which an increasing awareness of the loftiest problems of our time has brought forth. Their very number might have made us hesitate to add our own contribution, did we not know that the truth cannot be told too often if it is heard as a result. Men of good will must be allowed to replace the famous *Delenda est Karthago*, 'Carthage must be destroyed', with a more pacific motto: 'Europe must be built'.

On the other hand, we are not altogether happy that certain words borrowed from the sciences, notably 'mutation' and 'structures', should have caught public attention so successfully (and rapidly exhausted it). But it would have been presumptuous of us to coin new ones just for this book. Besides, we hope the public we are writing for will make contact with the thought itself, behind the words which are its vehicle.

While the book, which appears under our joint names, is the

outcome of teamwork guided by the very spirit of association for which we have long been pleading, it is also the result of dialogue (another word we apologize for borrowing from an overworked vocabulary) between Michel Drancourt and myself; a dialogue which both of us nowadays doubtless take for granted, without having to express it aloud. Perhaps the reader will discover traces of it, however, in the reiteration of certain key ideas whose various aspects he and I have developed alternately in the ensuing chapters.

Our collaboration, our sharing of ideas and work, is an old one; which means that we are getting old too. And the ageing process is a spectacle to which the young today are allergic. One of us is a grandfather, the other a father; we must leave the reader to judge whether we have stayed young in the way we think and express ourselves, in our respective departments.

What we want is to see our ideas taken up by those who will have to build the world of tomorrow, the team of fathers and sons; and our sense of the book's deficiencies enables us to present it to them modestly, with our sincere wishes that they will labour to better effect, and that their efforts will be crowned by success.

Louis Armand

We wish to thank those who contributed their help to the making of this book; notably:

M. Jean-Paul Pigasse, for his very active share in its documentation; and M. Darnis-Gravelle, who kindly went through the whole manuscript.

CHAPTER ONE

EUROPE
AND PLANETARY¹ REALITY

Europe is no longer Europe but just a piece of the world; not a special place any more. It can no longer do what it did in the past: define itself in its own eyes, in its own way, and then impose itself on others. To retain a personality of its own it is obliged to take stock of world reality and deduce the place it is capable of occupying within it. It is closely dependent on planetary trends but, in compensation, has the chance of influencing the development of world civilization.

This is obvious now but was by no means so clear twenty years ago. At that time some people aspired to see Europe built up into a third continent, holding the balance between the United States and the Soviet Union; they visualized it as a kind of structured super-nation, a top and crown to the existing nations. The venture was bold and the impulse behind it generous.

This draft of the future at once wrote itself into history by producing an irreversible effect on people's thinking. It was a decisive achievement, but one which is no longer adequate

¹ 'Planetary', meaning 'world-wide' or 'the world as an entity' in as much as many things, thoughts, techniques are shared in common. 'Planetary' and 'planetization' have been used as translations of the original French *planétaire* and *planétisation*; any use of substitute-words for these neologisms in English would have blunted the edge of the authors' message by blurring its main emphasis. (*Tr.*)

today. The fundamental data of Europe's problems are no longer what they were in the years just after the Second World War; they therefore require an approach on different lines.

They cannot be solved without taking into account the great laws of the technological age, the law of dimension and that of fluidity, which were formulated in the present writers *Plaidoyer pour l'avenir*.

In the older countries, organization is lagging behind equipment. Technique is evolving faster than structures and we are in danger of being carried away by it. Countries younger than those of Europe are better at adjusting themselves to new technique, and get more out of it.

The use of modern production methods presupposes the possession of means (men, capital, research and commercial strength) on a scale which no one European country can hope to command. The dimensions governing our century are, in most instances, planetary. It is in terms of facts like these that the new Europe must be built.

But when we talk of 'building' we certainly do not mean something as it were in reinforced concrete, to stand for centuries. From this time forward, one of the directives inescapably governing any attempt at political organization consists of combining great firmness in pursuit of the ultimate goal – the goal which Europeans have always had in view, a certain conception of man – with complete adaptability on the plane of action. Europe is capable of rendering cardinal services to mankind, but only on condition that it succeeds in inventing types of social relationship which take the fluidity of techniques and the demands of organization simultaneously into account.

PLANETIZATION IS INEVITABLY ACCELERATING

One of the points we emphasized in *Plaidoyer pour l'avenir* was that mankind was confronted by a ramifying, fast-moving evolution; a throng of transformations similar to those made familiar by biology. In pretty well every field of human activity the development-curve is exponential; hence the profound difficulty now being experienced by humanity in adapting itself to the flood of its own discoveries. In the years since we wrote the book, our picture of this evolution has been abundantly confirmed.

The three fields most characteristic of the planetary age are space travel, communication satellites and information techniques, which will be mentioned again and again in these pages; and in these three the acceleration has been particularly spectacular.

The first transatlantic cable came into service a century ago. Now we have started using communication satellites; those first little sputnik-bleeps in 1957 heralded more than could have been foreseen. Comsat has predicted that from 1970 there will be a system of four satellites in orbit, serving thirty television channels and offering 10,000 lines for transmission by telephone and telex.[1] By 1974 the figures will have risen to fifty-four TV channels and 60,000 lines; by 1980, to eighty channels and 180,000 lines.

Everyone's life and actions depend as much on what is going on in New York as in London, Paris, or Frankfurt. The micro-module produced in Tokyo is revolutionizing world electronics. Worldwide excitement is becoming a common phenomenon. Students everywhere revolt under the same slogans. In this context, the Russians and Chinese are seen to have been fighting out part of their quarrel in the streets of the Latin Quarter in Paris.

Shared experience, life in common, is what man is made for. Since the day when men gathered together to found the first city, the part played, the influence exerted, by society in every individual's life has been continually increasing. The progressive specialization of tasks multiplies the exchange between individuals and between enterprises, both on the national and, increasingly, the international scale. The development of collective organization, whether in transport, health or education, makes the day-to-day life of individuals depend continuously on services and institutions which are independent of frontiers. To draw up its weather forecasts, the Meteorological Centre in Paris makes daily use of information provided by seven foreign stations and some thirty French regional stations.

The reciprocal dependence engendered by planetization is very real, but its manifestations are insufficiently recognized.

[1] *Information et Documents*, no. 225, pp. 18–19.

It is not surprising therefore to observe that most endeavours both in social organization and in the political sphere still occur on the national plane despite the fact that an increasing ratio of political problems, particularly those of peace and development, belongs to the international one. Nor is it surprising to observe a shock-reaction away from planetary realities, in the form of a temptation to play the ostrich by retreating inside a system which seems authentic and original, but which in the long run is bound to cave in under the pressure of facts. This is a predicament with which scientists and technologists are familiar.

MANKIND, HAVING ENTERED THE PLANETARY AGE, MUST MOVE TOWARDS PLANETARY GOVERNMENT

Provided it does not commit suicide, mankind still has a certain amount of time left to live with its own problems alone. We now know, of course, that our solar system is uninhabited. There is no question of men finding in space, within any reasonable distance, similar beings whose existence would modify typical human relations (like the Martians in science fiction helping mankind to unite). The planetary age will be with us for a long time, and it is essential that we take the trouble to think over its consequences.

If Europe remains disunited, it will continue to go along passively with world trends but will no longer be among the creators of structures, and of civilization.

A world government would render it possible to institute a type of relationship more in conformity with the interests of all. We are still far from this goal; we must nevertheless tend towards it, even if its attainment seems so distant as to appear utopian at present.

Europe can play a decisive role in the coming history of mankind. By setting up a new type of active relationships between states and enterprises and societies it can both solve its own problem (that of adapting itself to the demands of size and of rapid evolution), and suggest, by force of example, an orientation susceptible of being adopted by all peoples seeking to combine more closely with one another.

If Europe were to produce a new system of political relationship between human groups and, in a kind of creative optimism, to achieve an authentic mutation, it would have a real chance of exerting an influence on major trends at the outset of the planetary age. Europe ought to support any project, even limited in scope, even perhaps mediocre, which is conceived on a world scale. It is better to try to sketch the outlines of possible future organizational forms than to throw one's imagination and strength into the service of forms already out of date.

Oppenheim's well-known remark that 'of all the scientists who ever lived 90 per cent are alive now' can be applied to most other fields. 90 per cent of all tourists who have visited a foreign country are alive now; the same is true of those who have received higher education, and, obviously, of people who have handled a camera. Realism is not on the side of those desirous of maintaining the structures and divisions of the past. The time is ripe to organize political society on a more than national scale.

THE NEW TECHNIQUES – A FACTOR MAKING FOR CLOSER RELATIONS

THE AIRCRAFT – A BASIC ELEMENT OF THE PLANETARY SITUATION

The aircraft is typical of the planetary age. It transforms geography. The speedy communications which it now offers enabled an American airline company, TWA, to base its advertising in 1968 on the theme, 'TWA presents a new river; the Atlantic.'

Because the aircraft homogenizes travel, flying indifferently over mountain, marsh, salt water or the Poles, we can regard our world as 'isotropic'. Land transport, on the other hand, is subject to the nature of the ground, which broadly determines the route and sometimes absolutely dictates it. The world in which land transport functions is 'anisotropic'. This is less true of sea transport, though ports impose a much greater limitation than airports.

Every year the number of air travellers increases. In passenger miles, the figure rose from eight thousand million in 1945 to 130 in 1962, from 172 in 1964 to 275 in 1967.[1]

These figures reflect one of the significant features of the planetary age, namely how much and how often people travel about the world. This has come to seem natural but is in fact recent. Not until 21 May 1946 did a European company (the Dutch KLM) start a regular service to New York; and the first regular round-the-world flights were begun in 1947 (by Pan American World Airways). Since then contact has been growing fast between the peoples of all countries, travelling either on business or as tourists.

TOURISM LEVELS DIFFERENCES OF OUTLOOK

Too little thought has been given to the implications arising from the tourist migrations of the present day. The situation offers Europe a chance – one of many chances – to make a bigger contribution to people's awareness of the realities of today and tomorrow. Mutations often crop up when several transformations are completed simultaneously; thus the transport revolution on one hand, and the shortening of working hours and the widespread introduction of paid holidays on the other, have engendered the terrific growth of tourism illustrated by the figures; both the French and the Germans, for example, have increased their expenditure on tourism outside their own frontiers by 300 per cent in ten years, though their gross national product during the same period only rose by approximately 40 per cent.

Evidently the chromosomes of the hunters of the reindeer and the mammoth are still exerting an influence! Palaeolithic man was always a nomad. Technical development produced the sedentary culture of the villages in neolithic times, but did not thereby erase the powerful ancestral urge for movement. This same urge, which has been responsible for the vocation of many professional soldiers, and which sent crusaders crusading and colonists colonizing, now provides the motive power of tourism.

All international aircraft and trains conform to identical standards. Chains of hotels cover the whole world. Often ac-

[1] The USSR and China not included.

cused of being alien objects imposed on the local culture, they can equally well be commended for helping to reduce differences in dietary habits and everyday behaviour. In any case the tourist is no longer someone to stare at; no one now says 'Are Persians real?'

This is merely one of the minor manifestations of the diffusion of a universal way of life. Progress of this kind alarms some people, particularly when it manifests itself in such matters as food and drink and town-planning. These fears are unnecessary. The world's former compartmentation into provinces, and later into nations whose intercourse was sparse and infrequent, gave rise to great diversity in artistic expression, techniques of production and ways of life. But development was slow. Folklore, incidentally, is almost always the result of arrested development. Today the creations of the human mind, while no longer rooted and confined in a given territory and seeming therefore to lack originality and flavour, are compelled to vary rapidly as the impetus of progress keeps sweeping along, so that variety is manifested in time instead of in space. Dress is the same from one part of the world to another, but evolves faster than before in its design, colours and textures. It would be easy to multiply examples of this sort.

The call of the outside world resounds in every country, including those which – notably under Soviet rule – have always sought to prevent contact between the society they are trying to build (or maintain) and external influences.

The more a country is shut in on itself, the greater the importance assumed by such contacts in its people's eyes. Hence those who fear the planetary stage in man's development are under a powerful temptation to imitate the tortoise and protect themselves with a scaly shell. Man, however, is not descended from the tortoise or from some species of armoured fish! Approached in this way, evolution is bound to become regressive. Anyone who rejects what is outside is led to barricade himself in more and more, though in some instances this defensive huddling is disguised by assuming a personal form and inspired by an apparently innovating philosophy. On the other hand, when in such a situation you start pushing down one of the barriers the danger is that outside influences will rush in like an overwhelming tidal wave. Given that contemporary transport and communications make light of frontiers, it may be foreseen that, in the long run, only police states will be able to minimize contact between man and man.

SOCIAL 'CAVITATIONS'

A continually growing number of men and women having visited the same countries, various of the world's crossroads have acquired similar associations for the visitors in question. The latter may not all react in the same way but at least their reflections are based on much the same data.

On the other hand, a deepening gulf separates the traveller from the non-traveller. At a time when transport and communication would appear to be wiping out old frontiers, new ones are arising by reason of the 'insulators' – zones, that is, whose inhabitants do not share in the prevailing intercommunication. The under-developed countries are the chief example of this phenomenon.

A similar 'cavitation effect' (taking as an analogy the phenomenon which prevents adhesion between solids and the liquid in which they are free to move) also appears between generations. The young are always travelling, and always going farther afield than last time. The world-as-intercommunication is a medium which it comes naturally to them to enter. The not-so-young, on the other hand, often have to make a big effort to get used to this new condition of life. Sometimes the unit of difference is as small as half a generation. In other words, mentalities follow the new equipment – aircraft, telephone, holiday camp – but always at a distance, lagging; the young are steeped in progress and impatient of its meagre fruits; the rest find these too rich – progress shakes them up. As for social structures, they are still far behind.

A given item of equipment evolves in the same way anywhere but is not necessarily used in the same way everywhere. Situated as we are at the threshold of the planetary age, we see different epochs cohabiting; as during the several thousands of years when the sedentaries, at that time the party of progress, co-existed with nomadic societies.

FEDERAL STRUCTURES SUPERIOR TO SINGLE UNITS

Equipment is a factor making constantly for planetization, but it also does much to develop infra-planetary exchange at regional level or between neighbouring countries. More and more, the city has become the centre round which life is organized, and cities are connected by a dense mesh of means of communication. The Greeks linked their archipelagos by ship; it was the sea that enabled them to have political relationships. In our age, European cities may tend to federate amongst themselves because of their 'megalopolitan' communications.

So then, even though the great migrations of nineteenth-century type (such as those which populated the United States) are not repeating themselves, human beings are acquiring through their transport and communications an ever greater chance of meeting and getting to know each other, and of thinking together and in concert. But their very varied contacts and their aspirations towards ecumenicism, life in common, have not so far led to any significant political rearrangement. What really seems to be happening is that travellers are all potential champions of an open world but, when they get home to their respective nations instead of to the units of a federal structure, as those nations ought to be, they sink back into ways of life which their travels have shown to be no more than relative. Techniques and economics are bringing people closer together; differences in outlook, living standards and behaviour are a bias which has been accentuated and ingrained by the habit of living in separate political units. Nevertheless, only federalist structures can transform the material associations between men into lasting emotional, spiritual and political bonds.

BIG SHIPS, GEOGRAPHY AND PRODUCTION

Rational exploitation of natural resources in energy and raw materials cannot be carried out except on a large scale. Evolution is being helped forward by a change in the size of ships and an increase in their radius of action, which is now on the planetary scale. Supply of the economy's basic requirements has to be managed in terms of world dimensions.

In *Plaidoyer pour l'avenir*, in order to explain that huge arrangements for production and transport had had to be set up before petroleum could be brought into general use, we quoted the size of the *Sitala*, at that time (1959–60) one of the biggest tankers in the world, with a maximum load of 70,000 tons of oil.[1]

Why this giantism (to borrow a medical term)? Nowadays it is a much better economic proposition to expand into a small number of large units than into a large number of small ones. Running costs do not increase proportionally with the size of the ship. For example, profit is raised by something between 15 per cent and 30 per cent per ton transported, depending on the length of the voyage out and back, when tankers of 80,000 tons replace those of 40,000 tons. But any further significant rise in profit depends on making a big jump, namely to 180,000 tons, and thereafter to 500,000. In view of the predictable demand for petroleum products of various kinds, this race for the giantism stakes can be expected to continue. In principle at least there is no reason why ships should not go on getting larger, though in practice some routes will be closed to them because there are straits too shallow to take vessels of such draught.

PRODUCTS OF ALL KINDS ARE CONCERNED, OR WILL BE

The Suez Canal was the first victim; its closing merely accelerated a process already going on. Suez *versus* the Cape is a contest likely to be won by the latter, though the partisans of the former used to think they held a permanent monopoly. By making distance unimportant, modernized transport is simultaneously preparing the way for the bulkheads dividing mankind to be dismantled.

Fertilizers are a typical example. Farming used to depend on natural manure, and no field inaccessible to a cart could be cultivated. Then came the epoch of fertilizers imported from specific geographical points of origin: nitrates and guano from Chile, potash from Alsace. Agricultural output was no longer limited by the amount of manure available locally. A further

---

[1] The *Sitala* has since been put in the shade by tankers of 200,000 tons such as the *Magdala*, launched in France by the Chantiers de l'Atlantique on 3 March 1968.

stage has been reached with the use of fertilizers originating as by-products from sources of energy; American nitrates are an example. Transport is an ever decreasing fraction of the selling price. Any farmer, if there were no customs barriers, could buy his fertilizers from any part of the world at the lowest figure available at the time.

Another new factor is that freighters specially designed for specific tasks and regular service have made certain coastal areas more suitable for the manufacture of base-products than the areas round the mines.

Transport progress affects products of all kinds. In addition to large, specialized vessels for coal and grain there are freighters for sulphur, bauxite, chalk, shingle, kaolin, paving-setts, nitrates, oil-cake; for gypsum, cement, phosphates, sugar and salt; for alumina (aluminium oxide), often equipped with special unloading apparatus based on the special property of alumina of becoming fluid under the action of a blast of compressed air.

The future outlook is one of expansion. Ships will certainly get bigger than those we now regard as enormous. The use of atomic power to drive them will become widespread and they will be able to spend even longer periods at sea than at present. As the progress of telecommunications enables them to navigate in all weathers they will be able to keep on the move continuously or almost so, apart from periodical overhauls. The epoch of ports without brothels has begun.

THE STANDARDIZATION OF TRANSPORT

Progress in shipping has been matched by corresponding progress in port facilities (handling and warehousing), in which the influence of the dimensional law can likewise be seen at work. Ports have to offer every facility for the maintenance and repair of ships, whose machinery and equipment are steadily becoming more complex. Only a few ports are able to do this. To provide the necessary installations everywhere would be expensive and mistaken; organization at European level is required. Perhaps 'graving docks' (to use the old term) will even be provided on a world scale in future.

The appearance of containers and their rapid development

means that manufactured goods too will be affected by decisive changes, rendering factories progressively more independent in the matter of location. This trend will even extend to products with a low market value.

The container, once merely a crate like those used by removal firms, is turning into a planetary tool, transportable by ship, rail, road or aircraft from anywhere in, say, the United States to anywhere in Europe, Japan or Australia. World standardization of transport will influence the whole policy of packaging and stock management (which latter will be increasingly carried out by computer, an admirable aid to stock control). This will inevitably produce changes in distribution and commerce, and corresponding changes in existing patterns of equilibrium must be expected in many quarters.

The chance a given product has of doing well in the world market will depend far less on its transport costs than on its production characteristics. Geography will cease to put a brake on competition.

Improvements in refrigerating techniques are contributing to a much enhanced flow of trade in foodstuffs. The people of Paris and Stockholm are acquiring the habit of eating oranges all the year round, and bananas as if the trees were just outside the front door. Modern man is becoming less and less dependent on his own country for his food; even the Japanese are eating more and more wheat. He thus has a better chance of overcoming the deficiencies of the local climate, unlike the inhabitants of the under-developed countries, who are conditioned in grim fashion by the areas in which they are born, live and die.

It is likely that, in time, physiological differences will become blurred under the influence of trade, and of the planetization of eating-habits based on dietetic principles. Everyone concerned with the implementation of agricultural policy will do well to study this possibility. Uniformity of taste is going to become increasingly prominent.

Man used to be shackled to geography and confined to one climate. Tomorrow he will be free to choose his place of work in the pleasantest parts of the planet. His food will come from the gardens of the world, and he will create sources of energy – industry's daily bread – wherever he likes, in the form of nuclear power stations.

DEVELOPMENT DEPENDS ON CAPACITY FOR
ORGANIZATION MORE THAN ON NATURAL RESOURCES

The raw materials on which nineteenth-century industry was based were coal and iron, and neither of these was transported over any great distance. War (for example the Franco-Prussian War of 1870) was waged, or started up again (as in 1914), partly at least for possession of the iron ore deposits in Lorraine. Energy-producing raw materials were transported up to a distance of a hundred miles. Today they are transported hundreds of miles, and in the future this may become thousands.

Japan offers a good illustration of this trend. She possesses no natural wealth. At first she set about acquiring resources by conquest (war in Manchuria). But after the Second World War she entirely reversed her strategy, making her factories and ingenuity take the place of military power. She entered fields which appeared to have been sealed against her by nature, such as the steel industry, in which she is now the third largest producer in the world. Rapid transport has enabled her to overcome her natural handicaps. Her big industrial centres – Osaka, Tokyo–Yokohama – are on the coast. In Japanese terms, this is the answer to the challenge of industrialization. In world terms, it is a pioneer effort heralding a complete change of outlook. Previously, it was customary to build an industry in the areas where its raw materials happened to be found. We are now beginning to learn that they can be cheaply transported over greater and greater distances in less and less time. Sea-water is taking over the role of canal and river, and the ocean-going freighter that of the barge. Activity is shifting outward to the coast. In Europe, it is clear that the Ruhr of the late twentieth century will be situated between Dunkirk and Rotterdam; not only because oil is now reaching that area by sea but because large deposits of natural gas have been discovered there.

Oil is in fact, at present, the chief means of man's liberation from geographical restrictions. Petroleum gushes from the earth in four main areas: the United States, the Middle East, the Caribbean and the Soviet Union. Occurring frequently in arid places and rarely being refined on the spot, it causes an endless coming and going of ships on all the seven seas. It represents an average of more than half the annual tonnage transported, and the carrying capacity of the shipping which serves it is doubled on an average every ten years. The world is consuming more and more energy: twelve million kilo-calories *per capita* in 1953, over twenty million today. Most of this increase is attributable to oil, which accounts for 60 per cent of world energy-consumption. In 1965 the world consumed five times more hydrocarbons than in 1938.

FROM 'MARE NOSTRUM' TO 'OCEANUS NOSTER'

The oceans, covering four-fifths of the earth's surface, play the same part in communications in the planetary epoch, and notably where oil is concerned, as did the Mediterranean in antiquity; they are specially important because they enable oil to be transported. The *mare nostrum* of antiquity has been succeeded by the *oceanus noster* of the great industrial countries.

Europe, that huge peninsula of the Euro-Asian continent, is lapped by the seas and oceans of the world in the same fashion as the Peloponnesos, jutting out like the prow of a ship, is lapped by the Mediterranean. We should remember that commerce, insurance and banking were all born on the isle of Delos, whose tutelary deity Apollo was the first chairman and managing director in history – a development of which an account has been given by Indro Montanelli in his *Storia dei Greci*.

TRANSPORT, TRADE AND HUMAN SOLIDARITY

The time is approaching when the economy of any medium-sized country will no longer be able to depend on local resources, but on that country's ability to make use of materials and energy imported from elsewhere. The most competitive countries will be those with the greatest capacity for organization.

The growth of transport is also having the effect of rendering trade more multilateral. No country can really afford to confine itself to one source of supply or one market. No economy has anything to gain from a proliferation of bilateral agreements which create impossible tangles obstructing the balance of trade and which often result in economic contradictions. France, for example, has been known to import Polish textile goods at a time when her own textile market was saturated, for the sake of being able to sell cars and machinery to the Poles.

Links of solidarity between societies are increasingly woven as trade is multilateralized. Planetization of goods is accompanied by planetization of economic problems and of economic togetherness. International trade is increasing powerfully: 265,000 million francs in 1938, 492,000 million in 1948, 2,000,000 million in 1968. But the increase is mainly confined to the most advanced countries. The twenty-one OECD countries alone account for 65 per cent of world trade, the East European countries for 10 per cent. This is no coincidence. The more advanced an economy becomes the closer are its links with others.

Above a certain level of production, trade becomes indispensable, an imperative. Above a certain level of living-standards – the level of the 'consumer society', so much abused yet so ardently desired – crude authoritarianism and state control are powerless to alter the fundamental motivations of the individual. Authority may frown as it will on the proliferation of private cars, but everyone still wants a car. But trade, like the car, contributes to a closer knowledge of other countries and social structures and hastens the advent of suppler, more versatile methods of organization than mere rigid planning, a method suitable only to early stages or hard times. It becomes an act of heresy to hold an economy back in the stage of autarchy when it has already accomplished the big, basic tasks of modern organization and entered on the period of consumer choice and individual satisfaction.

This new orientation of life is the result of three things: the specialization of labour, the infectiousness of technology, and the inherent virtues of trade as a generator of productivity.

THE BREAK-UP OF ECONOMIC FRONTIERS

The application of large-scale mass production methods, rendered possible by specialization, frequently compels firms to seek a market far larger than that enclosed by the frontiers of a medium-sized country. To recover the capital invested in the Caravelle one hundred and fifty of these aircraft had to be sold, which obviously could not be done in the French or even the European market alone. Any limitation placed on trade also limits the degree to which standardization can be applied in production. The need to export forces the producer to achieve efficiency. If he was sure of a protected market he would not make the effort to improve his goods and lower his prices. The standard of living would suffer accordingly. This actually happened for years in France, because certain goods were so highly protected.

But specialization, an inseparable aspect of large-scale mass production, tends to increase the dependence of small or medium countries on others. When Italy began forging ahead in the manufacture of refrigerators, in which she is now responsible for half the total European production, she could not look to the Italian peninsula alone as her outlet. The ships coming off the stocks one after the other in Japanese shipyards would be impossible without a world market in view.

New products and techniques are crossing frontiers with ever increasing rapidity. If Du Pont de Nemours or Bayer brings out a new man-made fabric which can be manufactured quickly in large quantities the whole chemical industry is on the alert. This is all the more the case because the big firms have a network of subsidiaries through which new techniques can be diffused.

Agriculture, varying according to soil and climate, still tends to differentiate those who work on the land in one place from those in another. But industry, because it practises solidarity everywhere however closely guarded industrial secrets may be, generates uniformity. Railways are a good instance of this: in every part of the world, the railway industry revolves around similar technical norms. Hence the close mutual understanding of railwaymen from all over the world, the similarities between them, and their readiness to get together at the drop of a hat.

Apart from improvements in the quality of many foodstuffs, the main form taken by material progress is the emergence of industrial products whose characteristics are international. There is no such thing as a regional refrigerator or a local nylon stocking. The very contents of the housewife's shopping basket reflect the same tendency. The greater the rise in the standard of living, the more markedly are the products typical of this improvement designed with an eye to the world market.

The result ought to be a world-wide homogeneity of standards to which a given industrial product is subjected; this would give us articles which were cheaper to buy and more convenient to use. On the contrary, however, all sorts of protectionist devices, often more onerous than actual customs duties, are devised to hamper trade.

Nevertheless progress is continually being made. The metric system is at last becoming universal; even the British, the ultimate diehards, have decided to adopt it and the first British decimal coins have already appeared. They are beginning to extend it to all their machinery, and the Americans are to do the same. It is safe to prophesy that the system will be planetized in the end, except in aviation; in that field habits acquired during the war, because of American superiority, will persist for some time.

The vigour and intellectual impetus of the Encyclopaedists was the cause of the original triumph of the metric system. The French monarchy had tried to unify the various measures used in the provinces. There were hundreds of them; the *pinte* of wine, for instance, was one quantity in Paris and another at nearby Fontainebleau. But the attempt fell through because the susceptibilities of the provinces towards one another were as prickly as those between the countries of Europe today. The metre was adopted enthusiastically precisely because it has no connection with any of these jealously preserved measures but only with mankind's common habitat, the earth, and with the terrestrial meridian, and hence with scientific progress.

Examples of this kind from the history of progress encourage optimism: they make it possible to envisage new structures, new associations, to be created by Europeans for common ends. There is such a weight of new data pressing in on us all, and it is always easier for men to associate effectively round new elements – such as the language necessitated by the computer – than round traditional ones.

For many years past, international intercourse has been fostering economic growth and development. As the historians have shown, technical advance is often quicker in 'open' fields than in a closed *imperium*. Throughout historical evolution, the milestones have been the victories of the seafaring, trading countries over the land-based countries, with their emphasis on the state and its affairs. No doubt the struggle between protectionism in all its forms and the open frontier amounts to a constant, something which is always with us; but the long-term tendency is towards the suppression of customs barriers and local obstructionism. Exchanges between nation and nation, moreover, go much wider than the mere exchange of goods: increasingly, they include services, patents, intellectual activity. The importance of the grey matter of the brain rivals that of raw materials in this continual interchange. In any context anywhere, technical know-how is the key, indispensable alike to the oil prospector and to the firemen summoned to a blazing well. Everything, even the mechanics of management, is now an export article: tomorrow we shall be seeing businesses in Marseilles sending off their accounting, *via* satellite, to be done in New York just as easily as to Paris or London.

Because of this accelerating evolution, every economy is becoming more and more sensitive to events taking place beyond its national frontiers.

POLITICAL ORGANIZATION LAGS
BEHIND EQUIPMENT

Although economic reality has become planetary, organization is still far from being so; for example, on the monetary plane.

Under the system set up at Bretton Woods at the end of the Second World War, nations are required to settle their debts to one another in gold or dollars, the latter being made equivalent to gold. Even if we grant that the actions of the United States have proved profitable to all parties, especially in times of reconstruction, we cannot help noting that the bias in favour of the dollar injects a national ingredient into a mechanism which is not national but planetary. The system's functioning is partly bound up with the policy of a single state, doubtless the most powerful state but not the only one. And we know what difficulties this contradiction has produced. Moreover the International Monetary Fund, which is prepared up to a point to grant credits to debtor countries, is far from having the means at its disposal which would make it a real central bank for the world's economy. The highest experts are in agreement about the path to be followed: economic reality is international, and a system must be sought which fits it. What they all want – while reserving their right to disagree about how to get it – is an organization of a planetary character. Having made the transition from regional to central banks (the Bank of France acquired issue rights as recently as 1848, the Bank of England more recently still), we now need to make the further transition from national banks to a world bank, whose policy regarding the issue of currency and credit would be directly based on the needs of the world's economy. In the proposals to be set forth later in this book we shall look at some of the constructive developments which could be set in motion to this end.

But time presses.

Every time a country suffers an economic crisis it shows a tendency, despite the real though informal solidarity which exists between industrial societies, to export its difficulties. To some extent, action of this kind was involved in the catastrophic course of events in 1929. It could still be a source of accidents even now, when industrialization and technical progress are tending to produce universal prosperity.

In this context as in others, we have to realize that we have moved into the planetary epoch and that we run the risk of severe shocks and upheavals if we fail to deduce the correct consequences from that fact. In this situation, Europe must choose between concentrating exclusively on her own affairs (and risk suffering the repercussions arising from phenomena and decisions over which she would no longer have any control), and coming out of her shell to co-operate in the building of structures of a planetary character.

We shall have much more to say about this.

THE 'NOÖSPHERE'[1] OF KNOWLEDGE

In one of the most interesting books recently published, *The Computer Age and its Potential for Management*,[2] G. Burck and the

[1] 'Noösphere': the name used by Teilhard de Chardin to denote the community of minds, corresponding to 'biosphere', the community of living organisms.
[2] Harper & Row, 1965.

editorial staff of *Fortune* repeat the following anecdote, dating from ten years ago.

Charles Miller, head of the civil engineering department of the Massachusetts Institute of Technology, set his first-year students the problem of designing an access road to a flyover junction. With the help of a computer and a special language devised by Miller the students took twenty minutes to solve it, and one of them expressed the general feeling by commenting that it was 'much too easy'. In real life and under conventional conditions the same problem would have demanded considerable expert study, and it had never been given to first-year students before. It seemed that, at any rate on a job of this kind, beginners armed with a computer were more efficient, probably several times more so, than an expert without a computer. Burck goes on to say: 'When logic can be tapped as readily as electricity, similar results may be expected at all levels from grade to graduate school and beyond. This is intelligence amplification with a vengeance. Man appears finally to be on the verge of using the full powers of his mind.'

Of all the revolutions we are now experiencing, this 'amplification' of human intelligence is undoubtedly the greatest. Thanks to the computer, which enables him to multiply his cerebral abilities in the same way as the steam engine and its various descendants have enabled him to multiply his muscular strength, man is in a position to exploit his own intelligence on a hitherto unprecedented scale.

THE MOST DECISIVE CONTEMPORARY
REVOLUTION OF ALL

The computer will impose itself as imperiously on our lives as the machine has done. It will transform every intellectual activity and every kind of human organization, from teaching to industry and business.

But it also confronts us with a vital choice. Will it be put at the service of the worshippers of that Moloch, an omnipotent state; or will it be used to give the individual greater freedom of choice and allow him to develop more fully as a human being, in a society whose functioning it is destined to simplify?

Without assuming the prophet's mantle, it is already safe to say that by setting up a properly equipped information service it would be possible to replace existing social structures with new ones, in the way in which the introduction of machinery made it possible to transform the workshop into the factory. Europe, thanks to its age-old tradition of respect for the individual, ought to be capable of making the right choice at the great fork in the road with which our century is presenting us.

In an extremely short time the computer has become an extremely powerful instrument. The law of fluidity and acceleration has never been more strikingly confirmed.

The ordinary public is beginning to become aware that there have already been three generations of computers. The first computers worked with valves, like an old-fashioned radio receiver. At that time – namely 1946 – it seemed that in order to build a computer with a complexity roughly comparable to that of the human brain, the whole of Niagara Falls would be necessary to supply the electricity and the same water would have to be used all over again to cool the valves. This was a very soothing thought for the kind of people who are always frightened by progress: there were too few Niagaras in the world for a plague of electronic brains to be an imminent prospect! The birth of the second generation was a somewhat haphazard affair connected with the studies in crystallography which resulted in the discovery of semi-conductors; this led at once to the development of transistors which, after ten years of research, were to revolutionize both electronics and information science (1958). The third generation (1964) was produced by the development of integrated circuits. The advance represented by the generations can be described as limited but immediately accessible memory, intermediate memory and omnivorous memory; three stages very similar to our dealings with the telephone – we carry a few numbers in our heads, write down a somewhat larger batch in a notebook, and look up the rest in the directory.

Even in the early days of cybernetics people marvelled at the machine's ability to 'remember' the entire contents of a book.

Today, in principle at any rate, it is capable of storing the contents of all the libraries in the world. And the rate of access, the speed at which electronic dictionaries, as it were, can be consulted, is measured in micro-seconds or even hundredths of micro-seconds. Out of the sum total of human knowledge to date, the machine can extract any item or quantity of items in ten seconds, and the main outlines of any such item or quantity in less than a hundredth of a second.

These few pointers are enough to convey the scale to which memory has now been magnified. Memory is knowledge's arsenal, providing that two conditions are satisfied: that the knowledge is easy of access, and that it can be manipulated in a logical way. To electronics, both of these conditions are child's play.

At the same time as the computer was being made more powerful another potentiality was also being developed: 'tele-treatment', which enables a computer to deal successively with different problems on behalf of the firms or other organizations in different parts of the world which subscribe for the use of the computer.

Unlike the steam-hammer, which could function only in the setting of a big factory, the computer does not oblige its users to collect round it. They can be dispersed over any distance, it makes no difference to the computer if some are in America and others in Europe. It is perfectly possible today to handle information not merely on a continental but on a unitary, global scale.

To find an example of mutation comparable to that represented by the computer we should have to go back to the invention of printing by movable type.

Before the invention and diffusion of writing, the human memory was the only instrument for storing knowledge. Possibly the reason why poetry played so great a part in those epochs was its power as a mnemonic device. As most people know, the professional bards of ancient Greece, in a tradition extending over hundreds of years, carried the entire works of Homer in their heads; and the medieval troubadours performed similar feats. In some countries this prowess has survived into our own day: in India, the British found men who could recite the entire *Mahabharata*, which is longer than the *Iliad* and the

Odyssey together, and which at that time had never been written down. These men personified the functions of conservation and distribution.

Writing was a step forward in both the storing and the distribution of information. It is not surprising that the first texts, and the initiated who were capable of using them, were regarded as sacred. It was early and widely realized that the conservation of the written word was one of the major functions of society; hence the great libraries of antiquity.

The development of information science in our own day presents a striking parallel.

PROBLEMS OF INCREASING COMPLEXITY, AND TOOLS OF INCREASING POWER FOR DEALING WITH THEM

The widespread use of computers, the cybernetization of the world, as we might call it, has taken up and extended a process which began with automation. Essentially, automation consists of designing machines capable of repeating a certain number of movements and producing a stream of identical objects, such as gramophone records or cars. Technical progress has now advanced beyond this stage; improvements to automated equipment have made it better adapted to actual production conditions.

Rolling mills, for example, turning out sheet steel from ingots, no longer have their rollers rigidly adjusted; they are now designed to take the qualities of the metal, its hardness, temperature and so on, into account from moment to moment; the temperature, and the pressure on the rollers, are registered by an electronic brain. In other words, external factors are applied to regulate the automatic process and to ensure optimum functioning. In the same way, we can imagine a number of small electronic brains in a chemical factory, registering pressures and temperatures and causing valves to open or close so as to regulate flow and to control the composition of gases or the mixture of raw materials. In proportion as new modifications are introduced into manufacturing processes, and electronic equipment is used to implement these changes, cybernetics is playing a more and more influential part. Whereas man often has to simplify a problem in order to solve it and may thereby distort and falsify it, the computer can co-ordinate a much larger mass of data and treat them with extraordinary promptness. This makes it possible to work in 'real time'; that is, to take immediate cognizance of information received and modify the procedure accordingly. Gunners used to aim a shell at a target in accordance with the available data; the power of the charge and the direction and elevation of the barrel being given the resulting trajectory was given too; nothing could alter the course of the shell once it had started on its way. Today, the fantastic speed of cybernetic calculation makes it possible to control the flight of a rocket after firing; its exact position in the sky can be checked and, if the position is wrong, the trajectory can be calculated afresh and the requisite message transmitted to the rocket-motor to ensure correction. It is obvious that the same principle can be applied in other fields besides war. The organization of society at European and world level could derive nothing but benefit from these possibilities of feedback and self-regulation.

One of the characteristics of cybernetization is its generality. Whereas many other technical changes are specialized, affecting only a few branches of activity, cybernetics affects every intellectual procedure which forms part of human society: technology and production, social and organizational structures and laws and regulations. All these can now be examined anew, because cybernetics is everywhere capable of offering new solutions.

But this mutation, the scope of which is far greater than that of any previous one, must be set operating on the planetary plane; especially in view of the fact that cybernetics now operates on scales greatly transcending any national scale. The need for abolishing national frontiers has never been so cogently indicated by anything as it has by cybernetics.

CYBERNETIC SOLUTIONS TO MAJOR EDUCATIONAL PROBLEMS

Up to now, most teaching has been done in classes, with the pupils gathered round a teacher and progressing at a tempo which is that of the class as a whole (the class has sometimes been diversified by 'streaming', which has its advantages but has also been much criticized for its drawbacks). But we can now see our way to using computers educationally from an early age in an entirely different style of teaching. The computer will communicate data to the pupil and explain them to him; the pupil will then have the opportunity of asking the computer questions. Better still, it will be possible to use the computer as a control; meaning that the pupil will teach the computer, which will ask him the sort of questions which might be expected from a slow or inattentive learner. Knowledge will thus be checked in the simplest possible way, since the first condition for teaching anyone anything – which means making him understand it – is to have understood it oneself. As soon as a pupil has mastered one section of a subject he will be free to go on to the next. Equipment of this kind, which is now being brought to the point of practicability, will eliminate the over-emphasis placed on streaming; and it suggests a picture of what may be done in the future. Such a fundamental transformation of educational means and methods, in conjunction with the necessity for permanent education (education continuing intermittently throughout life), gives us some idea how comprehensive is the mutation of education that we now have to undertake. It is quite impossible to make a success of it on the scale of any nation of European size. We must rise at least to the European scale, taking an example from America: in New York they have already used the 'terminal' of a course where the computer is in California.

Contrary to what is still too often thought, the computer, though complicated in itself, is perfectly simple for anyone with a 'terminal' at his disposal to use. Besides, the child will get accustomed to it at school and will thereafter have recourse to it as a normal part of his life. Anyone wishing to take part in laying the foundations of tomorrow's society will have to have cybernetics as his mother tongue.

The foregoing exposition shows what a difference the appearance of computers and tele-treatment has made to our lives.

It would be a mistake to bother too much about the difficulty of manufacturing these new items of equipment. What matters is knowing how to use them, how to apply their almost infinite possibilities to the better organization of society. A problem of such scope demands to be studied in relation to the world scale.

ELECTRONICS IN RELATION TO ORGANIZATION ON THE PLANETARY SCALE

Electronics is compelling human society to adopt the planetary scale as its frame of reference, but at the same time is endowing it with such means of information-handling as to multiply its cerebral power.

By storing larger and larger amounts of information, computers enable human brains to tackle more and more complex problems. In a study communicated recently to the Société d'Economie Politique, Charles Salzmann, an expert on data-processing, forecast that this new potential would eventually be realized in practice in every relevant field.

A medical data-bank (several are already in action in the United States, but none on a world scale) can 'remember' the cases of millions of patients and reproduce this multitude of facts in a few seconds. The case-history of each patient includes his medical history as a whole, all recorded clinical observations about him, the results of all tests, details of all diagnoses, the treatments prescribed, with results and secondary effects, etc. By consulting this collective memory any doctor can inform himself of what has been done in cases similar to those with which he is confronted at the moment, and is thus in a position to benefit from the experience of thousands of his professional colleagues. Of course this possibility depends on the reliability of the data entrusted to the computer; it must be objective, accurate, and free from misleading inessentials.

There is every reason to believe that the same thing will be achieved in other fields and that professional data-processing organizations, both national and international, will offer their subscribers the services of an information-bank embodying not only the fundamental references but also the extra material provided by the latest published research. It is in fact essential that all new knowledge should be made available in published form.

There are even proposals for putting computers into orbit, so that they can be consulted in any part of the world. In the words of the magazine *Planète*, 'Libraries will rise into the sky.'

THE ENCEPHALIZATION OF SOCIETY AND THE
DAWN OF THE NOÖSPHERE

One of the potentialities of information-handling is that any human group wishing to do so will be able to contact a computer by means of a combined telephone and television set, about the size of a viewer for transparencies, and get the information it wants.[1]

Technically, it is possible already to provide any user of a tape-machine or telephone, whether at home or in his office, with complete or partial access to the most powerful computers. Of course the cost of the computers is a consideration and always will be, but as the number of users will always be increasing, the expense will eventually be shared among thousands of participants.

There are all sorts of ways in which this technique can be applied. One American telecommunication firm decided that its own growth and prosperity were bound up with the development of information-banks. So it set up a 'bank of juridical data' for barristers, solicitors and company legal departments. There has even been talk of 'judiciary information-banks'. It is in fact obvious that the future of jurisprudence is interwoven with that of the computer. The latter will inform courts of the precedents they need as a basis for their decisions. It will be possible to interrogate the computer, as in the classroom, and to spotlight any inconsistency in a proposed verdict. Finally, computers will compile a systematic register of laws by classifying them in terms of a variety of criteria, thus making it possible to iron out inconsistencies in law as a whole.

In the administrative world, the nerve centres of the information system will probably consist of urban, rural and industrial information-banks. Economic information-banks will also be created. Other specialized information sources will become indispensable to engineers, teachers, chemists, physicists, dietitians, insurance offices, business men and financiers; in short, to a growing number of those professional groups which constitute the complicated fabric of our modern society.

The procedures outlined here will be valid for many other

[1] Cf. *Planète*, no. 38, 1 February 1968.

sectors whose increasing expansion is susceptible to control by computer. This will cut out the unruly jungle of complication which the modern world would be doomed to inhabit if methods of government and management were to remain unreformed. The computer has come in the nick of time to save us from getting more deeply bogged down in bureaucracy, that curse which is one of the reasons for the rejection of society by modern youth. It is ridiculous to squander the time saved by mechanization on wrestling with the difficulties resulting from the maladaptation of structures to equipment. The duty of cybernetization is to enable us to beat those difficulties, and to ensure that increased productivity is harnessed to social progress and individual development. To sum the situation up, nothing more strikingly characterizes the possibilities now offered to us on the world scale than the computer, with its possibilities in every field from medicine, which brings life, to the atomic missile, which deals death. Nothing demonstrates more clearly than the computer that what seemed visionary only yesterday can become a practical possibility today.

However extensive the changes required in our social structures, they are certainly not as great as the difference between 1 and 10^6 (one million) or 1 and 10^{12} (one billion in British parlance, a million millions in American). These are the figures which represent the multiplication of brain-power which is now within our reach. The development of living creatures in the age-long course of evolution is characterized by increasing encephalization (development of the brain), ensuring control over an increasingly complex organism. In just the same way an 'encephalization of society' is now taking place and putting at the disposal of mankind as a whole – given the will to make good use of it – the information enabling us to design our present behaviour in the light of past experience, through knowledge of the facts and how they arose.

EUROPE'S TASK IS TO INVENT THE TRANS-NATIONAL STRUCTURES REQUIRED BY THE PLANETARY AGE

The optimism with which we have argued our thesis so far must not be allowed to obscure the fact that the future development of the computer *could* take place as an adjunct to, and under the pressure of, a political system; and that if it was forced into the service of authoritarianism and hemmed in by technocratic control, the individual would be crushed under foot.

This is where Europe can and must come in. She has fallen behind in the sphere of equipment; she must catch up by showing high intelligence. She must invent the structures of the planetary age. If this is to happen, Europe must show a certain originality in the use of the computer. This originality could arise from our becoming fully aware of the trans-national nature of cybernetics, which is a force making for federation more powerfully than any force has done before; and because of this federal aspect, cybernetics ought to become one of the leading elements in European creativity.

THE WORLD FORUM
OR THE NOÖSPHERE OF THE VISIBLE

The Greek agora and the Roman forum were the setting in which man functioned as a political animal. It was there that the institutions and attitudes which were to remain typical of our history for so long were first formed. In our own day, a world forum can be said to be emerging.

SATELLITE TV WILL MAKE ALL MEN NEIGHBOURS

In the closing days of 1958 a human voice, for the first time, made itself heard to all mankind at once through the medium of space: the President of the United States sent out a Christmas message to the world. A little later, visual images also began traversing intercontinental distances: satellite TV had been born, evoking the same reactions from millions of human beings simultaneously and creating new bonds between them, comparable to those created in the ancient forum. Radio, blocked by the language barrier, had been unable to do this.

Previously, however, there had been no lack of sceptics and pessimists to predict that whereas radio had become international, TV would remain national because its waves were propagated in a straight line, like light, and would therefore cover only a limited area. It was true that, as early as October 1945, A. C. Clarke, in the British magazine *Wireless World*, had envisaged the use of artificial satellites to provide world-wide TV transmission. But this presupposed the fulfilment of various conditions: the use of rockets and satellites under electronic control, achievements which many apparently well-informed people thought were still far off. These people were wrong; simultaneous world-wide TV is now an accomplished fact, and is becoming part of the fabric of our lives to a degree which is still largely unobserved. Watching the news on TV at eight o'clock in the evening, the typical French family remains fairly unmoved to see the correspondent of the state radio and TV organization appearing in New York, or the French delegate to UNO. And technical improvements in this field have by no means reached their limit.

Obviously we must be alive to all the possibilities opened up by world TV, and in particular the possibilities for visual propaganda. The Russians, for instance, have announced their intention of putting a satellite station into orbit to cover the entire continent of Asia, simultaneously flooding the market with TV receivers at a very low price. This dual operation is perfectly feasible in a state where everything is subject to planning and it is therefore possible to put a single make of set into mass-production on the biggest scale for years on end, without holding up the flow even for modifications which would improve reception.

Thus, world TV represents a massive enlargement of the forum. For centuries, the public square was where the citizens repaired for news and entertainment. Napoleon, like Caesar, could never address a crowd of more than a thousand or so, and those standing at the back heard nothing.

UNIVERSAL SHARING OF EXCITEMENT AND IMAGES

By contrast, what is the position today? Three hundred million people watched the burial of President Kennedy and, on 4 October 1965, saw the Pope at the United Nations Assembly speaking with simplicity, emotion and the awareness of making a gesture which was nothing short of world-wide. He spoke of peace: 'Never must there again be war, never. ... Peace is what must guide the destinies of all the peoples of mankind.' Since then, TV sets having become commoner, there has been a still larger audience to share the tragedy of Robert Kennedy's last hours, in June 1968.

The visual image pulls more weight than any commentary, despite the fact that the use of simultaneous translation is now commonplace. This is why the Vietnam war has become a reality to the people of every country in the world. The Americans, because of their conception of political life, feel themselves to be involved with a very large public; hence every episode of the war which it has been possible to film has been shown on the small screen. These pictures have been retransmitted all over the world; if American information had been censored there would have been fewer of these pictures, and the war would have been less tangible to millions of people who now condemn it because they have seen it.

'INFORMATION' VERSUS 'PROPAGANDA'

Obviously, one of the major issues thrown up by television is that of the very real influence exerted by the visual image on political behaviour. No fundamental alteration in the foundations of democracy has been brought about since the liquidation of illiteracy or, of course, since the appearance of radio and TV. The latter, however, has definitely altered the conditions of public life. A politician or head of state can be seen by millions of people simultaneously. Political meetings, the modern descendants of assemblies of the crowd in antiquity, have had much of their significance cut away from under them. But there has been a change worth noting: audience-contact on TV is different from that built up at a meeting. Televised utterances are received by individuals, at home, in a family setting, not by a crowd. The speaker is speaking, in fact, to one person, whom he must convince by means of his presence, his arguments and the tone he adopts. He has at his disposal none of the artifices both used and abused by orators to wield power over the assembled masses. Television should therefore contribute to creating a more informed climate of political opinion.

The planetary forum now coming into being because of TV is, of necessity, vaguer and more diffuse than the national one. The difference is like that between loosely and closely woven cloth. But the planetary backcloth undeniably exists, and the national one, however much closer in texture, forms part of it and cannot be detached from it. Moreover the visual medium is likely to have effects which a purely verbal medium, spoken or written, cannot produce.

Cardinal Suhard used to say, 'Television has endowed man with a new instrument for achieving unity.' It will in fact by-pass the linguistic barrier and, as television spreads all over the planet (but it must be noted that the spread is uneven), enable all mankind, Russians, Americans, Englishmen, Japanese, Indians, Brazilians, to share in the great adventures of our century, and to become aware of the grave dangers by which our universe is threatened.

SPACE-TRAVEL AND PLANETARY UNITY

When, on 4 October 1957, the first Sputnik began circling the earth, its bleeps were heard by everyone who could get to a radio set.

This was a triumph for the Soviets, and was regarded as 'one up to them' on the political plane. But four months later, on 31 January 1968, the Americans replied by launching the first Explorer. It then became increasingly clear that man's venture into space was something much bigger than a competition between the two super-powers; it was of importance to everyone in the world.

Later experiments have been followed with the liveliest attention on all sides; the points chalked up by the two rivals, and the failures as well as the successes of their navigation in space, have been felt to be the concern of all the inhabitants of the earth. When the three American astronauts Virgil Grisson, Edward White and Roger Chaffee were burnt alive in the cabin of their Apollo spaceship, during its launching on 26 January 1967, and when the cabin of Soyuz I, manned by the Russian astronaut Tomarov, crashed on 24 April 1967, only those with blinkered minds regarded these calamities as an American and a Russian setback; everyone else understood that they were dramas conducted at planetary level.

Is there anyone who does not still remember the first photograph taken of the planet Earth by a human being?

While, of course, we know that what lies behind this gigantic undertaking is man's curiosity, the thirst for adventure translated into planetary dimensions, we also know that military preoccupations are implicated. Here again, technology will bear good or evil fruit according to whether it is applied to good or evil ends.

On the good side there is the satellite, which is partly the result of war but which has brought about a wider diffusion of information and, by allowing facts and emotions to be shared, will foster the emergence of a planetary attitude to life. Hitler's V2, after all, was the origin from which men of peace set themselves to fashion this new tool, a tool which is among the first elements of the noösphere conceived by Teilhard de Chardin.

On the other side, the same inventiveness has thrown open the possibility of espionage by satellite, the twentieth century form of the sword of Damocles: the missile-carrier capable of orbiting perpetually round our globe as a reminder of man's mortality.

Between this best and this worst, the adventure called space will continue to excite intense interest; particularly among the young, who, we must hope, will find in it a source of hope to offset their disappointment at the progress of another adventure, that of a new society, on which their elders have so far embarked so ineptly. Adolescence, the transition from childhood to adult life, is disappointing at the best of times, and is quite enough to explain the crises which have occurred lately among large members of the young.

STRIDES TOWARDS PLANETARY AWARENESS

It was not long ago that hunger was still a common phenomenon in Europe. The last great famine in France took place in 1709, but at the beginning of Napoleon III's reign a quintal of wheat cost a hundred days' wages, which explains (while it does not justify) the fact that until the middle of the nineteenth century a man could be sent to penal servitude in the hulks for stealing a loaf.

Today we think of the Indians or the Africans whenever the spectre of famine stalks before us; what was once a preoccupation bearing on our own lives has now been projected on to other people's. Of course not all of us think daily of the ordeal of the under-developed countries; yet it makes its presence generally felt, whether consciously or otherwise, as a major problem. It seems to impugn not the Western individual as such, but society itself.

In this respect the visual image plays a decisive part; a film of starving children is more eloquent than any amount of speeches about them. And there is another factor: speed. Information is spread so quickly that as soon as hope arises in one place that suffering can be relieved and life prolonged, that hope becomes universal. It took less than twenty-four hours to establish the fame of Professor Barnard, the first surgeon to attempt a heart-graft on a human patient.

ATOMIC TERROR AS THE CEMENT OF WORLD UNITY

Fears regarding the possible use of the atomic bomb are more acute in heavily-armed nations than elsewhere. Nevertheless, images of potential destruction are arousing in the minds of people everywhere an anxiety which is becoming planetary in character. It would be best, moreover, for it to spread yet faster and be felt more thoroughly. The complete documentary film material on the bombing of Hiroshima and its consequences was not publicly shown in Japan until February 1968. There could be nothing more salutary than to show it on every screen in the world.

The atomic danger is now nearly twenty years old (as early as 1951, Karl Jaspers was pointing out that 'humanity could commit suicide'). But what really underlined the mortal nature of the danger was the arrival of China in the ranks of the nuclear powers.

Pierre Sudreau, in his book *L'Enchaînement*[1] has expressed the anxiety of the world today in plain terms: 'Ever since mankind's earliest days there have been wars. History is war. People have always made war in order to have peace, but they have never found any other way of getting peace than winning the war. War is the fact, peace the fugitive dream. War is what happens, peace is what we seek.'

Practical experience of the use of nuclear armaments has so

[1] Paris: Plon, 1967.

far been confined to the explosions at Hiroshima and Nagasaki in 1945. At a time when the heaviest bomb carried by an aircraft contained a hundred tons of TNT, the two American A-bombs were equivalent to 15,000 and 20,000 tons of TNT. With conventional means the same effects would have required 20,000 one-ton bombs carried by 2,000 bombers. Two aircraft were enough to kill 105,000 people and injure 110,000: 4,600 dead per square mile at Hiroshima, 6,500 at Nagasaki. Since 31 October 1952, when the first explosion was carried out at Bikini, there have been thermonuclear bombs as well as A-bombs. One H-bomb of one megaton produces an effect comparable to that of several million conventional bombs.

The United States and the USSR possess devices of from fifteen to twenty megatons. In October 1962 the USSR set off a fifty-megaton device. The mechanical and thermic potential developed by such a bomb is fifteen times greater than that exploited at Hiroshima.

Not only are the bombs themselves extremely powerful; the radius of action of the various means of carrying them is increasing. The bomb-and-satellite combination, which is now practicable, means that the danger could become continuous, and emphasizes its planetary character. The threat could in fact be suspended over any country whatsoever by means of an armed satellite crossing the sky several times a day.

And there are other, equally formidable, tools of war besides atomic explosives, derived from electronics and sophisticated contemporary chemistry. We shall have something to say about these later.

So the suicide or ruination of mankind is becoming an ever more real possibility. The resources of soul and spirit required to avert it must be sought, and found, on the planetary scale. Many people are still far from admitting the danger, or even becoming aware that it might exist.

There is an enormous gap between technical reality and political behaviour.

Still, changes are beginning to appear in the conduct of peoples towards one another. The Vietnam war is significant in this respect. None of the antagonists has been willing to assume the onus of declaring the war official. All the same, the capital of the country which has been denounced (by the

Americans) as the aggressor has been bombed, and regular troops have attacked towns not within the frontiers of their own country.

Somehow we must break out of the dangers of 'enchainment' (the word seems more appropriate than 'escalation'). But the question is how?

KNOW-HOW IS NOT PROGRESS, BUT IT MAKES PROGRESS POSSIBLE. ORGANIZATION MUST BE RAISED TO THE SAME LEVEL AS EQUIPMENT

In our book, *The Case For the Future* (*Plaidoyer pour l'avenir*), we dealt at considerable length with the huge problem of adapting contemporary structures to contemporary realities.

Equipment is continually developing, and is carrying us forward into the planetary age. Mental attitudes follow behind. Children are not born nationalists, or reactionaries, or racists, or enemies of the computer; they become these things because, and only because, the structures of upbringing and education are a step, or several steps, behind the facts. Even grown-ups are often closer to acquiring the planetary attitude to life than is admitted by those whose power depends on preserving the existing structures. It is true that public opinion frequently blames technical progress as the source of all its woes; but this is because no one explains to the public what technical progress is up to, so that the public remains unaware that the ills of the modern world are mainly a matter of retarded development, in which social progress lags behind economic, and cultural behind social. Because it does not develop fast enough, organization lags behind technology, which, abandoned to its own devices, goes sweeping torrentially forward. Technical advance makes progress possible, but does not in itself constitute progress.

Quite apart from the repercussions of technological advance, it sometimes happens that the forward movement of civilization itself places obstacles in its own path, obstacles to the attainment of closer community among mankind. At the time when governing circles in Europe, in their respective countries, were fashioning the European body politic, they all spoke the same language; which happened to be French. But the further this formative process was carried the higher rose the fence created by language-differences. Simultaneously two things, conscription and the introduction of universal suffrage, stimulated the growth of nationalistic feeling, which was certainly stronger than it had been in the eighteenth century.

The visual and audible forum provided by world TV is capable of helping us to surmount this dangerously divided condition. But organization, animated by a mood of political creativeness, must also take a hand in this vital matter.

The contrast is more than ever striking between the greater physical closeness of individuals which has been brought about by technical progress, notably in the sphere of transport and communications, and the gulf dividing us from our fellow men. We are closer to one another than ever before but we are still not neighbours.

The lack of communication is all the more glaring in the light of the fact that we can now move from one quarter of the earth to another in less than a day.

This freakish discrepancy naturally shocks some of the young, who forget that present-day attitudes are an inheritance from a still recent past in which compartmentation was the rule not only between countries but even between classes, deeply separated as they were by educational contrasts. The young accuse society of having done nothing to render the world more coherent and meaningful; they accuse the grown-ups of having been more alive to the progress of technology than to the inadequacy of structures. It is true that adults are still slow to take full advantage of the pleasures of holidays, travel, home movies, whereas the young take all that for granted and turn aside impatiently to whatever else remains to be seen or done. The result is a sharply defined gap between the generations, a gap which Europe must strive to overcome by mobilizing everyone of good will and channelling the idealism of youth into the search for new structures.

THE DAWN OF EUROPE COINCIDES WITH THE
DAWN OF THE PLANETARY AGE

A short-term world government is unthinkable. This stands out all the more clearly when one reflects that none of the present types of government would serve as a model for it. Their constitution and the way they work and think all date from the era before television, the computer, the jet plane and even the spread of literacy. Any rational organization of humanity as a whole, on the other hand, necessitates using information techniques which belong to the planetary scale, and whose crowning achievement is world-wide simultaneous TV.

The horizons opening before European thinking at the present juncture differentiate it sharply from the thinking which emerged at the end of the war. That was chiefly dominated by two ideas which, though elementary, were apposite to that particular time: reconciliation after all the internal conflicts by which Europe had been ravaged, and the possibility of making Europe into a 'third power', between America and Russia.

A new conception must be elaborated. We must re-make our idea of what Europe is; re-think Europe in her new context. If her destiny were fashioned in any other terms she would cease to have any meaning and, indeed, would not be viable; there would be no future for her. The time for mutual forgiveness and the 'third continent' has passed; we have reached the time for imagination and example.

European thought and initiative must register their influence on the world by taking the rapidity and fluidity of the world's present development into account.

The dawn of Europe must coincide with the dawn of the planetary age.

CHAPTER TWO

AMERICA AS A FACT OF LIFE

Today, as we stand on the threshold of the planetary age, the United States is the greatest of the world powers. It is consequently playing a fundamental part in the development of planetary society, which, however, behaves towards the States rather like an adolescent in a hurry to cut loose from the adults' leading strings, and yet incapable of dispensing with adult help.

With an industrial production constituting more than a third of the world total, with the highest average standard of living (twice as high as that of the French), with a third of all the cars now on the road in the entire world, 90 per cent of existing pipe-lines and 80 per cent of the computers, the United States since World War Two has felt compelled to adopt a policy of intervention abroad for which it was unprepared.

AMERICA THE STANDARD OF COMPARISON
FOR ALL INDUSTRIAL SOCIETIES

America's destiny as a great power was none of her own choosing. America is an empire which has never had an emperor and which has found itself engaged (to quote John F. Kennedy) 'with a struggle we did not start, in a world it did not make'.

But having evolved a corpus of organizational technique which is more effective than anything of the kind elsewhere, the United States has become the prime standard of reference for industrial society in general, the example from which others take their cue more or less well, more or less clearsightedly, and more or less of their own volition. Since equipment and organization engender a way of life, the much-heralded 'American way of life' has penetrated far afield, mingling with local practice in a great many places. The Americans, after having so long imitated others, have in their turn been pillaged by all. In one way or another, the whole world bears the marks of their influence: some 50 per cent of American-type organization is visible in German society, perhaps 25 per cent in French, and traces can be found, though in smaller amounts, in countries such as India or Mali, although their style of civilization is totally different. The Americans, our distant cousins, characterized from an early stage by their wish and hope to be popular, have now become the heads of the family, at once feared and envied. And their activities in the present-day world have excited both admiration and hatred, servility and jealousy.

Hence American leadership in this, the initial phase of the planetary age, a leadership which might have been the leaven producing a new mode of togetherness among the collectivities on our planet, is contributing, in the present state of affairs, as much to division as to federation.

Europe should make it her concern to remedy the insufficiencies engendered by the orientation assumed by American policy. This she will not achieve by trying to be a second United States or a third continent. In that way she would in fact create new openings for disagreement and perpetuate struggles for influence; she would still be outstripped as a power by America and probably also by Russia, which has greater ideological cohesion and (what is more important) more land, more room. The right road for Europe consists of inventing a federal form susceptible of universal adoption, which is the case with neither the American nor the Russian.

WHY AMERICA IS A SUPER-POWER

The Americans laid their national foundations in a manner which is historically most unusual: several of the States, and not the least important ones, were acquired by purchase – Louisiana from Napoleon in 1803, Oregon from Britain in 1846, California from Mexico in 1848, and Alaska from Russia in 1867. Their principal war was internal, not a war of conquest. But above all they 'gained ground', in two senses, by their technical skills, paralleling, at a distance of ten centuries, Europe's great victories over marsh and forest. They have done the same thing on their own scale, helped by a powerful arsenal of tools and the internal combustion engine. The United States is a phenomenon which will remain unique in history: within the space of one hundred years a mixed population, pre-occupied with its own problems and turning its back on the rest of the world, has risen to the position of a dominant nation through economic strength, rapidity of development and talent for innovation.

The stature and vigour imparted to science-based techniques in the American organizational field have been underestimated by historians and sociologists. It should not be forgotten that in the early days of American history the pioneers, who were eager to become independent of British industry and manu-facture, had difficulty in becoming so. Philadelphia's liberty bell, one of the first to be cast, cracked because the bell-founders lacked the knowledge possessed by their colleagues in the Old World. One of the first silk fabrics woven on American territory, on which were printed copies of the Constitution, has fallen a victim to time and decay. These examples aptly demon-strate the distance covered between that time and our own, when the United States, as the indisputable pioneer of tele-vision and the computer, is the leader in at least two of the fields which are destined to revolutionize the world and thrust planetization upon us.

If we are to understand at once the development of American society and the reasons for the influence now exerted by it on the rest of the world, it is essential to throw as sharp a light as we can on the principal factors which have contributed to its leading position. These are: productivity; dimension (i.e. size and scope); selection; and the world wars, especially World War Two.

In the United States humanity has always been scarcer than land, whereas in Europe it has long been the other way round.

So, from the beginning, the Americans had to turn to the machine for help. Automatic barriers at level crossings, for instance, were installed very early, at a time when crossing-keepers' cottages were continually being built in Europe as the rail network was extended. They were also quick to replace telephone operators with the automatic telephone, which is still not universal in France. As early as 1880, 80 per cent of their wheat was harvested by machine.

Whereas in Europe calligraphy was long regarded, as in China, as a sign of elegance, politeness and the hallmark of official documents, especially legal documents, the Americans adopted the typewriter as soon as it was invented. In its early days it did not produce very handsome results, and many Europeans made no secret of their opinion that the use of such barbarous letter-forms carried the risk of destroying both personality and culture. But the Americans, lacking retired soldiers or gendarmes to become official clerks and give the world the benefit of their copperplate and curlicues, cared nothing for such criticism and, in this sphere as in others, put their money on the machine.

After trying various writing pianos and printing telegraphs, Christopher Sholes brought out, in Milwaukee, in 1867, the first typewriter worthy of the name. In 1873 Remington launched the first factory-produced model, mounted on a standard sewing-machine, and Thomas Edison, wishing to lighten the typist's labour, built the first electric machine, mass-produced by IBM in 1930.

Thus did the United States give birth to typewriting, a force which has left its mark on modern society – as, more recently, has the tape recorder, the successor to shorthand.

Plenty of other examples could be quoted: in 1874, the replacement of millstones by steel rollers, in flour milling; in

1931, the adoption of the Barber Green road-surfacing machine which enabled roads to be repaired quickly and did away with the slow, laborious work of road gangs. These and other innovations demonstrate the Americans' precocious confidence in the machine, their ready acceptance of the disciplines it imposes, and their determination to benefit fully from it. In Europe, on the other hand, fears of unemployment made the machine a source of apprehension in more than one stratum of society.

Although in countries like France science has always been the aristocrat and tools the vulgarians, faith in the tool as much as in science was bound to result in mass-production and Taylorization.

Therefore in 1909 I announced one morning, without any previous warning, that in future we were going to build only one model, that the model was going to be 'model T', and that the chassis would be exactly the same for all cars, and I remarked: 'Any customer can have a car painted any colour that he wants so long as it is black.'

This memorable declaration from Henry Ford's autobiography[1] records his decision to build cars for the maximum possible number of customers. He wanted the public to be astonished that they could be 'given so much for so little money'. He reckoned that if the product and the price were both right, profits would automatically follow, and mass-production would acquire its natural economic significance. But reaching this goal had demanded gigantic labours of simplification and standardization.

After setting up a complete production line by boldly applying all the ideas and experiments of Whitney, Cyrus MacCormack, Taylor and Ramon Olds, Ford succeeded in doubling his workers' wages; from $2.50 they went up to $5.00. Mass production had proved that it could engender mass consumption.

This was in January 1914. The United States was already the second industrial power in the world. By being quicker than other countries to apply the industrial methods made possible by technical progress, it enabled itself to establish a lead which was to be maintained for a long, long time.

[1] *My Life and Work*, Garden City Publishing Co., 1922.

THE LOGIC OF TECHNOLOGY AND INDUSTRY, AN
EARLIER DEVELOPMENT IN THE USA THAN ELSEWHERE

Because human beings were in short supply the Americans grasped, at an early stage, the importance of time as a factor in the economy. Mass production of standardized products also became necessary in America because of the mixed population. To get Irishmen, Italians and Poles working together in spite of language difficulties, the practical solution was to break the work-task down into small, definite sections, making it easy for everyone to understand what was expected of him. Similarly, the best bet for the development of sales was to go for products which were easy to recognize and designed to appeal to the largest number of customers; any product had to be as it were reduced to the smallest possible denominator: in a word, standardized.

This 'logic of technique' took hold more quickly in America than elsewhere; so did the widespread recognition that, where the products of industry were concerned, quantity was the mother of quality, thus reversing a principle which had previously remained impregnable – a change depicted in *Plaidoyer pour l'avenir*.

The idea of quality has been extended to become the idea of total reliability, which is specifically American. A tool or working part or mechanism has to be so designed and made as to continue functioning satisfactorily at all times and in all circumstances. This is imperative in astronautics, where some minor fault in one of the thousands of mechanisms constituting a satellite and rocket assembly is enough to endanger human lives and a costly programme. There is an escalation of quality which is gradually affecting all materials and most products. Domestic heating, for instance, whether by gas, oil or even coal, can now automatically be regulated with such precision and safety that it can be left permanently turned on in country houses. Soon it will be possible to regulate it by putting through a telephone call direct to the thermostat.

The Americans have been forced in this direction by a chronic shortage of repair workers. In the States there were too few trained hands for many of them to be diverted into repair work; they were needed for production.

In short, lacking qualified people to overcome the challenges presented by their territory, and without manual and social traditions, the Americans have not hesitated to make use of the possibilities offered by modern techniques. They threw themselves into the tasks of organization at the very juncture when those techniques were demanding new methods of rationalization, and when anyone with the requisite technical knowledge was faced with expanding prospects.

Europeans have indeed tried to follow the same road – often, however, on the cheap; which has unfortunately resulted in lending a certain weight to the reactionary view which fails to understand the way progress is moving, and pleads the cause of the past in the name of quality.

LEARNING THE LAWS OF DIMENSION

The United States has been built up in a territory whose standards of measurement were larger than those previously known to history. The latter were centred round the horse. The United States has been modelled round the railroad and the dollar.

The American plain stretches some fifteen hundred miles from north to south and a thousand from east to west.

In a few hours one can move from the fjords of Maine to the coral shelves of Florida. The USA's northern frontier is on the same latitude as Lyons, the southern on that of the Hoggar massif in the Sahara. In the East, the summers are humid and very warm, the winters icy (Niagara Falls are frozen, and New York is as cold as Berlin despite being on the latitude of Naples). In the Middle-West, the lack of mountain chains allows the blizzards to sweep down from Hudson Bay in winter, and the hot winds to sweep up from the Gulf of Mexico in summer. These contrasts in temperature make for strong winds; hurricanes are endemic from Texas to New England.

In order to carry on working normally in any environment, and to create pleasant conditions for family life, the American has recourse to modern know-how, as in other things; and he does it systematically, so that surroundings both professional and private have been standardized from one end of the country to the other. He consequently benefits from a considerable advance in comfort, so much so that any way of life based on contemporary facilities looks like a plagiarized version of America. And indeed it must be admitted that Europeans, without the rigours of the trans-Atlantic climate to excuse them, sometimes deserve this criticism; they transplant appurtenances and devices into their surroundings which they do not need. Air conditioning, for example, which is imperative in Texas or Alaska, makes less sense in Toulouse or Geneva. The things we take from America are not always the most useful she has to offer; we sometimes ape habits our environment does not justify.

It should be underlined that, in Europe, man has long been bound up with nature and lives in partnership with her. He has often regarded the development of modern skills as an offence against natural living, unlike the American who is indebted to these same skills for having made his life possible. On our side, modern technique is synonymous with mutations which are often hard to accept; on the other side it has proved to be the necessary condition of life.

To the American, everything born of technology and the factory has an aura of trustworthiness. What is natural and comes from the soil, on the other hand, is regarded with some degree of circumspection: there was, for example, a period when it was compulsory to print an exact description of the composition of flour on the sacks containing it, but not to list the ingredients of a medicine on the packet. In France, on the contrary, distrust of technical mysteries causes far stricter regulations to be applied to medicines than to flour; anything made from the fruits of the earth is sure to be good.

Geography and climate have compelled the Americans to think big. In overcoming the handicaps with which they have been faced they have forged the tools which make them better at accepting the challenges specific to our century. The original Brooklyn Bridge, which stopped Manhattan from being an island, was made possible only by using the newest technical developments of the time, whereas de-islanding the Ile de la Cité in Paris or connecting one bank of the Thames to the other had merely obliged the carpenters of those remoter epochs to take timber from the surrounding woods. In America it was necessary to work in a largely untraditional way, in Europe it was enough to rely on the skill and thoroughness of traditional craftsmen.

USA = RAILROADS + $

In the United States, generally speaking, production and commerce have sprung up after transport has facilitated access to raw materials. The development of modern transport began in 1803 with the entry of Ohio into the Union and the building of the National Road, which included the longest bridge in the world (320 yards). The process was continued by the building of the Erie Canal (1817–25), which helped to open up the West and lowered the cost of transport in that direction by nine-tenths. By 1850 there were 800 steamboats on the Mississippi, carrying a tonnage greater than that of the entire British merchant navy.

But what really brought about the conquest of the continent was the railway. It connected the Atlantic provinces, steeped in English puritanism, to the Pacific, tinged with the influences of Spanish Catholicism, and provided a link between two different worlds.

Those in the present day who reject the quest for closer association between different collectivities, on the ground that civilization depends on maintaining a diversity of cultures, would certainly have claimed, if they had been alive at that time, that it was dangerous so swiftly to connect two so strongly contrasting social entities. Did not certain worthy souls in France stand out against the joining of the Paris–Lyons and Lyons–Marseilles lines, on the ground that it was against all reason to think of oneself moving in twenty-four hours from the world of cooking in butter to the world of cooking in oil?

In 1828 the Baltimore–Ohio Railroad laid down its first stretch of line, a mere dozen miles long. Between 1850 and 1860 railway development proceeded at a rapid tempo, opening up the prairies and thrusting towards the Pacific. On 18 May 1869 the first trans-American rail link was formed when the Union Pacific and Central Pacific lines came together at Promontory Point (Utah). This achievement had been made possible by close co-operation between the United States Government, the governments of the different States involved, and private enterprise.

By 1893 there were five lines connecting ocean to ocean. The effect produced by the railways was almost as marked on the psychological plane as on the economic. As a historian has observed:

What Drake and his sailors in the Elizabethan age had done to give the British nation its superiority complex, Congress, the engineers and the Chinese and Irish platelayers did for the United States and for American confidence in the inevitability of material progress, by building the first railway across the continent.

With its roads, canals and navigable rivers, France had at one time possessed the most modern means of transport, adequate to ensure the economic unity of an area of 193,200 square miles. The United States was the first country fully to exploit the possibilities of the railway on a continental scale, whereas Europe, holding fast to the methods which had proved their value in the past, was content to develop the railway on a national scale only. At Peking during the same period a few members of the governing hierarchy visualized the railway as the possible instrument with which to effect the centralization of the Heavenly Empire, but Chinese traditional xenophobia rejected the 'foreign devils'' new tool. It is said that the advocate of the railway cause was exiled to Formosa (yes, even then!), on which island the first 'yellow' railway was eventually built.

As well as giving the Americans their springboard into a new dimension and leading them to embrace the intrinsic conditions of their century, the railway acted socially, as a powerfully integrative force. As the total length of permanent way in the States grew from 19 miles in 1840 to 187,500 miles in 1900, trade developed rapidly all over the Union. From 1870 onwards the use of refrigerator cars stimulated the prosperity of the prairies and the rise of Chicago, with its celebrated slaughter-yards, to be one of the world's greatest industrial centres.

Today, goods still do much more travelling in the United States than in Europe. For every ton transported in Europe there are seven in the States; and every ton transported in Europe travels an average distance of 135 miles, as against 512 miles in the States.

Transport alone would not have sufficed to create the

American common market: the dollar was necessary too. The one certain way of killing the American economy would be to compel each State to issue its own currency. Incidentally, is not monetary diversity one of the principal causes of Europe's weakness?

It has been said that the USA = railways + the dollar, just as Lenin gave the formula for the USSR as socialism + electricity. The real formula in Russia has turned out to be socialism + imported American techniques, such as tractors and TV.

Aptitude for mastering nature and setting up communications, whatever the climate and whatever the obstacles, has remained typical of America and also of the USSR which, in this sphere as in many others, has more or less copied America.

These observations supply one of the most striking explanations of American power. Organizing her own territory has compelled America to develop techniques which have proved indispensable elsewhere, whether to reclaim Canada's 'acres of snow' (Voltaire's famous phrase), to conquer wild regions and deserts, to build huge motorways, to lay out continuously serviceable airfields, to remodel big cities or to create towns at the poles, on the equator, under water or under ground.

A HUGE COMMON MARKET FROM THE LATE NINETEENTH CENTURY ONWARDS

Rich in natural resources, and eager to become independent of the Europe their ancestors had abandoned when they no longer felt at home there, the Americans aimed at becoming as nearly self-sufficient as possible by exploiting all their country's potentialities. The endeavour caused them to create a formidable internal market which so swelled and proliferated as eventually to extend to the rest of the world.

The American Civil War, coinciding with the transport revolution and the rise of the machine, put the economy into overdrive. When, in 1861, the Northern and Southern armies found themselves face to face for the first time, the United States was still not a great power. The war, by mobilizing thousands of farmers from the North and West, accelerated the mechanization of agriculture and caused an influx of immigrants, attracted by the facilities offered to settlers on American soil; the Homestead Act of 1862 granted the freehold of 200 acres to anyone undertaking to cultivate it for five years. In order to feed an army of a million men, the acreage under certain crops, such as maize in the West, was considerably increased. The total head of sheep was doubled. Industry, too, was boosted by the war. Wool production, which was quadrupled, garment manufacturing (after the invention of the sewing machine), leather goods (thanks to the introduction of mechanical sewing devices), tinned meat, not to mention naval shipbuilding and armament manufacture in general, profited greatly from the hostilities, all the more so in view of the reductions in taxes granted during the war period.

This was the time when the big cities came to birth. Michigan became the world's largest copper producer. Oil, which had been tapped for the first time in 1859 on Drake's estate at Titusville (Pennsylvania), became one of the United States' leading industries.

Nothing is more characteristic of the transfer of economic power from Europe to the United States than the development of petroleum exploitation. If the exploitation of coal was a European creation, that of petroleum, with its complex escort of drilling rigs, was American. 'Fuel oil', 'cracking', 'pipeline' – the very vocabulary speaks of American influence. Any foreigners wishing to contribute to this new technology had to settle in the States to do it: Houdry and Schlumberger, for instance.

The Civil War also gave much stimulus to scientific and technical education; between 1860 and 1870 fifteen colleges were founded, one of which was the famous Massachusetts Institute of Technology. And Foundations proliferated.

The war was also the period of the Gold Rush, which was accompanied by a silver rush (the population of Colorado increased from 32,000 to 100,000 between 1860 and 1864), and of the imminent development of the Federal banking system which was to lead the Americans over the boundaries of a vigorous internal market, out into the world market.

Subsequently, the Americans found it convenient to distribute their profits, in the form of overseas aid or long-term credits, all over the world. Among the results was an increased appetite for American products. At this stage certain American producers, even if only a minority, realized that the maximum expansion of American industry would not be achieved by their confining their attention to markets (Europe and Canada) which could pay for what they wanted, but by extending the conquest in advance to the markets of tomorrow, such as some of the South American countries, and even those of the day after tomorrow. Hence investment in under-developed countries; a big gamble on the future.

TWO MIGHT-HAVE-BEEN-USA'S: RUSSIA AND CHINA

Two other countries, Russia and China, were of American dimensions and could have profited from the fact in the same way. But Russia had an autocratic regime, structures rooted in the past, and a sense that her strength was derived from the Tsar and not from developing her territory and exploiting its resources.

China, as we have seen, rejected everything foreign, even the railway. She excluded the alphabet for the same reason.

The fact that Chinese handwriting consisted of ideograms, each a little islet of meaning in itself, led to a culture totally different from our own, which strings ideas together. A script which was synthetic instead of analytic precluded the kind of reasoning which has enabled European civilization to grow, and to grow up. Moreover the number of written characters increased and multiplied to about 80,000 and kept Chinese culture out of the reach of the masses, so that although printing was known in Peking long before Gutenberg it was never any use. The mandarins were capable of deciphering some 8,000 characters, but it cost them a lifetime's practice. Not unnaturally, they had little time left over for inventing anything new; Chinese culture remained fossilized for centuries. The China of Chairman Mao has at long last notched up a few successes in the scientific field, and launched out into industry, only because a number of Chinese have received an American or, recently, a Russian education and become accustomed to using the alphabet, sticking to it thereafter and doing their best to spread it among their compatriots.

Of the three continental-size nations, then, only the United States has been prompt to accept the scale of the technological era and to benefit accordingly.

But while the Americans have adjusted themselves, technically speaking, to the scale demanded by the inception of the planetary age, philosophically speaking they have failed to do so. Their equipment is planetary, their approach to political problems is not.

FROM THE PIONEER SPIRIT TO THE SPIRIT OF COMPETITION

The human and psychological climate in which America has been built up explains some of the guiding principles which have led to her holding two trump cards: selection by quality, and a population of mixed origins.

The making of the United States was achieved by Europeans who had left their native countries without thought of return. They had sentenced themselves to success. They may not all have been the most refined and sophisticated sons of the Old World, but they were certainly above average in energy. The man who steps out to try his luck in the wide world is a soul of hardier temper than the one who sits at home, warming his toes in the carpet-slippers of custom and tradition. Today we talk of the brain-drain; but there was a temperament-drain which started long before. Today, the pioneer spirit survives in the form of a fondness for taking risks.

Under the French economic system, the banks lend to the rich. Under the American system, loans are made to men.

During the last quarter of the nineteenth century, the ordinary American could hardly open his paper without encountering some magic name resounding with the chinking of dollars. The railroad kings, and their counterparts in the canning industry, or steel, or agricultural machinery, waged merciless war on one another. 'King' was the right word, in context; these men were in fact conquerors of a new type, and their conquests were founded on technology and organization. These conquests were led, with all drums beating, by the initiators of the gigantic enterprise which was in process of placing its stamp on the century. It was no longer a question of seizing new land for wheatfields or vineyards, or of increasing the heritage from generation to generation, but of developing a new species of action and organization.

This epic was a continuation of that of the adventurers seeking gold in the sixteenth century, or that of the Florentine merchants turned bankers (whose coin, the florin stamped with the fleur-de-lys, their city's coat of arms, dominated their age as the dollar dominates ours).

Let us recall in passing that the word 'dollar', like many of the ingredients that went into the making of America, comes from Europe: it corresponds to the hard form of the pronunciation of *thaler*, from Joachim Sthaler, a coin minted from silver from the mine of that name, now called Jachymov in Czech. The same mine also yielded the radium used by Mme Curie and, it appears, part at least of the materials of the first Russian atom bombs.

The centres of commerce and finance in the fifteenth and sixteenth centuries were also those of art, science and technology. A case in point is Florence, which gave a refuge to Galileo, so much in advance of his time, and whose cupola of Santa Maria dei Fiori represented in its own day a structural feat of unrivalled daring.

Thus there is confirmed a law of societies according to which, at a given period, the most creative collectivities are those which simultaneously mobilize boldness, intelligence and ability in organization, to make use of contemporary techniques.

The love of risk in the United States is accompanied by an urge towards output. Adventure is sought for the sake of some tangible result. The Americans know how to innovate, but refuse to change for the mere pleasure of changing. They distrust the intellectual satisfaction afforded by the creation of a large number of prototypes.

The criterion of productivity is the dollar, and is linked with another criterion, profit. The Americans have long admitted this. They judge a firm, and the men in charge of it, by its profits. It is profit which, permitting investment and technical improvements, unleashes the fundamental process which keeps America galloping far ahead of the other industrial societies and creates the various 'gaps' so much talked about in Europe, and often quite incorrectly explained. However much the notion of profit, which is inseparable from that of the consumer society, may be criticized by certain political movements, by the Chinese and by a section of the young, it nevertheless remains the foundation of human liberation. Without the profit notion and everything it represents, most of those who attack it would themselves be living at a miserably low ceiling of prosperity.

Of course abundance must be used in the right way, to liberate the human potential in every man, woman and child; it must be handled in a truly liberal spirit. But to subject it to polemical attack is to make a dramatic but sterile gesture, like the opposition of the Lyons silk-workers to the introduction of the power-loom. This denigration of material abundance is a typical case of the intellectual misconceptions which never fail to appear in periods of major change.

America's candid acceptance of profits and the profit-motive as a condition of progress is due in considerable measure to the fact that the pioneers came first and functionaries emerged only later. The Americans were under the necessity of building bridges before they had created a section of the engineering profession with specialized qualifications in bridge-building. Sometimes the bridges fell down, but that did not stop them from building more. In the USA, priority was given to action, and it still is. There is theoretical study too, but only because demanded by practical necessity. In this respect, it is curious to observe that the Russians were led to think of applying cybernetics to their railways by their conception of the world, in which man is nature's master; whereas the Americans came to it because they saw that cybernetics was a form of modernization which had money in it.

This is a far cry from a country like France, where the administration traditionally plays so large a part that, in order to develop the spirit of enterprise, it is necessary to indoctrinate not only the captains of industry but also the civil service, which would otherwise make clumsy fun of it and leave it to die.

NOTHING IS FOR KEEPS

The priority given in the States to the man who gets things done is accompanied by the rule, 'A fair chance for all and may the best man win.' Nevertheless, competition (which is the translation of personal liberty into economic terms) is subject to organization. The most prominent of the laws relating to this is the Sherman Act, the anti-trust law which compels firms to observe the principle of open competition.

This conception of the organization of economic activities has its origin in the very history of the rise and development of the United States.

The consequences it has for the economy as a whole are positive ones: by causing everything to be kept continuously in question – established situations, accepted ideas, men in power – it forces everyone to be efficient. Even the most powerful individuals are not securely enthroned. The practice which enables a group of shareholders to question the position of the directors if the company is not showing a big enough profit, and to propose their replacement by a different team, is a perfect illustration of the general attitude.

In the United States, the higher a man sets out to rise in the social hierarchy the more risks he has to take. The best jobs are not acquired once and for all by heading the short list at the age of twenty, but by accepting a wager of double or quits at every stage on the way up.

Admittedly, equality at starting is not quite as complete as it used to be in the States. But the educational doorways are far wider open than in Europe, and give everyone a chance to rise in the world. The story of the young telegraph operator who became a great industrialist (Edison) has not receded into the limbo of mythology. It remains equally valid for the industrious Italian as for the quick-witted Jew, who in many cases finds a suitable field of action in distribution, advertising or one of the service industries.

The fact that everyone has the chance of making his own life has tended to produce a high degree of mobility of labour, and still does. Mobility is even the rule inside big firms: though the presidents of eight out of the ten leading American firms have made their careers inside the organizations they now rule, they have all occupied a number of different positions and gained a wealth of experience in the labyrinth of the industrial world, that world whose size and significance have been so well emphasized by Albin Chalandon in his book *Leçons d'Amérique*: 'What strikes you at once, on coming into contact with American

life, is the primacy of industry: not only because it attracts
the country's best human resources but because, among their
various institutions, there is nothing the Americans look on as
more important than their great firms.'

THE INDIVIDUAL AS CREATOR OF THE COLLECTIVE

Another factor besides those just mentioned is the manner in
which the United States has acquired its population. Immi-
gration produced two consequences whose influence is still
much in evidence: the primacy of the individual, and the
conviction that the American system is the best.

The primacy of the individual: Over there, it is the individual
who has created the collectivity. America is the country where
the individual's name is put on the door of his office or his
working overalls; where churches run advertisements proclaiming the merits of their preachers; where citizens' contributions create, endow and enrich museums, universities and
foundations (those laboratories which mould the shape of things
to come and give birth to the future). By spotlighting the
individual and stressing individual achievement in every sphere,
America opposes Russian anonymity and French (not to say
European) technocratic arrogance. In Europe, universal suffrage is the heir of the absolute monarch who personally made
every decision affecting society as a whole, society being in
effect his property. Hence the state is generally speaking responsible for equipping society with all its major apparatus, for
the provision of education and even for culture and leisure. In
the United States the efforts of the citizens, in specific re-
groupings, are what produce and direct the state and shapes
the collectivity.

Public opinion, that is to say, the sum of individuals, counts
for more in America than anywhere else. Awareness of its reactions is a matter of continuous concern, so much so that the
holders of responsible positions are all too frequently inhibited
by it. Information in all its forms is overwhelmingly voluminous.
A quarter of the world's newspapers are published in the United
States and their circulation is one-fifth of the total. American
television has reached a stage of development which fascinates
the other industrial countries. The most diverse points of view

are expressed in the medium. The American is totally free to choose from the utterances directed at him from all sides, the difficulty being not to get the information he wants but to escape drowning in the flood. Advertising is equally ubiquitous, and expenditure on it *per capita* is six times greater than in France.

In the economic sphere the shareholder (which means Mr Average Man, since there are over 20 million shareholders in the United States) is a lively participant to whom the directors must account precisely for their actions.

The company or corporation, itself a collective organization, stands between two sets of individuals, its shareholders (as described above) and the customers. The latter receive far more consideration than in Europe, notably France, where the state monopolies, such as tobacco and telephones, and the various public services are taken for granted.

Team-spirit is highly developed in the United States and produces more extensive fields of solidarity than would otherwise exist.

Authority is functional instead of hierarchical. What counts is not rank and seniority so much as the efficiency of the group, it being understood that every member of it, while respecting collective discipline, also has the right to be respected by others; whence the far more egalitarian tone of American society as compared with European. During the war, it was a surprise to the rest of the world to discover that American admirals drew the same rations as the ordinary seamen.

Of course money creates inequalities. But it is regarded primarily as a means of exchange and as a factor of prosperity, for anyone and everyone. It is meant for circulation, not hoarding.

Confidence in the system: In Europe, the system under which one happens to live is something given in advance; imposed, not chosen. One may therefore find oneself tempted to scrutinize it and seek a reappraisal. An immigrant entering the United States, on the contrary, is assumed to accept the American way of life as it stands. To question its validity would be to question his own; the opposite attitude, criticism, is peculiar to the negroes, who did not choose their lot in life and accordingly constitute the revolutionary ferment in society.

The essential aspirations of American society – the pursuit of happiness, civic-mindedness, respect for individual liberty – would seem to be the noblest aims any political society can possess. Superior persons often regard these aims either as intrinsically contemptible or as being hypocritically exploited, a cynical device for papering over the cracks. But they are wrong; what they have failed to appreciate is the true depth of American thinking considered as a whole. The American attitude, and the nurture on which it depends, are simple and healthy, the antithesis of the preciosities which are the breath of life to 'Byzantine' or ideological societies. Campaigns of anti-American abuse are usually motivated by jealousy, not conviction.

For their part, the Americans cannot understand why others reject the ways they themselves follow with such success. They look on their way of running their society as an ideal for all. From this attitude, it is only a step to visualizing the happiness of other nations as being dependent on their adopting the American way of life – a step which a great many Americans have automatically taken, with unhappy consequences for mutual comprehension at the present time, when the peoples of the world are experiencing the dawn of the planetary age. Instead of encouraging fellowship within diversity, the United States is incapable of projecting any other vision of society than its own upon the world. This causes it to wield a divisive influence, usually unconsciously; although the whole of American history, and in particular the aid given both to a ruined postwar Europe, and thereafter to a Europe struggling to beat off the clutches of Stalinism, should have led the United States to promote federalism.

WAR, THE GIGANTIC SCHOOL OF ORGANIZATION AND ABUNDANCE

Global war is primarily an affair of organization, and both world wars were conducted by the Americans as huge industrial operations. Leaders of industry and business, experienced in commanding big organizations, tended to be made generals. It is no coincidence that General Doriot (a Frenchman by birth, as it happens) was quartermaster-general in World War Two and also Assistant Dean and Professor of Industrial Management in Harvard Business School.

Modern management practices were raised to a new pitch during hostilities. New methods were worked out, such as operational research.

When war began the United States had 6,000 aircraft; 300,000 were built in the next four years. Between 1939 and 1944, total industrial production for military purposes was multiplied fifty times over in the USA, ten in Great Britain, and five in Germany and the USSR.

The United States' fighting men are not trained on the classical lines derived from the prejudices of the nobility and the prescriptions of military law, but in accordance with the standards of industrial enterprise. The British Admiral Cunningham was badly off course when he predicted it would be a long time before the Americans had a navy: the US Navy was organized in less than a year, like a huge piece of civil engineering, and occupies today the position formerly held by the Home Fleet.

Many more examples could be quoted to illustrate this application of business methods to the needs of war. Experience shows, moreover, that the US Army, while excelling in the highly mechanized, highly industrialized type of war, encounters – as when fighting against Japan or in Vietnam – considerable difficulties in adapting itself to the methods of an enemy still at pre-industrial level, or uninhibited in the use of suicide tactics.

The fact remains that for the United States both world wars constituted a big leap ahead.

Whereas in other countries, in all periods, war has brought large-scale destruction, the effect of war on the United States, which has never experienced destruction on its own soil, has been to accelerate consumption and raise it to unforeseeable levels. Allowance being made for the rise in prices, American production in 1945 was higher by two-thirds, in real terms, than in 1939.[1]

After the war, civilian consumption took over where military had left off. Instead of collapsing soon after 1945, as predicted by Stalin, the American economy was characterized by wave upon wave of prosperity.

[1] Louis Franck, *Les Etats-Unis d'Amérique* (Paris: P.U.F.)

AMERICA INUNDATES THE WORLD

American inventions, methods and attitudes have overflowed the bounds of the United States. It is like what geologists call 'transgression': the engulfing of land by sea, either because the level of a continent has sunk or that of the water has risen. The opposite phenomenon is regression; which, unfortunately, is what is happening to Europe.

The old countries, of course, rebut this description, announcing at frequent intervals that while America wields enormous material strength, the riches of the mind are still their own special preserve. But this is to forget how highly American university degrees are prized in Europe; those holding them never fail to mention the fact, even if they have passed through the best European schools or universities, and if they have official positions in their home countries.

The dollar has replaced the pound, and Wall Street has overtaken the City as the world's leading financial centre. The US Army, whose style of waging World War Two we indicated in the preceding chapter, is, in effect, the biggest business in the world. Its chief of staff has his counterpart only in the Soviet Union. He heads an army of 3,400,000 men, with an annual budget of 63 thousand million dollars (of which 19·5 thousand million go towards materials, 20 thousand million towards personnel, 6·5 thousand million towards research and development, 1·5 thousand million towards building, etc.). He controls several thousand missiles with nuclear warheads, 40 submarines each equipped with 16 Polaris missiles, and 12,000 aircraft and helicopters. The greater part of American scientific research is carried out for his benefit. One American out of ten is employed on tasks connected with national defence; seventy-seven different branches of industry are directly concerned with it. The Pentagon, with 20,000 direct contractors and 100,000 civilian sub-contractors, is the keystone of the American economy.

'A dominant nation can be recognized from the fact that we copy it', wrote the Italian Marquis Caraccioli in 1777, during the period of French domination in Europe.

'Ninety-four per cent of the earth's inhabitants dream of being Americans,' echoed Lyndon B. Johnson in 1966. Exaggerated though this pronouncement may be, it contains a good deal of truth, judging by the signs of American influence on the world in such varied fields as economic production, the organization of modern society, and contemporary attitudes to life.

AMERICA HAS A FINGER IN EVERY PIE, FROM THE
LATEST TECHNOLOGY TO THE MOST
HUMDRUM ARTICLES

Products are the wings of ideas; method shapes our horizons; technologies mould culture. The ideas, horizons and culture of contemporary industrial society are not American but they look as if they were, because it is in the United States that they have been most spectacularly manifested, and this, moreover, in just those sectors which are characteristic of our times.

Homo automobilis, the modern centaur, was born in the United States. There are 81 million private cars on that country's roads, which means a car to approximately 2·4 inhabitants. No doubt the car would have appeared on earth without the United States, but it was there that it first emerged in a big way. Where the car is concerned, United States experience is certainly the general yardstick.

In its capacity for invading ordinary life on a truly planetary scale, the car is equalled only by television. But whereas television can be used for either of two diametrically opposite purposes – information or conditioning – and therefore requires an initial option for or against the individual (a question to which we shall revert in due course), the car, essentially, is a generator of individualism. It has a powerful catalytic action on transformations of outlook, and it penetrates everywhere; frontiers are porous to it. Begotten of technology and organization, it undermines ideologies.

Civil aviation, too, is something whose widespread everyday use was first developed in the USA. The economic and geographical size of the internal market, combined with military requirements, has placed the United States, and the USSR for that matter, in a planetary position which is in keeping with other American developments. The civil aviation fleet of any country intending to join the users of the great intercontinental air routes is bound to have recourse – as heads of state do for their official travels – to American four-engined jets, which are supplied painted in the appropriate national colours for the purpose. It is peculiarly symbolic that in this field, so heavily charged with status, the only suppliers in a position to compete are the world's two great military powers.

Photography, though not invented in the United States, is a typical instance of American influence on the world market and on the habits of modern man. American firms, producing over 12 million cameras a year, lead the world; the combined production of Germany and Japan, which come next in the list, is only half that of the US. Kodak is the biggest firm; in 15 factories and 250 other establishments scattered about the world it employs more than 100,000 people, 60,000 of these being in the USA. In 1966, with well over 25,000 products on the market, the whole group achieved a turnover of $2,150 million, a quarter of which was outside the States. Eastman, the founder of the original firm, had his eye on the world market from the start and deliberately chose a trade name which was easy to pronounce in any language. (In passing, note how early the planetary vocation of American industry revealed itself. Eastman-Kodak dates from before World War One.)

Food is going American too. The hot dog has become familiar even in France – much to the horror of connoisseurs of etymology, the expression 'hot dog' being, to the best of our knowledge, bereft of any etymological origin; a verbal mongrel without pedigree. Gastronomes are even more deeply scandalized. And most of these kinds of purist are unaware that firms like Oscar Meyer & Co. are manufacturing hot dogs in computerized factories at the rate of 36,000 an hour (see *Time*, 12 April 1968). The hot dog is catching on relentlessly; it is, so to speak, eating up Europe. But the most potent epidemic of all is the consumption of ices and iced drinks; a strikingly convincing example of the planetization of the sense of taste, and of taste. Children in all latitudes and of all races – which points to a certain unity of the species – are equally fond of these products which the United States did not invent but which, like the motor car, it has subjected to industrial treatment.

The same thing is going to happen with numbers of other food products. The American example will win: a certain way of life engenders a certain diet.

France will keep her culinary traditions going, but rather as an art reserved for special family or official occasions, and becoming gradually rarer.

The American presence in the world takes many forms.

The interval in any cinema programme anywhere may include an advertisement for 'Washmatic', followed by 'Twenty' make-up, one of the Ford models and Panty underwear. On the screens of the same cinemas, Walt Disney has emerged as the great story-teller on the planetary scale, the twentieth century's Charles Perrault or Mother Goose. Who could have prophesied, a good many years ago now, that a little character like Mickey Mouse was destined to become a world figure? Pop-singers from all over the world seek to crown their success by a successful tour in the States, just as film actors have long regarded Hollywood as the place which really counts. Many other American influences are at work, and they are typical of our times.

The whole question of American industrial domination is summed up in the fact that the United States is a long way ahead both in advanced fields, such as atomic development and space-exploration, and in perishable or semi-durable consumer goods, such as food and cars. There is no need to portray this phenomenon here; it has already been adequately stressed in *Les Clés du pouvoir* ('The Keys of Power')[1] and *Le Défi américain* ('The American Challenge'),[2] published in 1964 and 1967 respectively. But we ought just to remind ourselves that the widening gap between the United States and the rest of the world is visible not only in computers and other advanced fields, but in very simple things based on nothing more than a little imagination.

Jean Creiser, after investigating the dominion of the computer in the United States, declared in *Le Figaro* for 2 March 1968 that in ten years' time there would probably be more Americans with a knowledge of Basic (a special, simple language devised for conversing with a computer) than of French. The gulf that threatens to appear between the United States and a country like France involves not only the number of computers in use but the number of their users, who, in Europe, are a select few.

[1] Michel Drancourt, *Les Clés du pouvoir* (Fayard).
[2] J.-J. Servan-Schreiber, *Le Défi américain* (Denoël).

In the United States they tend to be a majority: schoolboys and schoolgirls, university students, trade unions as well as employers' organizations, business firms and libraries. There were 40,000 computers working in the United States in 1967 (as against 8,000 in Western Europe); 100,000 more will be installed over the next ten years. The computer is introduced into the stream of normal working activity without causing so much as a ripple, being regarded as a natural extension of mechanization. The Americans know that the computer does not of itself create good organization, but also that good organization is what enables the potentialities of the computer to be used to the full; and on this score they have nothing to fear. In France, on the other hand, because business and administration have not kept their standards of organization up to the level required by our industrial age, the massive arrival of the computer causes some degree of anxiety. It is as if the learner-driver of a bubble car had suddenly been put behind the wheel of a Ferrari.

Despite the strenuous efforts of forward-looking individuals in Europe to optimize the methods which allow computers to be used, it is highly probable that the United States will settle down to live happily with the computer both more quickly and more completely than other countries. Once again, we shall find ourselves having to copy those who used to copy us.

At the other end of the technical spectrum, America is still the pacemaker, the field laboratory, in the use of all sorts of devices and aids for simplifying the actions of everyday life; sprays, for example, for coating surfaces with a wide variety of substances, such as polishes or cleaning agents, on the lines of the old-fashioned atomizer. In that great country, any invention which lightens the load of human work, be it by ever so little, is sure of attention; nothing of this kind is left to go by default.

AMERICA'S PRESENT PREFIGURES THE FUTURE OF OTHERS

American influence does not only affect objects (bulldozers, scrapers, draglines); it also works in the key of organization, and thus affects structures and attitudes. Its impetus comes radiating out from America to collide with many of our habits. A defence-mechanism often adopted by conservatives is to camouflage their archaic mentality under a convenient cloak of nationalism. It does, after all, look better to pronounce in favour of what is Spanish or French and against what is American, rather than in favour of the past and against the future.

Anything coming from the United States can be interpreted either as a sign of foreign invasion or as the future knocking on the door; it depends on your point of view. Whatever opponents of America may say, the second interpretation is usually the one commanding more assent. The '1985 report' appended to the French Fifth Plan predicted that, twenty years from the date of writing, France would be in the same situation as the United States in 1965; the only variations, more or less realistically assessed, were in matters of detail.

ADAPTATION TO TECHNICAL ORGANIZATION, OR CONVERSION TO THE AMERICAN SYSTEM?

Let us look at some other terms, those referring to economic and social organization in a more general sense. If management was French, it would be called *science de la direction*; if marketing was French, it would be called *technique d'approche du marché*; if discount was French, it would be called *rabais*. But management, marketing and discount were not born in France (though they have infiltrated the French language): they are imports from the United States, like public relations (which has been domesticated into French as *'relations publiques'*).

The practical lessons in economic affairs today are reaching us from the United States and only from there. We have borrowed nothing from elsewhere, even from the other super-power, Russia – except planning, which we accept as an idea while rejecting its content.

The presence of American troops on our continent in the final phase and after the end of the Second World War might have taught the French to understand something of American power, both as to the value of its methods and the efficiency of its tools. But it seems all too clear that the French yielded yet again to their perennial assumption that they have nothing whatsoever to learn from anyone. The Germans reacted differently: contact with the Americans inspired them with a determination to become the Americans of Europe; no unreasonable ambition either, seeing that many of the good qualities of industrial America are simply a wider application of the German industrial genius, the genius of the Ruhr and the German chemical industry. The USA has been described as 'Germany without the Junkers'; if this is true, it was only natural for a Germany without Junkers to be fascinated by the USA.

It must not be forgotten that Germany was to Europe in about 1910 what the United States is to the world now. Germany had given a big new impetus to the main branches of industrial production and exerted a fertilizing influence on the field of invention, in heavy engineering as well as in what was practically her own creation, the chemical industry. In the years preceding the First World War, Europe's railways were virtually becoming a German system. It was German railway technique which was taught at Kharkov University and in the Balkans. Germany was extending her industrial influence into the Middle East, relying on the building of the Baghdad railway as the spearhead of her conquest. However, the representatives of the most advanced technical progress of the period, such as Haber (the inventor of the Haber process for manufacturing ammonia), were moving familiarly in the social circles of the Hohenzollern dynasty, who lived in an atmosphere of hunting trophies and military glory and indulged in the conviction that industrial might was meant for winning wars, blind to the far greater benefits it brings when harnessed to the needs of peace. Well do we know what consequences flowed from these dreams of domination.

The ruin of Germany after the Armistice of 1918 left such a technological void that, in the railway sphere, the French Government took the initiative in creating the Union Internationale des Chemins de Fer, and gave ample support to it.

After the Second World War, when the problem was not only to reconstruct Europe but simultaneously to modernize it, the ideas necessary for restoring productivity were inevitably taken from the lessons rammed home by the example of the United States.

Before the Atlantic had become a 'river', American influence was transmitted to Europe as it were by remote control and delayed action. Distribution provides an illuminating illustration.

1878 was the year when Frank Winfield Woolworth launched his stores ('nothing over five cents') in the United States. He started one in Liverpool in 1909. But the first Uniprix did not appear in France until 1928.

Self-service, based on the development of branded goods and originally known as 'cash and carry', was started by Clarence Saunders in 1916. It was first tried in France in the 1950's.

In 1930, in the depths of the depression, Michael Cullen[1] opened his first supermarket. The earliest French successes in this field are a mere five years old.

Finally, in 1948, Don Casto conceived the shopping centre ('no parking, no business'). It was not until 1955 that the first such centre was opened in Europe, at Vallingby in Sweden.

In future, American innovations in distribution technique will reach the outside world more quickly: hundreds of business experts now attend courses at the Dayton (Ohio) headquarters of the National Cash Register Corporation, to hear about the latest experiments in the USA and their results. Even if, on getting home, they say that what they saw in the States is unsuited to transplantation, they remain deeply affected by it. And there are always a few bolder spirits who dare to disturb their country's ingrained habits by applying the lessons brought back from Dayton. In many cases they are handsomely rewarded, for although they are at bottom merely plagiarizing the Americans, they find themselves thereby placed in the forefront of profitable progress at home.

There are certain fields in which American influence comes up against stiff resistance, but it will overcome this in the long run. Certainly we must hope it will. Consider, for instance, what can happen to the stock market. Either Europe will lay the foundations of a great financial market-place and, by operating it on Wall Street principles, will enable European capital to fertilize the continent; or, neglecting her opportunity, she will leave Wall Street to become practically the sole centre of world finance.

---

[1] Cf. Étienne Thil, *Les Inventeurs du commerce moderne* (Arthaud).

MANAGEMENT, THE MOST SPECTACULAR
INUNDATION OF ALL

In the present stage of development reached by our society, the main field in which American influence is making itself felt is the running of business and industry. American practice has contributed much to the thinking of those leaders in the business world who, finding themselves having to build up large industrial and financial complexes, want to make certain of having them thoroughly under control.

Management, in the contemporary sense of the term, is in a fair way to becoming the typical modern method of running a firm, and its basic principles were discovered and applied at an early stage in the United States. Alfred P. Sloan is usually regarded as being the father of management. As Durant's assistant before succeeding him as head of General Motors, he had been struck by the frequency with which Durant 'overloaded himself' with work.[1] 'Important decisions had to wait until he was free, and were often made impulsively.' Sloan came to recognize the necessity of discovering the principles of organization and the division of labour in industrial undertakings. It was observance of those principles which made General Motors the world's leading industrial enterprise.

Alfred P. Sloan soon attracted a following in his own country and, as time went on, in the rest of the world.

Marcel Demonque, the President of Ciments Lafarge, is accustomed to remark that a man is better at running a business in Europe if the firm has a branch in America. An increasing number of individuals in the upper strata of European business are striving to learn from American experience. Even though the environment with which they are concerned in Europe is different from that on the other side of the Atlantic, they are convinced that the superiority of American firms is chiefly due to greater organizing ability at the top.

Claude Labouret, on his return from studying at the Harvard Business School, wrote a short paper epitomizing the way his colleagues, in France and elsewhere in Europe, evaluate the mentality and outlook of the men in responsible positions in American business and industry.

[1] *My Years with General Motors*, by A. P. Sloan (Sidgwick). Roger Priouret, *La France et le Management* (Denoël).

Progress being the objective, business activity is aimed at the future, so that detecting the nature of the future is the main preoccupation of the men at the top. Conservatism and inertia lead to decay. Only movement ensures survival. The terms of the business vocabulary continually reflect ideas such as foresight, plan, objectives, research, creativeness and innovation. Anything obsolescent or worn-out is a bogy.

The first thought of those in charge must always be to detect market tendencies and weigh up their probable effects on business. They are then in a position, after taking a good look at their firm's weak and strong points and assessing the means and methods to be employed, to decide on a policy and define objectives in such terms as their fellow-workers will fully understand.

The Americans are pragmatic: an idea is of no interest unless it can be put to the test, and a programme is worthless unless it leads to good results in practice.

Practical ability – successful realization and execution – is more highly valued than intelligence in conception.

Progress is made in a sea of uncertainty. Risk is accepted as the price of movement and life. The business ethic includes the acceptance of loss and of a competitor's consequent gain, and is kept under careful scrutiny by the legal authorities.

Inconsistency and a lack of continuity in the line of action are regarded as a sign that events and circumstances have taken control, instead of being controlled. An adjective much used in English stresses the need to be 'consistent' with the policy and objectives of the firm.

A firm's prosperity, and the competence of those running it, are measured in terms of profit.

Profit is defined clearly as the difference between capital costs and the yield on investment.

The art of directing a business can thus be reduced to finding money at low cost and obtaining the highest return from it, which, after all, is simply the ultimate logic of what we call a capitalist system.

The report adds:

Europe, in its age and maturity, habitually believes that while America is on top as regards wealth, know-how and productivity, the Atlantic's eastern shores still have a monopoly of culture and inventiveness. It may be that this belief is becoming more and more illusory. History shows that culture and civilization accompany prosperity and political supremacy.

In exporting American organizational methods and the American system of industrial and commercial concentration, the United States is in fact broadcasting something much more than recipes for prosperity, since the firm is to modern society what the cell is to a living organism: the firm, quite simply, is what characterizes our epoch. We are not implying that society should aim at nothing but the smoother functioning of business activity, any more than the sole aim of an organism is to ensure smooth cellular functioning.

In spite of all the progress achieved in the United States the development of management is still far from having reached its end. Its foundations were pre-cybernetic. The next job is to create post-cybernetic management. If Europe were to grasp this task firmly she could make it her turn to be the teacher and force America to develop, and other countries too; though America would have fewer initial inhibitions to overcome.

AMERICAN FOUNDATIONS, LABORATORIES FASHIONING THE FUTURE

Looking beyond American business, it is in America's Foundations (with a capital F) that we can see a further cause of America's power and of the role she has assumed in our world. A considerable fraction of the profits made in business has been diverted into research and other intellectual activities, enabling thoughtful men to pursue their studies freely. These Foundations are the contemporary counterpart of the medieval monasteries and the regular orders (as distinct from the secular clergy), at the period when the temporal power of emperors and kings provided the material support which enabled St Bernard of Citeaux and other great minds to work towards the radiance destined to blaze forth triumphantly in the century after their own. In Chapters Five and Six, which will be devoted to our proposals for the European challenge, Europe's wager on the future, we shall return at some length to these Foundations – crucibles in which the future is prepared – and the need to create and develop their analogues in Europe.

Meanwhile, it should be noted at once that in America these Foundations work in a climate of freedom, whereas in the USSR, where there is the same preoccupation with the future, there is no thought of escaping from strict dependence on the state and the Party; a fact which automatically precludes certain hypotheses about the future and impoverishes the spectrum of research.

America's various Foundations have directly or indirectly inspired the best of that country's political actions (the Marshall Plan, programmes for liquidating poverty and under-development, anti-pollution programmes, and the study now being made at the Ford Foundation of the negro problem and urbanization). But, however open-minded, these Foundations are all tinged with Americanism, and their influence is correspondingly limited. To solve trans-national problems, our Foundations must be trans-national too.

THE USA AS THE MAINSPRING OF THE INDUSTRIAL WORLD

The thrusting expansion which, in a space of fifty years, has made the United States into the mainspring of the world of industry is in itself a success-producing factor. The surging advance generates optimism. And when the atmosphere is optimistic and development substantial, private interests are attracted to take a hand in the game for the advantages it offers them.

This expansionist American economy, through the liberation of its potential and the adjustment of its structures to fit the continental scale, demolishes taboos and conservatism. The results are therefore not far removed from those pursued under the Soviet economy, which takes the opposite route, making a clean sweep of the past and imposing innovation from above. Europe meanwhile has not got further than attempts at conversion and adaptation.

So it is not surprising that, in today's world, New York has come to be regarded as the capital of business enterprise, and Moscow as that of the state and its apparatus. Nor is it surprising that the United States serves increasingly as the standard and pacemaker for the rest of the world.

It would be a mistake to assume from this that those who admire or detest the United States necessarily have any understanding of the principles responsible for that country's success.

But both partisans and opponents find America far more engrossing than any other nation, even if only because of the flood of information poured out by the Americans about themselves and their affairs; whereas the USSR is very niggardly in releasing any very solid information about itself.

Prior to the Vietnam war and the explosion of the negro problem, the Americans were at peace with their consciences.

They are brought up to respect their institutions. They are subject like other men to the disciplines of work, and both in this and in their private lives they have a sense of being citizens. In their relations with the outside world they feel they have done their duty. They would like to do more; they would like to export happiness, as well as their structures and machines. But they encounter resistances which they cannot understand. When they think they are being generous they are treated as imperialists. Though full of good will, they provoke hostility.

It would be easier to forgive the United States for being wealthy if it were not also powerful and addicted to moralizing.

The American system is probably the most effective for ensuring material prosperity, but its transplantation to other, considerably poorer countries would require that the latter make a prodigious bound ahead to catch up; this, it is unrealistic to expect. Moreover, the exportation of America looks different from what the Americans themselves imagine. The Cadillac proudly flaunted by many dignitaries of the 'third world' is the equivalent of the royal mantle of earlier ages. What is normal in America becomes, in those parts of the world, a badge of wealth. The image of the United States gets twisted; the under-privileged peoples associate the Americans with those whom they see behaving in an American way in their own countries, that is, driving about in a Plymouth or staying at a Hilton hotel.

This reputation is due to the fact that, in the United States, luxury has been rendered democratic to an extent as yet undreamed-of on nine-tenths of the earth's surface; even in the European countries we have glimpsed no more than the beginning of the process. The Americans, in recommending capitalism to others, honestly believe they are offering the best thing they have got. But in many parts of the world, capitalism is a harder sell than communism.

In October 1967 the Red Square in Moscow was the scene of a huge march-past on the occasion of the fiftieth anniversary of the Communist régime. Not long after, on 17 November, *Time* devoted its editorial to 'Fifty Years of Capitalism'. In

reading it one sees all the difference between ideology and pragmatism.

That U.S. life has changed dramatically for the better in the past half-century is a commonplace. ... In the period before World War I, the garment industry was emerging from the era of the seven-day week and the $5 weekly paycheck. Today ... the average worker gets $2·60 an hour for a 35-hour week ... the worker in the earlier period had to work one hour and 35 minutes to buy a dozen eggs; for the same eggs now he spends twelve minutes on the job. A man's suit, which cost him 75 hours of labor then, calls for fewer than 20 hours now.

One key to this unprecedented prosperity is the astonishing productivity ... that has trebled since 1917, far outstripping the performance of workers in any other industrial society (in 1960, European workers, for example, roughly reached the level of output attained by the American worker in 1925) .... In 1917, when the U.S. population was 103 million, the nation's gross national product was about $75 billion (in prices adjusted for inflation) compared with about $800 billion now, for a population of roughly 200 million.

As the nation's wealth has soared, the distribution of that wealth has changed just as strikingly. Before World War I, only 4% of U.S. families earned more than $10,000 a year; today, 25% do.

... An infant born in 1916 had a life expectancy of no more than 52 years. This year's child can expect to surpass three score and ten.

The material rise is only part of the story. There have been cultural gains as well. With paperbacks in every drugstore, reading has soared. Thirty thousand titles were published last year. ... Magazine circulation has multiplied tenfold in 50 years. ... Early in the century, perhaps 4% of young Americans between 18 and 21 were in colleges and universities; now, roughly 45% are ....

To this evidence in favour of a system which has proved its worth more conclusively than Soviet communism, may be added the facts that, in the United States, seventy-five per cent of the national income is distributed in the form of salaries and wages, as against sixty-five per cent in France; and that those 'capitalist hyenas', the boss-class, have been replaced by managers who have won their positions solely on merit. America's outstanding social evolution has eliminated, or at least considerably reduced, the defects of which Karl Marx accused the capitalism of his day. Nevertheless the habit persists, and not only in communist circles either, of picturing American capitalism as the Big Bad Wolf. But, though there is doubtless a long way to go before everything is perfect in the United States, it is an unmistakable fact that the American system has given the world a very striking and positive example of social development.

In spite of all this, however, fifty years of communism were celebrated with much more of a flourish than fifty years of capitalism. Why?

While the structures of American industry and business constitute a yardstick for the best firms in the rest of the world, the political structures of the United States cannot be said to have the same exemplary value.

American policies can be seen to be getting more and more out of phase with the functioning of industrial society. The organization of the American firm is far better than that of the state. It is not surprising that the economic structures of the United States are envied, while its political practices are criticized.

For the same reason, the pressure of American capital is regarded in some quarters as a more intolerable kind of interference than the military attacks of the old countries on their neighbours.

THE ACHILLES' HEEL OF THE
AMERICAN GIANT

For many years the Americans held fast to the Monroe doctrine, which can be summarized as 'Don't come bothering us, and we won't bother you'. The basis of this position was, of course, a vigilant desire to safeguard the smooth functioning of American society by avoiding any involuntary entanglement in the affairs of the outside world. The immigrants, after all, had left Europe to escape not only from the poverty but from the conflicts and abuses of their home countries. But the policy contained a contradiction, in that the preservation of American security might demand political action outside the territory of the Union, a fact clearly grasped by the Americans in 1917. After the great conflagration, the hope of preventing a recurrence inspired in some of their leaders, including President Wilson, the noble vision of a world order based on the League of Nations. As we know, American public opinion did not support the idea and America did not join the League, the failure of which was largely due to her absence. In 1944 America took the lead in founding the United Nations Organization, in which she placed great hopes. But she was mistaken concerning the intentions of Stalin. She possessed, in the person of President Roosevelt, a great leader who envisaged the organization of the world as an expression in four terms (USA, USSR, Great Britain and China), and who doubtless, at heart, saw it as an American world. He was reckoning without Stalin. Where the Soviet dictator was concerned, America moved abruptly from excessive confidence to the policy of containment. Wherever the communist world wanted to build a new bastion, in Greece, Berlin or Korea, America set up a barrier.

To avert the poverty which breeds communism, she carried out in Europe and Japan an active programme the generosity of which was accompanied by an eye to her own defence. For which no one can blame her. What the United States wants, in fact, is to see the foundation principles of her own civilization maintained intact in the countries which stand as ramparts about her. She is thus induced, at decreasing intervals, to intervene against someone or something – always against; a style of action which promotes division between peoples, rather than association.

A philosophy of action based on free enterprise and anti-communism is even less of an answer to the problems of the planetary age in that, even in the United States, the facts no longer fit the ideas which, so to speak, constitute free enterprise's engine-power; and recent political development is such that anti-communism no longer adds up to a coherent view of the world.

AMERICA'S INTERNAL CONTRADICTIONS, OR THE AMBIGUITIES OF FREE ENTERPRISE

'Free' enterprise in the United States is as enterprising as ever, but 'free' has lost a good deal of its pristine purity.

State intervention has become ever more frequent and more pregnant with consequences, the latter being the result of socialization-phenomena which are themselves the outcome of technical progress. In our day, even the most liberal-minded state cannot help intervening in one way or another, whether to provide capital equipment for some important collective undertaking, to fight pollution, to take charge of some sector of public education, or to provide security for the old. Nor can it avoid participation in the launching of new technological endeavours. Research and innovation are so expensive that the necessary funds can be supplied, in one form or another, only from the public purse, the most usual method being taxation to finance investment.

Until the 1929 depression the Federal Government intervened only rarely. Its aim was to hold the ring for competition, the effect being to stimulate the growth of a market economy and to force business to be efficient and progressive; and that was about all. As for the individual states, they confined themselves to such matters as the police, justice and a certain amount of social welfare.

The 1929 crisis and the need to counter its effects forced the Federal Government to come out of its shell and lend support both to the development of mass consumption and to the encouragement of business, and it has gone on doing so ever since. Prosperity breeds prosperity, and when the producers find themselves without a market the Government steps in to re-open the blocked outlets, either by creating new activities or by redistributing revenue. The great thing is to get the stalled engine running again. As President Eisenhower told his compatriots during a recession, almost in as many words, 'Consumption is your duty'.

But the resulting state intervention goes far beyond slight, transient adjustments; it directly influences the orientation of industrial and economic structures.

The signal for this new departure was the creation of the Tennessee Valley Authority in 1933, and the Federal Government's development of the hydro-electric resources of that valley.

The Second World War forced the state into a deep involvement in industry, and even more so in scientific research.

The Manhattan Project, which developed the A-bomb, brought over 7,000 scientists and engineers into close collaboration. At the end of the war there was a brain drain into the private sector until, under the MacMahon law of 1946, the AEC (Atomic Energy Commission) was set up, and responsibility for nuclear programmes passed from military into civilian hands. The national laboratories regained their denizens, and from 1948 onwards the nominal roll of the Commission's scientific and technical personnel was bigger than that of the Manhattan Project had ever been.

The AEC has been given a special structure of its own: political command is entrusted to five members of the Board, assisted by a General Committee with advisory powers. Nominations to all these posts are made by the President of the US in person, including that to the chairmanship of the Commission. Once a year the President decides on the quantity of fissile materials to be manufactured and the Commission sees that these are delivered to the armed forces, and authorizes the latter to produce or acquire nuclear weapons.

Private firms had a share in these activities from the start and still have, which has been good for their profits but has certainly not strengthened the principle of free enterprise.

Apart from the Atomic Energy Commission, the prime movers of the United States economy at the present time are NASA and the Pentagon. The Department of Defence (DOD) is the mainspring of the country's scientific and technical activity. The Defence Department's policy is to invite research-workers to submit projects and, if these seem promising, to subsidize them. A directive from the President in 1965 having recommended a wider institutional and geographical spread of this financial support, the DOD has been encouraging 'specialized programmes connected with national defence tasks' in a large number of universities.

The main purpose of NASA is to maintain American supremacy in space. It is at present developing the equipment and technique which will enable an American to land on the moon[1]. Having put out nearly ninety per cent of its research and development work to private firms, it has to co-ordinate the activities of several thousand contractors and sub-contractors. It also finances scientific work in universities and gives research grants to a number of students working for their doctorates. In 1967 its budget totalled 4·5 thousand million dollars of which 612 million went on fundamental research, 648 million on applied research and 3 thousand million on development.

Since the publication of the remarkable report of the Scientific Affairs Committee of OECD, it has been known that, because of its emphasis on military expenditure, the United States Government is partly responsible for the financing of about two-thirds of American research and development. The private sector, which finances the remaining one-third, carries out some eighty-five per cent of the work, a fact which demonstrates better than anything else the state's determination to help American firms, and its wish to associate them in all the country's large undertakings. Fundamental research, on the other hand, is still largely the concern of the universities.

In 1980, 46 thousand million dollars will be devoted to research, amounting to about 3·4 per cent of a gross national product of 1,600 thousand million dollars. (In 1965, expenditure on research and development was 21 thousand million dollars, as against 2 thousand million in Great Britain, the leader in Europe in this field.)

In a space of twenty years, expenditure on research and development in the United States has been multiplied by fifteen,

[1] Since this was written the Americans have of course landed on the moon. (*Tr.*)

while the gross national product was multiplied by three and expenditure on education by ten. Expenditure for military purposes and the maintenance of the 'balance of terror' is still absorbing the greater part of the country's finances. But during the last few years the amounts allocated to the 'environmental sciences' – health, culture, and working and living conditions – have been growing rapidly.

THE INCREASING PRESSURE OF STATE INTERVENTION

The conviction held in the United States is that economic efficiency demands the maintenance of free enterprise and the encouragement of competition, even in the field of public contracts. But it is impossible for life under organized competition to remain altogether 'liberal', particularly when the technological advances on which firms depend for their most important developments are tied in with the plans and activities of the state. The latter, moreover, is extending its actions in many fields, as is shown by the fact that in 1967 President Johnson appointed a Federal Minister of Transport; legislation concerning transport had previously been the responsibility of the individual states. The only wider authority had been an Interstate Commerce Commission, with functions something like those of a trade tribunal on a large scale. This arrangement, however, had become inadequate for the proper handling of the country's transport problems.

The United States is still a federal country where many problems of secondary importance are concerned, but tends towards centralization on essentials (with the exception, fortunately, of education).

In 1929 there were 533,000 Federal Government employees and 2,532,000 local government employees. By 1964 these figures had risen to 2,438,000 and 7,153,000 respectively. Whereas in 1929 there were 4·3 Federal and 20·8 local employees for every 1,000 Americans, in 1964 the figures were 12·2 and 37·2.

Thus the United States is becoming increasingly national and central in structure and moving away from the local, federal structures which are what the world needs most.

THE LIMITATIONS OF ANTI-COMMUNISM

American foreign policy is dictated by two motives: the quest for an understanding with the USSR so as to avoid atomic war; and the resolve, already mentioned, to contain communist influence. The second objective was clear and definite so long as communism had a single centre, the USSR, striving to extend its influence in Europe. But clarity has been succeeded by confusion because communism now has two rival centres, Moscow and Peking; because the USSR is equally concerned with raising its standard of living as well as extending its influence externally; and, most important of all, because some peoples are accused of communism when what they are really struggling for is freedom and independence.

In a clearsighted essay, *Pax Americana*[1] Ronald Steel has put his finger on the limitations and dangers of American policy as at present conceived. 'Although she possesses greater power than any nation in history, the United States cannot impose her will even on a technologically backward society of a few million people.' By attempting to do so she has bogged herself down in military operations and aroused the hostility of peoples who ought on the contrary to be on terms of mutual understanding both with the United States and with one another.

A return to isolationism would be no solution. 'America is fated to play a dominant world role during the remaining decades of this century, and perhaps for a good deal longer.' If America declined to play that role there would be economic collapses in various parts of the world; and the USSR would be the only world power left facing China. Hardly a recipe for international amity.

Arguing from this situation, some Americans preach a return to the old idea of spheres of influence. But that arrangement tends to tie the weak to the apron-strings of the strong; which runs counter to the idea that the natural diversity of human beings should be developed to the benefit of all mankind.

There would be a danger of whipping up nationalistic rivalries and strengthening them, just when they need it least and are becoming the dominant world ideology. Anti-communism finds itself totally defeated by nationalism; communism

[1] The Viking Press, 1967.

itself is sometimes powerless against it. 'Not only is there no longer a single source of authority, nor are there even, as there were just after the Second War, several centres of authority; now, every nation is in some sort its own bishop.'

There is even a proliferation of nuclear power, which, as everyone is aware, is one of the great challenges of the modern world.

In the final part of his study, Ronald Steel suggests that his country abandon its worn-out myths, including the cold war. But, like many other analysts of the contemporary situation, he does not really open any new paths into the future. Though understanding that a policy on the planetary scale is required, he fails to transcend the American dilemma: which is that if the greatest country in the world is to become still greater, it must transcend its own limits and work on a plane beyond that of nationhood.

TOWARDS A REVISION OF THE CONCEPTS BEHIND AMERICAN POLICY

In the programmes carried out by the Americans after the war to save the worst-hit countries from tyranny and ensure their economic recovery, and in those they applied in the spirit of the good Samaritan to the under-privileged countries, they failed to recognize one of the essential phenomena of our times, in spite of having shown such appreciation of it in their own undertakings: namely, the pace of present-day development.

Technology is developing so fast as to revolutionize the preconditions of politics and world relationships.

The Americans, the 'founding fathers' of the atomic bomb, had not foreseen how soon the USSR and China would join them in the possession of nuclear armaments, and that the United States would become vulnerable from two sides at once; Chicago, after all, lies between Moscow and Peking.

This very fact should be enough to convince the Americans how wrong they are in presuming to take the fate of the world solely in their own hands, and to rescue them from the temptation which is ever the pitfall of the strongest party – the temptation to isolate themselves and 'go it alone'.

Simultaneously they must revise the general philosophy of liberal capitalism, which, under present conditions, must inevitably be capitalism-with-controls. They must also take better cognizance of the growth of huge firms whose radius of action goes far beyond the scope and implications of the national market, the home market. Systematically to support them is to invite the charge of imperialism. But to leave them to their own devices is to negate the need for superior political organization, above economics, and to risk seeing the world shaken by economic crises which no organizational entity would be capable of foreseeing, averting or containing.

Technical advances in the information media have made the American negroes more conscious than ever before of the gap between the haves and the have-nots, and have set their sensibilities on fire. The negroes have realized that the position they have been occupying within the Union is that of an underdeveloped people, and they have displayed the typical symptoms of that position: the touchiness, the grabbing insensitivity in the pursuit of just claims, the refusal of all advice, coupled with a demand for courtesy and consideration; the whole seasoned with an aimlessly vindictive spirit and a certain amount of straightforward jealousy.

The limit towards which all these difficulties tend, the point on which they converge, is this: American policy needs to be renewed, inside and out, without distinction between home and foreign policy – since what is due for overhaul and replacement is the whole outfit of concepts and methods.

Otherwise, and despite the technical drive towards planetization on the one hand and, on the other, the gradual drawing-together of the two great powers – not so much to ensure the best as to avert the worst –, the combined action of the USA and the USSR will have the effect of accentuating the division of the world into two camps, until such time as China and the general resurgence of nationalism shall plunge mankind into some kind of international anarchy.

ONE OF THE GREAT TASKS FOR EUROPE:
TRANSPOSING THE AMERICAN APPROACH INTO THE
WORLD KEY

With the situation as it is, in what direction ought we to be steering the future as from this moment?

The new course to be set must take two things into account: (*a*) the superior efficiency of American society, which nobody denies; and

(*b*) the necessity of dissociating planetary affairs from those of any single country, however powerful and modern, and however useful to the rest of the world it may be. The architects of the future must reject this monolithic construction, because it puts the future in pawn to the caprices of public opinion in the dominant country. Experience has, moreover, proved the inability of both American and Soviet Russian society to create a form of organized international life corresponding to the needs of the planetary era.

The true solution demands the presence of Europe as the intermediate agent.

Taking it as proved that the USA/USSR division of the world is insufficiently constructive, and also that the American mentality is one which cannot be assimilated by other countries without preliminary adaptation, Europe becomes the indispensable political filter, the medium through which will be derived those new types of relationship between peoples which will foster their endeavours towards federation.

The example set by America will be one of the ingredients passing through this filter, and could not possibly be left out; but the final result must embody new standards and a new outlook, adapted to the planetary dimension.

It is clear that from whatever side we approach the great problems of political orientation in the planetary age – whether from the technical side (Chapter One) or that of United States influence (Chapter Two), the conclusion we reach is that Europe must return to her age-long tradition: she must give up imitating and once more become creative.

CHAPTER THREE

WHERE EUROPE STANDS NOW

At the moment when the world is moving into the planetary age, Europe's position is that of a collectivity losing speed, running down. Europe clutches her former ambitions about her like mourning robes.

Bearing the scars of her past, bruised and shaken by the wars she herself has occasioned, she conducts herself in a manner which, seen against the background of the contemporary world-dimension, is merely provincial.

She who was once the active ferment in civilization can now assert her individuality only by decrying the economic power of the United States and the military might of the Soviet Union, and by trying to make herself look big in the eyes of the smaller or weaker members of the family of nations.

It is true she has 'never had it so good', and may therefore choose to think that she still has a real and important part to play; but that is an illusion. To be influential, it is not enough to be prosperous. The designing and construction of the future (assuming the fundamental material problems to have been solved) is a task demanding much more than that recipe for greater material well-being which has in any case already been perfected by the United States and, where other countries are concerned, now remains only to be applied.

If, in the various European countries, there still are a few men capable of thinking and acting in terms transcending their national frontiers, they lack the economic and political power which alone would enable them to propagate their influence on a contemporary scale, the world scale.

The only way Europe can heave herself out of her intellectual doldrums is to become sharply aware of the imperatives of our epoch and accept the necessity of organizing herself in a new and different way. She must stop fobbing herself off with mini-realizations.

Frontiers constitute a preconception which must be abandoned in face of the technological challenge, a challenge which no European country, not excluding Britain, is capable of meeting alone.

No longer is Europe entitled to speculate whether her new role can be played within the framework of her traditions or whether it demands a new one. She must either set about building that new framework herself, or resign herself to meaninglessness.

Of all regional collectivities, she is the one best suited, by her very weakness, to bring the genuine transnational spirit to birth; having lost her leadership, she is in a position to establish federal connections between the world's collectivities without arousing the same suspicions as the USA or the USSR. She is, after all, just as anxious as the rest of the world to escape from the patronage of either.

EUROPE IN DECLINE

THE EFFECT OF TWO WORLD WARS

Though Europe has been able – with American help – to wipe out the material traces of the two wars by which she has been devastated in a quarter of a century, her moral strength has still not recovered from them. The wounds inflicted by Nazism have still not entirely healed.

All, or nearly all, of the European countries are suffering in common from the complexes begotten of the two wars; all or nearly all are, in effect if not in appearance, in the same position as Germany, divided between two rival power blocs.

After the storm of 1914–18 France felt herself to be the leading world power, and on the military plane this was at least apparently true. Taking as her premise the fact that industrial supremacy had not sufficed to save Germany from defeat, France mistakenly concluded that peasant values were the true values, superior to all others, and the Chamber of Deputies, enveloped in a cloud of wishful thinking, turned its back on the capital modernization which the country's circumstances demanded.

Again, so far from admitting that her defeat in 1940 was the result of the enemy's technical superiority, France took refuge in a 'back to the soil' attitude and a mistrust of 'materialistic civilization'. After the liberation, the majority of the French recovered their connection with their country's past either by simply regarding the 1940 collapse as an exception, or by affecting to think that by participating in the final phase of victory France had regained her status as a world power. Only a very few understood that traditional values had vanished in the recent storm of destruction, and that the irresistible drive of modern industrialization could no longer be resisted. There is no need to look further than this for the cause of the sometimes bewildering reactions of France on the threshold of the planetary age. She would have preferred that age to begin about 1910, when she would have been in a position to take a leading role.

Great Britain lost her empire after winning the Second World War. Her victory practically ruined her and she has never really recovered since. Her monetary difficulties, which force her to adopt austerity measures even now, in 1968, have their origin in that postwar exhaustion, despite the time-interval. But, just as France in 1918 stood aside from the huge changes taking place, Britian since 1945 has staked her future on the Commonwealth, not the Europe of the Six.

Italy was no less terribly shaken by the war, going over from one camp to the other while hostilities were still at their height, running the risk that she would lose her relatively recently acquired national unity, and losing part of her political structures as a result of the adventure.

The repercussions of the war have not left Spain wholly undamaged; they have accentuated her withdrawal into herself caused by the civil war, in which she had lost 1,200,000 men.

As for the East European countries, Poland, Hungary, Rumania and Czechoslovakia, the war's impact upon them has been more than a psychological trauma. After forming part of the old Europe they were brutally severed from it.

This accumulation of events might have helped Europe to formulate ideals which would have knit her peoples more closely together. But the currents flowing in this direction were not powerful enough. Economic materialism gained the advantage over political maturation, and for want of a genuine ideal the social groups of Europe have entrenched themselves in particularism. Instead of devoting themselves enthusiastically to constructing the future they have even, as in Belgium for example, mobilized their energies against it. This is a regression-phenomenon, one to which a number of countries are undoubtedly subject. It is visible in Scotland and Britanny; there are premonitory symptoms in Croatia and Slovakia; and signs of a recrudescence of Catalan separatism.

If Europe wielded an influence on the world scale her internal antagonisms, as factors of diversity, might produce positive effects. Provincialism is useful in a federated structure. But in a nationalistic Europe, provincialism augments the existing weaknesses and absorbs the energies so badly needed for moving forward.

THE CONSEQUENCES OF DECOLONIZATION

For a number of countries with the ocean at their doors, such as Spain, Portugal, Britain, France, Belgium and Holland, colonies, for many years, provided both an outlet for expansion and added savour and variety to life at home.

The colonies were a training-ground in teamwork and effectiveness: for a country's most effective troops, most popular leaders and boldest administrators. European literature and the cinema are full of colonial heroes.

On losing their empires the European countries were deprived of the bases which made them feel they were the masters of the world. Simultaneously they forgot the ardour and enthusiasm which, along with the sordid and sometimes repellent side, were involved in their colonial undertakings.

To the American, adventure is something which happens at home, an economic or technological game to be played and won. The European, dreaming of bridges to be built in some remote wilderness, is less allured by the prospect of spanning his home valleys.

All in all, Europe has huddled back into herself emotionally as well as physically. She cannot get over the fact of her own absence both from the theatres where the drama of the future is being played, and from the colonies of the technological age – the immensities of Alaska and much of Canada and Siberia, in which enormous resources lie untapped. And what rubs salt into her wounds is that these reserves are owned or controlled by the USA and the USSR, both of whom, not for the first time, she sees advancing along trails first blazed by her.

No doubt Europe's enfeeblement has accelerated the course of planetization, in so far as her internal wars have touched off world-wide reactions; it has also involved the United States in political intervention everywhere, including Europe; strengthened the foundations of Soviet power; and dismantled, much more quickly than could have been foreseen, the crumbling bastions constituted by the colonial empires.

For Europe, however, all this is cold comfort.

EUROPE'S IDEOLOGICAL DIVISION

Europe is divided between West and East, both materially and on the plane of ideas.

Western Europe is affected internally by the antagonism between those political parties which look towards America; those which look towards Russia; and those which still look towards the national past or even urge the cause of provincial separatism and the revival of a local language. Eastern Europe is subject to Soviet organization but is increasingly coming into contact with the influences of the 'liberal' countries.

Every country has its own internal tensions, which are a good thing so long as they result in healthy competition. But the tensions by which Europe is agitated hinder progress and produce a retrograde development, because they themselves are the product of fundamentally external influences. To use an electrical analogy, we may say that Western Europe (which ought to be creating the new political world set-up, and in which therefore we are principally interested) is in circuit with the United States yet simultaneously undergoing the influence of the East (Russia and the Iron Curtain countries) by induction. Western Europe not only lacks original thought, capable of influencing the rest of the world, but is caught between contrary pressures. What is more, it does not always select the best, most efficient aspects of the leading powers for imitation.

What do we take from the United States? Its Foundations? Copious information-supply? Faith in progress? No: we take automatic vending-machines and bad films, thereby adding fuel, all too predictably, to anti-American feeling.

Similarly, what we take from the USSR is not the discipline of its workers, or the courage which chooses to go short of consumer goods in order to develop the sputnik. In the West, many trade unionists daydream of transplanting the Soviet system into their own countries – which is odd when you come to think of it, the function of the unions in the USSR being to dragoon the workers and forbid strikes.

The example of France is a good illustration of Western ideological inconsistency. Plenty of Frenchmen voting Communist have no desire to see the Party's programme put into execution. And the French communists, whose living-standards are decidedly superior to those of most communists elsewhere, show no desire to go and live in Russia. They adopt Russian communism *minus* the technology and the discipline. All that is left is the spirit of antagonism, the ferment of social division. Just when it is more essential than ever to develop the spirit of enterprise, French-style communism obstructs this development by encouraging the anti-profit mentality. By so doing it forces the state to intervene, thus producing further antagonism between those who hope to benefit from *étatisme*, and those who are against it.

EUROPE EGOISTICAL

The last thing we want to do is to decry the desire for a higher standard of living. To increase the overall volume of wealth, and to divide it more equitably, is a necessary task and, at

times, an exciting and uplifting one. The increase in material
well-being is one of the better sides of Europe's history since
the war. Unfortunately, however, it is accompanied by a
temptation to take refuge in mere comfort and to refrain
from the effort required for solving the big problems of our
century.

Germany, particularly the kind of Germany symbolized by
Professor Erhard, affords a pretty sharp illustration of this
attitude. The reactions and protests of the German students
prove that the most dynamic section of the public, and especially
the young, find it unsatisfying.

Germany takes little part in the study of development problems except when she herself is directly concerned by them.
The agreements she makes for helping under-developed countries, for instance, are generally hung about with financial
strings, obliging the recipients to buy their capital equipment
in Germany. She seeks American support so as to arm herself
the better for her subsequent undertakings in the European
market. Her industries prefer links with American corporations
to intra-European alliances. She shows a lack of interest in the
problems of European organization. It was a long time before
she consented to participate in the joint study of plans for
European unity. In the Common Market, she tends to stress
'market' and forget 'common'. In this, however, she is not alone.

After the reconstruction period, Europe plunged with a kind
of passion into a spree of consumer spending. For want of a
philosophy and of some broad, overriding objective, the arguments exchanged in the meetings of the Common Market
Commission are more often dictated by the wish to defend
national, regional or sectional interests than by a determination
to win the battle of the future.

The economy is a convenient refuge for those who are unwilling to assume political responsibilities. Such people delude
themselves that they are building Europe within this narrow
frame of reference. They pretend not to know that whoever
contents himself with purely economic considerations
remains in bondage, whether he likes it or not, to political
forces beyond his control. By not conceiving a line of action
of our own, we submit ourselves passively to the actions of
others.

EUROPE COMPLEX-RIDDEN

Most Europeans do not accept industrial society; most Americans and Russians do. Not all of those Europeans who do accept it are resigned to identifying it with American society. While some manage to get more or less used to the idea of Europe as a satellite of the United States, others revolt, albeit in their words rather than their actions, against the prospect of seeing the American pattern stamped on the future and moulding European and world society. Both attitudes, resignation and fear, have raised a crop of complexes in a Europe already suffering from the aftermath of two world wars and the disappearance of the colonies.

Europeans really must become conscious of these traumas and their implications. From the start, the crisis has involved everybody in common, and it still does; surely the effort to overcome it must be made in common? This effort implies a modification of structures. Europe, in fact, is suffering even more from a failure of adaptation at the level of her structures than from the necessity of having recourse to external sources for her equipment. In order to integrate contemporary techniques into her way of life she will have to advance from the nineteenth century type of organization which she created round the steam engine, and which bore the mark of her own special genius, to that projected by the dawn of the planetary age. This necessity adds to her problems. It demands massive conversions and adaptations. To demolish and rebuild is harder than to build from nothing, in a clear field.

IN THE MATTER OF EQUIPMENT, EUROPE IS TRAILING

To such a point is American influence predominant in Europe, where business, industry and the economy are concerned, that we not only adopt American equipment without asking ourselves whether it will suit our environment, but show an increasing tendency to reject any equipment which has not already been tried in the States.

When the new airport at Orly was still in the planning stage, someone suggested connecting it with the Gare d'Orsay – in other words with the centre of Paris – by means of the existing railway, with suitable modifications, using fast self-propelled coaches; these would have had customs officers on board so as to save time on controls as well as transit. The idea was contemptuously turned down, on the score that the Americans had long since given up their railways and now swore by motor-roads. This example was followed, with the result that travellers have to start a couple of hours earlier in order to make sure of catching their planes. Since then, the Americans have discovered that some connections in or between cities can be made more rationally and effectively by rail than road. It is highly probable that by the time the Americans have linked their airports and city centres by rail, the Europeans will start thinking about doing the same thing.

Some European countries, thinking to display a slightly more emancipated turn of mind, try to build equipment of their own after the American style. This reaction we might christen as 'the nationalism-at-top-prices syndrome'. Britain and France suffer from it pretty constantly, but on the whole the results in both cases are disappointing.

When a country shows a systematic determination to repeat – on a small scale and at higher cost – things which have already been done in the United States, we can hardly help feeling worried. Nothing but transnational endeavour will make it possible to avoid copying America at exorbitant cost. This same transnational co-operation would liberate us from too close an adhesion to American methods, and in particular from American demands in the matter of patent rights. It is common knowledge that, in order to use American patents, European firms are frequently obliged to cede exclusive rights in their own discoveries to America.

Europe's inadequacy induces the state, particularly in France and Britain, to try to act as a counter-poise to America. But government intervention is more apt to lead to rearguard actions than to encourage initiative; it tends to put industrialists into a defensive state of mind. They wait for officialdom to forge them a buckler before committing themselves to the fray, and tacitly leave themselves with the option of compounding with the 'enemy' in the event of the buckler proving inadequate.

Negative nationalism is no less harmful than top-price nationalism. In the eyes of negative nationalism, American methods of any kind are dangerous, and even sinful. A few home-grown pioneer achievements are lauded to the skies to show that the old country's technology is the equal of anything from abroad. At home, this succeeds to the extent of turning a few heads; but abroad the effect is the opposite of that desired.

The young in France are unaware that the Serre-Ponçon dam, presented as a great national achievement for their admiration, was designed in accordance with an American technique (a gravity-dam with earth as the bulk material) and that almost all the equipment used in building it was American. Neither do most of them know that the Caravelle's electronic equipment and the computers for France's atomic energy establishments are of American origin. By this kind of deception they are given the illusion that their country can achieve anything and everything by going it alone. On discovering this to be untrue they are astonished or angry, or, worst of all, retreat into indifference. It would be better to tell them the facts, without trimmings, so as to enable them to gauge just how much a medium-sized country is in a position to attempt. The Americans are pretty shrewd about the real value of the 'national' feats so loudly trumpeted in various quarters in Europe, and they acquire a certain scorn for the nationalists of the Old World; which, it must be emphasized, does not make for good international understanding, despite the fundamental solidarity between the American people and the peoples of Europe.

By such play-acting the Europeans not only use up their money but also undermine such standing as they still possess in the eyes of world opinion.

Failures and disappointments lead to the brain drain or a fit of the sulks. Bewildered and at bay, Europe's brightest people go off to seek their fortunes in the USA, or relapse sourly into isolation, or abandon themselves to the fantasia of communism.

THE BURDEN OF RE-ADAPTATION

As we showed in *Plaidoyer pour l'avenir*, Europe was the champion of the first phase of the Industrial Revolution (coal, steel, railways); but the things which once constituted her strength have now become a source of difficulties.

While America is advancing and the USSR tries to catch her up after making a clean sweep of the past, Europe remains stuck in the mud of superannuated structures. Leaving constructive progress to others, she divides most of her energies between conversion operations and rearguard actions against them.

The British cast of mind was well suited to structures hinging on a system of world trade dominated by the English language. The essential thing then was to derive as much advantage as possible from British superiority in technology and energy-utilization by setting up efficient trade outlets more or less all over the world. It should be remembered how important Britain's shipping was to her at the time when British coal, which was largely responsible for the expansion of her empire, dominated the world market. British power was also much indebted to her cotton industry, which had grown enormously.

But the problem today is to sell to customers who are no longer convinced of the superiority of British goods, and to industrialists who no longer believe that the adoption of British machinery and habits is the ultimate badge of economic progressiveness. Coal and the cotton industry no longer rule the roost; the British have partially sacrificed the latter in the hope of keeping part of the Commonwealth, but in vain.

The face of German industrial power has changed no less markedly. The throes of re-adaptation are apparent throughout the factories of the Ruhr. Various parts of Europe on which the Ruhr once depended for its economic strength have now turned into a handicap.

In order to stand up to technical progress and American competition, those in authority in the various European countries preach industrial concentration. This is unquestionably valuable in itself. But it is also necessary that the new firm be more efficient than those which were regrouped to form it; and that the policy pursued should not be allowed to paralyse initiative. The state, always glad to intervene, is in fact more at home with large concerns over which, if things turn out badly, it can seek to gain control, and whose directors are often in closer touch with the administration or the political world than with their colleagues in firms of medium size. Industrial conversion, and structural reorganization in business, are not the most difficult adaptations to execute; to reshape administrative and political structures demands far more complex changes in the conduct of higher authority and of the officials directly affected. Governments, under pressure from the facts of present-day life, busy themselves about economic reform but show far less willingness to apply themselves to the reorganization of the state. Paradoxically, moreover, the demands imposed by economic readaptation are such as to increase the powers of a traditionally-minded administration.

NATIONALISM AND GOVERNMENT PLANNING

The consequences of reinforcing the conventional, classical state are several: a covert reinforcement of nationalism; growing complexity of administrative life, which becomes excessively bureaucratic; and, in compensation, the development of an anarchical spirit, hostile both to industrial society and to those who run it.

The necessary conversions need to be carried out in a European, not a national, setting. Inside each country, the requisite changes cannot be made without the risk of severe social upheaval or, alternatively, diluting them to the point of ineffectiveness. If mutations are to be executed without bringing the students out into the streets, to be followed sooner or later by their elders, external factors must be brought into play. The economy is a visible reminder of the fact that rules which would not be accepted within the framework of any one state are found perfectly palatable when they constitute the law common to several.

Unfortunately, the nationalist mentality is often blind to this obvious fact. Nationalism today represents a confluence of different currents, in which the country's historic heritage mingles with provincial particularism, inferiority complexes, socialist ideas distorted by certain technocrats who exploit them for their own ends, and state intervention in the name of progress.

The desire to look as big as Mr Big induces some countries, as we have pointed out, to go in for expensive installations and organizations which can be supported only out of public funds. The further they travel along this road the more inexorably are they condemned to see the state intervening heavy-handedly in their economic life. For in fact it is only the state which, in face of American and in default of intra-European enterprise, has the sheer brawn for the job. This does not mean that the money the state invests in its prestige operations yields as high a return as that previously invested by the evicted firms. Laying out capital is one thing, drawing up the balance sheet another. A further drawback of nationalization (so-called) is that it tinges with chauvinism – that is to say with a degenerate form of patriotism – branches of production which in an economy such as that of the United States are governed by purely commercial considerations.

State intervention in the economy manifests itself not only through money, but through human beings. Para-functionaries are becoming a new caste in Europe, especially in countries whose industrial structures are weak. In Italy, Spain and France, senior officials occupy high industrial posts and bid fair to constitute a state within the state. When called upon to make their undertakings a paying proposition they ally themselves, even if unconsciously, with functionaries properly so called – the civil servants – in order to ensure that the main cost of the necessary reorganization and re-equipment shall fall on private enterprise. Their own undertakings are loaded with more and more burdens, which they are able to discharge only by drastically raising their productivity. The public and semi-public services, for their part, content themselves with spending more without bothering much about making every possible economy. As they are part of the state, and as the state wants to set the example of bigness, they start by extending their powers without first asking themselves whether, in order to reach their prescribed targets, it would not be better to overhaul their methods.

THE ILLUSIONS OF SOCIALISM

State intervention, largely caused by war and its consequences, by the demands of modernization, and by fear of international enterprise, would not have occurred so frequently and been pursued so systematically had it not been interpreted as a sign of progress by the upholders of socialism.

The socialists think the best protection against the American 'capitalist' system is to strengthen public action (government action); whereas the communists are satisfied if they can watch organizational structures being built up which they would be able to take over if the time came. But the result of socialist economics is to open the door to political nationalism.

Few, as yet, are the socialists who can be got to admit this. Many socialist ideas, conceived in terms of a certain situation, are applied only after the context has altered completely, and are thus out of phase with reality.

Here again, modernization is necessary, on the intellectual level this time, leading to a re-examination of the problem of nationalization.

Many European countries, having nationalized a sizeable part of their economic activities, are in danger of sliding towards a national-socialized (as distinct from National Socialist) régime, which might appear to offer some defence against American dynamism. But this is a dangerous illusion, for once an undertaking has been nationalized it is hard for it to associate with undertakings in other countries in order to attain the size required for efficiency. And without that size, competition on the world scale is impossible. Hence attainment of the size typical of nationalization is risky; it may be a step back, perhaps the first step in a whole retrograde development. People have got used to rigid state controls because there was a period during which they were necessary; and because of the Russian example; and because, in the eyes of a certain number of intellectuals without experience of the economy, the application of controls tends towards the elimination of profit, which they regard as an ideal. All this toleration of *dirigisme* depends on psychological mechanisms of a simple, naïve kind, and is based on obsolete doctrines.

The foundations of the socialist philosophy go back to an earlier period than the age of industry and the functional hierarchy, and (what is pertinent here) than the management age. In other words, socialist ideas, which are the only political doctrine in harmony with the slide towards nationalization, state control and all that they represent, date from a period when industrial and business undertakings had not assumed their contemporary form. Those ideas have lost their justification in our time, when businesses are passing more and more out of the hands of the boss with the big bank balance and into those of salaried managers who are paid for what their work is worth. To hold socialist ideas, in the forms in which they are still expressed, is to be out of tune with the times in which we live. Cybernetics, which will make it possible to carry out the necessary calculations for the more equitable distribution of wealth, will enable us to 'socialize' more efficiently than by means of nationalization. A partial solution of the problem can already be seen in action in such countries as the United States and Sweden.

Socialism requires to be re-thought in terms of the type of organization which has to be created today, a type much closer to the associative mechanisms of federalism than to the centralist practices which were in order some time ago.

So great has the discrepancy between ideologies and social structures become that the former really must be revised. This would entail distinguishing between socialization, an inevitable phenomenon, and the frequently delusive myths of traditional socialism. Socialization is the multiplication of links between the different individuals in a collectivity, and the augmentation of the part played by the life of society in the existence of each individual. Socialism, on the other hand, consists all too often of the temptation to subject the individual to the demands of the majority, the mass. Many ideas on socialism were expressed in a period when the most important thing was to secure a fairer distribution of wealth, at which time they were very justifiable. With the equipment now placed at the disposal of production, everyone has much more to gain from better organization than from merely tilting distribution this way or that to provide fair shares. There have been so many advances enabling work to be performed ten times as productively, or more, whereas merely amending the division of the rewards of labour can never do better than double them. If every Frenchman were to receive the same income, his salary cheque, in the present circumstances, would be that of a skilled artisan; whereas, if we had an economic framework similar to that of the United States, it would be twice that amount.

DEMOCRACY REACHES ITS CEILING

Making-over an old system into a new one is always a battle. War must be waged on all those who, from a variety of motives, persist in championing the past against the future, even though, in some cases, they preen themselves on being the standard-bearers of progress.

The innovators, confronting this opposition, are divided amongst themselves. Because the present-day organization of society precludes the co-ordination of their efforts, every group and administration puts forward its own make-over programme. The Plan, when there is one, does not always arbitrate swiftly and effectively enough in favour of one of these programmes. The party of the past is united, the party of the future is only a coalition. Democracy of the approved pattern, democracy as we know it, does not always give the latter its proper chance. The forces of demagogy are arrayed against it. All over the world the democratic system is under attack for its inability to solve the problems confronting modern societies. This is strikingly so in Europe, of all places, whose pride it was, for so many years, to have been the cradle of democracy.

Many European countries looking for a constitution have tried one modelled on the British system of parliamentary government. But the dramatic adventures witnessed in Europe not many years ago showed up the underlying weakness of political structures conceived in the eighteenth century for countries with fairly small populations and a life mainly pivoted about the farmer and the artisan.

Europe, in which the liberal British monarchy and the French Republic used to set the example of stable government, or at least of well-established political structures, contrasting so favourably with Tsarist reaction and Chinese muddle, now finds herself stubbing her toes against the obstacles to political effectiveness in her trauma-ridden countries, which are in the throes of a continuous making-over process. On the political plane, battling for the future is less profitable than defending entrenched interests. Since the majority is conservative *de facto*, if not politically labelled as such, and rebuts the changes demanded by the situation, the only way left of effecting those changes is direct administrative action; otherwise the prospect is one of political crises and counter-crises.

The pre-eminence of the administrative power, which does its best to turn the executive into its colonial subjects – despite having been appointed expressly as the executive's instrument in running the country – is against both the requirements of efficiency and the aspiration towards a fully human life. An individual can no longer express himself and seek his personal validation in the same setting as hitherto. He needs an environment of productivity-structures which encourage initiative by giving him the means to unfold his gifts. The social value of an individual consists of his imagination and his ability to get people working together on a constructive task. Neither in France nor in Britain is there much awareness of this development as yet. In many cases it is held in check by the administrative power; which is not to deny that individual officials necessarily lack a feeling for progress, though in all too many cases they are the prisoners of their professional environment and its atmosphere.

Prince Philip said roundly, in a TV interview on 20 March 1968: 'People talk about a tolerant society, but the British have never been so much regimented: you practically need a permit to breathe.'

In general, as we shall continue indefatigably to repeat, the existing structures were conceived for other times than ours, and administrations were designed for running countries whose development was slow. The existing organizational forms take no account of the prolongation of human life and the necessity of appointing young men to certain responsible positions. Many adolescents eager to integrate themselves with their own times find themselves blocked and immobilized from the start. This is one of the causes of the antics in which we have seen them indulging lately.

Europe is suffering from a lag in her social morality which is dominated by a sort of bourgeois conformism that has no equivalent in America, and by the expiring energies of the military hierarchy, long regarded as the noblest hierarchy of them all. These hang-overs from the past do not mix well with planetization and socialization.

Relations between the administration and the government are a problem everywhere, but particularly in France, because of its long administrative tradition and because political upheavals have not decapitated the state apparatus, as in Germany and Italy.

The major defect of the traditional type of administration is that it is now frequently an obstacle to the development of the society whose affairs it was created to run. The interdependence of science and technology (which latter includes organization) is accelerating the evolution of society, but its effect in administrative circles takes the form of more and more complications, of which the better-equipped departments take advantage to increase their own power. These two opposite effects engender a pernicious disequilibrium, which underlies reactions ranging from student unrest to antipathy towards the machine.

But in addition to all these signs that democracy has reached its ceiling, there is another which is still more disturbing and which must be emphasized accordingly: the limitations imposed on free information.

MISDEMEANOURS OF THE STATE IN THE SPHERE OF INFORMATION

One of the means increasingly employed by the administrative power in certain countries to retain its holds over public opinion is the control, direct or indirect, of information. We have got used to state-run radio and television, an arrangement which we are told keeps the sources of information pure. This is a very serious matter. Freedom of information, and progress in information methods, are part of the development towards 'one world'. The countries which had reached the highest democratic levels were proud to think that one of the characteristics of democracy was the freedom of the Press. Countries which had not yet conceded that freedom could not claim to be democratic, and the word 'censorship' is abhorrent to Europeans. All the same, if censorship itself has been abolished, television and part of broadcasting depend in many countries on a public corporation. Radio and TV, particularly the latter, exercise a decisive influence on the masses, if not on the elite. Previously, the way to put across a policy was to secure the co-operation of the elite, who were strong partisans of freedom. What is needed now is the support of public opinion, which the state seeks to mould; if the elite object they can have some of their powers of opposition, and some of their means of influence, withdrawn.

The mixture of universal suffrage and monopoly control of audio-visual information is contrary to the purpose of those who made that suffrage an institution. If, through lack of competition between different channels of information, opinion is subjected to a conditioning process during the run-up to voting day, elections become more like a plebiscite.

Countries which used to pride themselves on their free press now practise monopoly control over the audio-visual field, and thus contradict the principles of democracy while appearing to continue supporting them. In this matter, moreover, as in some others, archaic socialism finds itself at one with nationalism. '*Contestation*' ('highly critical radical opposition' would be the nearest equivalent in English) is a word much bandied about in supposedly left-wing circles, but some of their leaders have nevertheless been moving towards a reduction of freedom of information: they are fanatically in favour of the state monopoly of audio-visual information and, in fact, of the press as well, which they would like to see converted into a public service. Freedom of the press and internationalism, once so typical of the left-wing spirit, have given way to the information monopoly and nationalism: a typical example of the way a great historical trend can become perverted.

Having failed to perceive that democracy's methods must develop along with technical progress, we are now abandoning, without realizing it, some of the great democratic principles which were once the glory of our European countries. We are going over to centralization and state tyranny without any real discussion of this new orientation. Control has been laid upon just that means of expression which most affects the mass of the population, and which is most capable of falsifying democracy.

LEAD US NOT INTO MACHIAVELLIANISM

Machiavellianism is the usual weapon of the back-to-the-nation school. The line is, 'Since we can't be as powerful as the USSR or the USA, let's be cunning instead.' It needs to be said, however, and as loudly as possible, that no one has ever built the future by basing himself on Machiavelli. There is no truly grand strategy, no 'action of great pith and enterprise', to be found in Machiavelli. His book is no foundation-stone for those who wish to build the future; its mediocre counsels are meant for those who wish to keep themselves in power in non-evolving societies, whether by convincing the people that everything in the garden is lovely, or by providing themselves with the means of keeping the people in check.

Machiavelli and his intelligence and artfulness notwithstanding, the Italian princes never rose to the stature of the century they lived in – which meant, then, the stature of France. Translated into contemporary European terms, a policy of Machiavellian type amounts to saying: 'With such means as I am in a position to take to myself, I shall never be as great as the great powers; but I carry just enough weight to tilt the balance in whatever direction I wish to travel. And can anyone stop me changing sides if I find it advantageous to do so?' This policy enables one to subsist, but not to construct. It represents a certain degree of ambition, but not ambition of a type that wins respect.

In this connection, it is necessary to mark out quite clearly the limits of the idea of a *nation* in the planetary age. A country is anxious to acquire and assert a personality of its own for two main reasons:

(*a*) to feel free – not towed along in the wake of others;

(*b*) to have enough power to exert an influence on the development of the world's affairs.

These are legitimate objectives, but they can no longer be attained in the same ways as hitherto, especially by countries of medium size such as France, Britain or Germany. Hierarchy between the nations, like hierarchy among men at work, is something which changes character as time goes on. Today, anyone in a responsible position finds himself alternately commanding and being commanded. A colonel who is a rocket specialist is heard with greater respect than a general who is not. There is more scope for development, more of the future, in association, than there is in the old, rigid type of hierarchy. Of course, there has got to be one man in charge, to say what to do or not to do; but one of the aspects of liberty in the modern world is that we choose that man ourselves, and if he gets out of step with his job we can sack him. This rule holds for countrie as well as for business, industry or any other enterprise. A system of association must be invented in Europe which will give everyone his own share of responsibility – provided he earns it by his abilities, his effectiveness, his coefficient of adaptability and innovation – and which will give him higher rewards than if he worked in isolation.

If those who call themselves nationally-minded were truly ambitious, they would realize that it is hopeless expecting to be one of the nations which really count in the world's affairs while clinging to obsolete preconceptions. The only solution is to rise to a higher level, a European dimension.

THE LOST VALUES

We have said that with her imported equipment, her complex-ridden mentalities and her worn-out organizational structures, Europe can never do more than turn herself into a bad copy of America, while grasping at certain Soviet myths as a counter-poise. Even this would be better than the alternative prospect, namely to follow a regressive path which would deepen her divisions and confirm her incapacity to present the world with the ground-plan of a system for the planetary age.

We are not overlooking the efforts already being made towards a united Europe, and the bodies already in existence, which will play their part in bringing it about; we shall have more to say about these in Chapter Five. But despite all that has been accomplished so far, no real re-creation of the European spirit, in new terms, can as yet be seen.

Europe has not yet re-created the values on which her growth and her greatness were based and which have now been left behind, devalued by the march of development. She is without new philosophical and political foundations. The very notion of patriotism has been severely shaken. Hitherto, patriotic feeling has found its clearest expression in defence against an enemy, generally an immediately neighbouring country.

French patriotism, German patriotism and so on existed, and everyone knew what they were like. But have they been re-placed today by a '360° patriotism'? [*un patriotisme tous azimuts.* The reference is to the '*défense tous azimuts*', defence directed all round the horizon and towards any and every point in the sky, ordained by General de Gaulle, when President of France, as the keystone of French military preparedness. *Tr.*]. What about German patriotism today, has it really progressed beyond its old ideas, as dangerous as they were simple-minded, of yet another attempt at conquest in the east?

Patriotism was still a sane and healthy thing as long as it referred to a certain conception of the nation. But the time-honoured concept of the nation is no longer in harmony with technical and political realities. Europe's menfolk feel, whether consciously or confusedly, that if ever they should have to gamble their lives on something it would be on some other principle or principles than 'the nation'. Unfortunately, whatever the new principles may be – a certain concept of liberty, or progress, or humanity – they have not yet been clearly enough defined to be translated into political terms. And yet at the dawn of the planetary age, when what is at stake is the life and organization of the world as a whole, nobody has any doubt that some broader idea of patriotism is what is needed. But because we are not making it our business to study the problem in its real dimensions, and because defence, in every country, persists in remaining 'national', chauvinism is gaining the upper hand over patriotism. The resurgence of chauvinism – which in the economic field is nothing less than retrenchment and the costly employment of capital in the pursuit of unprofitable prestige operations – is symptomatic of regression. It tends to the creation of new frontiers in a world where old ones have been burst wide open by the advance of technology. It pushes governments and their administrations to turn their states into so many Bastilles, and to employ the most modern instruments, such as data-processing techniques, to that end.

It is pertinent to inquire how much is left of the other great values which have inspired Europeans for several centuries, such as the quest for progress.

Of course, the thirst for progress still exists; but the content of the term is coming to be regarded with scepticism. In a number of countries – in France, Britain, Spain, Poland, there are plenty of people who declare themselves against modern society on the score of its being American. They criticize it, but their attacks are tinged with a kind of masochism which leads them to declare inevitable the development carrying us towards it, to the detriment of all that Europe represents. In other words they regard Europe as being irremediably defeated in man's endeavour to become a master of technical achievement, and thereby of nature.

By denouncing 'machine civilization', even while using it to advantage (without its help, many of its critics would have died before reaching adult years), and by falling behindhand in the task of paving the way for the post-industrial society, we reinforce the present intellectual disarray to an alarming degree. By condemning technology and consumer-values without suggesting anything to put in their place, we eventually cause the black banners of anarchy to appear.

Being, in their hearts, by no means proud of their position in the modern world, the Europeans look round for alibis to salve their discomfiture. We can label them. Alibi one: make monuments out of molehills – score a minor success of some kind and set it up as a major one. Alibi two: decry thy neighbour – exaggerate other nations' difficulties until you succeed in convincing yourself that their successes need not be envied. Alibi three: the humane culture ploy, which consists in asserting that Europeans are more civilized than others – despite the fact that there is a considerably higher percentage of university students per head of population in the United States than in Europe, and that the human sciences have been developed much further in that country than elsewhere. Alibi four: the future – shuffle it all off on to the future, treat the future either as an ideal state, a wish-dream to lose yourself in, or as doom, a decree of irresistible fate. Alibi five: the complacent self-satisfaction gambit – keep telling yourself how much progress we are making. To which it might be objected that when every industrial country in the world is raising its production by from three to five per cent annually it would be odd if we were to stand quite still. Sixth alibi: Europe, the new entity under construction in the setting of today's 'European institutions' – which serve, only too often, as a camouflage-screen for all those who in fact reject Europe but award themselves certificates as good Europeans on the pretext of their being strict observers of the Treaty of Rome.

Believing in Europe is not Utopian – it is a wager on the future, as we shall show; what is Utopian is believing in the possibility of cultural and moral cohesion inside a superannuated framework. The old arrangements need not inevitably disappear but must be reduced to the proportions of the part they play, which corresponds to that of the former provinces rather than to that of nations. Recent experience in France – ten years of apparent stability, followed by the explosion of spring 1968 – shows that the restoration of political authority on such traditional foundations as national pride does not produce ideals capable of attracting a deep and lasting allegiance.

The only conceivable road is the federal road. As we pointed out in our contribution to *Le Défi américain*,[1] and in the early pages of the present volume, we have reached the planetary stage. What part is Europe to play in this situation?

Economically Europe must be, as regards both quality and quantity, strong enough to operate in the world market. This does not mean that she must put competition above everything. Economic independence is an idea the content of which has altered completely. The word 'independence' has lost the simple, straightforward meaning it used to possess. Economic life now is a matter of exchanges, of 'flow' as a scientist would say. We must seek to be as indispensable to others as they are to us. Europe is not rich enough in raw materials to rely only on her own sources of them. Until such time as the industrial use of the elements of nature (air and water) enables her to overcome this handicap, she must concentrate on the full employment of her immense technical gifts.

If we tot up Europe's resources country by individual country, we become aware how limited they are. But if we consider Europe as a whole we see that her potential is on the world scale. She must therefore move forward to a federal position; in other words, organize herself with a view to the common economic and political activities which will enable her to be competitive.

POOL WHAT IS NEW

The golden rule for progressively introducing the requisite structures of federal type is as follows: 'Let us develop in

---

[1] See the Réflexions by Louis Armand in Jean-Jacques Servan-Schreiber, *Le Défi américain*.

common whatever is new, and leave on one side our inheritances from the past, whose unification would take up too much time. Let us create "federal structures"; for instance, let us create the legal basis for transnational companies for the exploitation of European patents. We need not unify our existing university degrees and other special qualifications, but, rather, organize them in such a way that those which involve the newer disciplines shall be valid in all countries.'

If we make up our minds to develop all the new technologies, and have sufficient impetus to do this in common, in accordance with a deliberate plan – instead of resigning ourselves to doing it piece-meal – there is no reason why, after about fifteen years, Europe should not regain a leading position in the world in a certain number of important fields.

But if we want Europe to have a character of her own, the fact of her taking an active part in technological intercourse will not, though indispensable, be enough. Europe must show originality on the sociological plane. She must have an ethic, a philosophy, produce a living body of political thought. We are in danger of letting our technological backwardness mask from us a much more fundamental inadequacy, something much more general: our backwardness in organization. Europe as a whole does not know what she wants; and as long as she does not know she will be incapable of playing a guiding role in the world.

The absence of original European thought is even more evident than the absence of a specifically European technology. Europe gazes wistfully and jealously at America's wealth in more senses than one.

This mental squint in space, across the Atlantic, is accompanied by a squint in time: Europe is loath to forget the ages in which she was great. This reluctance only betrays how unsure of herself she feels.

A mutation of mentalities and attitudes is imperative. It will not occur spontaneously, under the mere pressure of material progress; it will demand men of resolution and will-power. They will have to be practitioners of politics, statesmen. So let us give absolute primacy to politics; meaning, of course, political strategy, not the agitations which are its epiphenomena.

The power and extension of the zone of action of equipment

are drawing the various national collectivities closer together. The citizens, notably the young, will adopt a spirit corresponding to this planetary phase of human development. Politico-economic structures, on the other hand, will be seen to lag behind. This, indeed, is the classical sequence: equipment develops rapidly, overflows national frontiers, and changes the attitudes of the young; but economic and political structures fail to follow suit; hence equipment and structures get badly out of phase, and the older countries become debilitated accordingly.

Europe, having fallen behind in equipment, owes it to herself to be more intelligent with regard to structures. Provided she shows the necessary political will-power, she is capable of placing her own stamp on all activities specifically concerned with shaping the future, from the sciences of man to business management.

It is impossible to envisage, in this planetary stage of development, a world political structure being arrived at by a mere extension of the existing national system. Mankind will be forced to pass through a federal stage.

But Europe will first have to become a federation herself in order to play a part at all; for her this is an absolute need. By so doing she will put herself in the van, since she will be in the position through which all humanity must subsequently pass. America feels no compulsion to envisage a type of federation transcending her own sovereignty, nor does Russia. It is for Europe to set the example. And it is high time. For these are the only ideas which can really capture the interest, conscious or unconscious, of the young; they are also the only ones capable of reducing the considerable dangers hovering over the world at the dawn of the planetary age.

THE CASE OF FRANCE

One of the difficulties in the way of constructing the future Europe arises from the 'personality' of present-day France.

France, in fact, faced with the necessity of a Great Leap Forward into industrial maturity, does not know what to do with herself. The events of May 1968 illuminated both the deep-seated desires for change which are present in her, and the reflexes of fear and recoil with which changing times are greeted, even, in many cases, by those who think of themselves as progressives. Let us see, therefore, how the considerations which apply to Europe generally apply in particular to France.

THE STUDENT REVOLT

The revolt of the students, and of the young in general, in May 1968, was partly a reaction against the fossilized mentality of French university authorities and the stick-in-the-mud, backs-to-the-wall and backs-to-the-past attitude of authority as a whole. But what it also brought to light was a rejection of certain collective disciplines. The motor-car, for instance, exists, as a thing to be used or abused; yet the natural consequences of automatization are not accepted. The young believe, or affect to believe, that the wealth produced by industrial methods can be taken for granted, a never-failing cornucopia, the pre-supposition from which one sets out to remould industrial society into the society of the heart's desire. But they overlook the fact that some people want one thing, some another; desires vary. They also forget, in their search for happiness and the poetry of life (incidentally, the word 'happiness', *bonheur*, has a slightly bourgeois ring, which the young also overlook), that for the vast majority of people the same search connotes, if not coincides with, material success and satisfaction. 'Machine civilization' is rejected root and branch; and indeed some people in positions of authority volubly support its detractors, in order to keep power in their own hands. But how on earth are we to satisfy the human need for advancement, for equity, even for culture, without fully exploiting our machines and their benefits?

America is pilloried as the symbol of the society the rebels reject; yet at the same time, the aspirations which come to light are in many cases curiously akin to American realities. Thus, when the students demand the autonomy of university faculties, they are rediscovering a system which works excellently on the other side of the Atlantic. Again, when specialist cadres demand a share in decision-making in business, they are envisaging, though without admitting it to themselves, the correct application of American principles of management. And when the

wage-earners demand to be treated as men instead of mere
numbers, they are urging, without knowing it, the adoption of
the principles of 'public relations' as practised for many years
in the USA.

Only, because everything from over there has a whiff of
capitalist brimstone about it, people shrink from seeming to
have absorbed the lessons it can teach and claim to have worked
out instead an original system, half-way between the American
ethic and the classical communism of Moscow.

There thus arises a disturbing conjunction between the most
dynamic of the intellectuals, the most adventurous of the young,
and authority at its most hidebound. For the latter opts for
independence as the nation's goal, meaning, by independence,
the pursuit of national originality. This desire for originality
serves in part to mask an anxiety to maintain certain thoroughly
French traditions such as distrust of business, contempt for
technology, insistence on egalitarianism, admiration for emi-
nence when it is political or intellectual and contempt for it
when it is economic.

Unfortunately, it is much to be feared that all reference to
American achievement as a standard of comparison will be
rejected, and that the French experiment will be compromised
in consequence. We are, in fact, in danger of sacrificing productivity to a certain conception of society. Projects will be launched
by us for the happiness and dignity of mankind, without our
having the means to put them into effect.

Efforts to achieve better social relationships come up against
the inhibiting influence of the state. Some people attack the
machine and therefore, indirectly, business and industry also,
while forgetting that the most potent factor in making individuals feel like mere members of the herd is the administrative
machine. Centralization is primarily a political thing, a matter
of laws and regulations. In the present circumstances, therefore,
we must call in question the very foundations of the state if we
are to move forward at all. In France, this is just what the vast
majority are unwilling to face and what a few over-vehement
minorities attempt to do, only to end in complete nullity; where
there should be a conclusion, there is a vacuum.

American methods, as we have seen, offer solutions to many
of the problems we find ourselves formulating. But, if it is clear

that yet vaster advances must be made (and the Americans themselves are keen on this), it will be more to the point to ask ourselves questions at European level than within the national framework. If industrial society is sick, the remedy cannot be a national one but must be both conceived and applied at the level of industrial society as a whole.

This revaluation offers an opportunity for a common endeavour between the peoples and is capable of giving new impetus to their sense of solidarity. Youth, and practical enterprise, and the search for objectives of civilization which are worthy of free men, and eagerness to construct new organizational forms for collective living – all this concerns every country which has attained a certain level of technical development.

Marxism, in its time, and the spirit of the Encyclopaedists at a much earlier one, rendered useful service in pointing out that the biggest problems are posed in terms wider than those of the merely national framework: an observation which is more pertinent today than ever before. The technical advances associated with the advent of the planetary age have caused so much commotion that a new type of organization must now quickly be discovered, to restore equilibrium and calm. This is the direction in which Europeans must aim their endeavours; the alternative is to sink into civil disorder. Faced with imminent anarchy, authority will assume special powers, alleging that its tasks of innovation render them necessary, but it will be no more successful than before in satisfying those who wish to see a genuine evolution of society; the result will be to sow the seeds of future revolts, more serious than those we have witnessed in the universities and certain factories. The shocks of 1968 will be succeeded by full-blown revolutions.

But of what does progress consist, if not precisely of foreseeing evolution and of so ordering it as to avert revolution?

FRANCE INDISPENSABLE; IMPOSSIBILITY OF
GENUINELY CONSTRUCTING A NEW EUROPE
WITHOUT HER

We are paying special attention to the case of France in this book, not only because we, the authors, are both Frenchmen, with a natural concern for the future of our country, but also because it is hard to conceive that the new European structures, and the mental attitudes to make them work, can be developed without France. This fact is generally recognized and has already been confirmed in a number of instances. The Americans, like the Russians, accept it as a fundamental item in their political data.

This gives the French a special responsibility.

France was for centuries the leading nation in the world, and occupied the second place throughout the nineteenth. The problems facing her correspond to those preoccupying Europe as a whole. Moreover, having developed to its highest pitch a certain form of state organization within a national framework, France has become the symbol of the nation-state, with all the advantages and defects which this implies. She suffers from a permanent temptation to become preoccupied with her own past, and to persuade herself that such an attitude renders her more capable of planning her future. She is a country endowed with excellent natural equilibrium: the population-pressure is slight, and the accumulation of wealth is big enough to ensure a substantially higher level of wellbeing than might appear from a casual scrutiny of industrial indices. It was natural that for many years she felt no need for rapid development.

Nurtured in the atmosphere of their country's military glory, the French still retain illusions of greatness. The period in their history which marks the beginning of their country's relative decline, namely the Napoleonic adventure, is presented to them in the guise of an epic; nor would they accept any other version. A certain number of their national structures, and a few of their underlying motivations, still date from that time.

Having undergone more big changes since World War Two than in the preceding hundred years, and having been suddenly thrown into a market economy after a long and habitual reliance on autarchy, and having begun to learn, with surprise and anxiety, the economic rules of technical progress, France is now passively undergoing technical mutation, rather than actively controlling it.

She is still a state first and an economy second. This is doubtless the most profound feature of her character; and it is also, in present circumstances, her gravest handicap. We must detect in this fact one of the reasons why the younger generation are dissatisfied, both with their country and with the way she is coping with the novelty of our time.

THE INFLUENCE OF THE STATE AND THE SPIRIT OF COMPETITION

The increase in the size of the market is forcing French firms to climb into the ring against the world champions in their respective fields; a much harder matter than merely competing with one's neighbour. Two attitudes are possible in face of this situation:

(*a*) to take a cool look at the facts and discern the sectors in which French technology is capable of coming out on top, but at the same time to avail oneself of foreign technology where necessary; or,

(*b*) to strive to create, in all or nearly all fields, a specifically French technology.

The second attitude has so far been regarded as the answer in France, but, as French firms do not possess sufficient resources to make out on their own, the state seeks to compensate for their inadequacy by direct intervention; whereas in the United States it does it indirectly, through the firms. Hence it comes about that, in order to hold its position in the market economy we have now entered, French industry is tending towards a condition of semi-control by the state.

In France, state and nation have become so far merged that even when the French are at loggerheads with the state they persistently call on it to intervene. This habit is largely to be accounted for by the fact that our society had reached maturity before the industrial epoch. It also derives from the fact that the whole of our recent history – particularly the two world wars and their aftermath – has favoured public enterprise and official intervention.

INITIATIVE COMES FROM THE TOP

It is customary with the French to transpose the methods of the military and the administration to the economic realm. To them, initiative is something which comes from above. In the days of the French monarchy, the country's activities were organized along lines selected and proclaimed by the sovereign. Industrial development was even in many cases the direct handiwork of the king and his agents, and, later, of emperors and governments; in short, of the state.

In France, attention is constantly focused on the state, on what it means to do and how it means to do it. Very naturally, the administration considers it its duty to assist the government in selecting objectives for the economy, whenever it does not actually select them itself, and subsequently to verify whether the French people are duly carrying out the programmes adopted. Ministries like to look on themselves as the guardians of the people.

Everyone insists that the purpose of economic measures is abundance. Simultaneously, however, there is persistent failure by those in the highest state and administrative circles to dissociate themselves from the attacks launched on the 'consumer society'. They allow doubt to be cast on the very economic system they have made it their mission to develop, and which they say they will improve by using political means to keep individual aspirations under proper control. Despite the intention to support the economy of the West they incline rather to the methods of the East, with which they feel themselves curiously in harmony: it is not uncommon for a French civil servant concerned with economic affairs to be more at his ease with a technocrat in the Kremlin than with staff members of some multinational industrial group.

The tendency towards rigid state control causes politicians and government officials to exert an old-style stranglehold on production activities; which is not the best thing for progress. Moreover, economic nationalism is still visibly in action, still developing, at the very time when the logic of industry is leading to trade on the planetary scale.

Civil service traditions lead to a liking for monopoly. But, to take one example, it is hard to see any cogent justification for it in the case of the telephone. Monopoly has not been good for the development of telecommunications in general (the choice of fields for investment being made from above, by men with little or no understanding of the high priority which ought to be given to communications); and has it really produced much of a bargain for the subscribers?

Our technocratic shortcomings are aggravated by our 'scholocracy', our educational fetishism. 'We must choose our men and constantly check the results they get,' said Lenin. But, all too often, we choose ours on the strength of their paper qualifications and are persuaded to go on trusting them, even after repeated failures, merely because of those bits of paper.

Centralization leads to aberrations. Strict adherence to the loftiest principles can be a dangerous thing; it is sometimes in their name that the most crashing blunders are perpetrated. French morality, tinged quite as much by the principles of officialdom as by the peasant outlook, militates blindly, indiscriminately, against profits and wealth. And unfortunately it must be admitted that behind this morality a complex lies in ambush: the complex of jealousy. In France it is not uncommon for a man to declare himself a left-winger when the truth of the matter is that he is jealous, just as some people are nationalists because other countries' successes have put their noses out of joint.

The opposite of this psychology of jealousy is the psychology of competition and business. In the United States, competition is, broadly speaking, synonymous with the sporting spirit; whereas in France competition is something which is good enough for the other fellow, or is regarded as a means of securing some kind of permanent privilege.

PRIVILEGE IS AN ENDEMIC TEMPTATION

In earlier times, the sovereign rewarded services rendered by granting privileges. From this there developed the practice of selling rights of various kinds to augment the royal revenue.

The wish to acquire a permanent income has become a widespread ambition. The French threw themselves into the Revolution in order to abolish the privileges held by a few of them; thereafter they all began longing to acquire the same privileges, or at least some special advantage or other.

In industry, this mentality shows itself as a quest for the featherbed of a well-protected monopoly; in agriculture, as the demand for guaranteed prices; and in ordinary life, as intrigues for a licence, such as that for a café or a tobacconist. The state behaves as if it was the owner of all that exists or may exist at any future time, and hands it out in a slightly arbitrary fashion. As for the employees of big enterprises, especially in the nationalized sector but also in the private or semi-private sector, insufficiently exposed to competition, such as banking and insurance, they often behave as if the institutions for which they work had been created for the sole purpose of supporting them. The idea of business and the market, which implies the existence of other people, is a minority idea. The commonest view is the belief that, since the state has all the power, it must also have the means to satisfy everybody's wants.

The deficits incurred by public undertakings, or by the Securité Sociale, are not felt to be problems that concern every private citizen but only 'Them', the state. A certain income, a certain guarantee against the whims of fate, and a certain standard of living, are regarded as so many dues which the state and, where applicable, the enterprises over which it has power or ought to have it, are bound to pay.

It is a matter of considerable psychological difficulty in France to get it recognized that the fate of every individual is primarily in his own hands, and only secondarily in those of the state. Paradoxically, the state is criticized and the civil service written off as intolerable and oppressive at the same time as a clamour is raised for liberty and, at least to judge by what people say, a strong desire for *laissez-faire*. These are not exclusively French shortcomings, but they are symptomatic of a state of mind still sufficiently widespread in the country to impede the change-over to a competitive economy and the necessary critical, continual revaluation of the existing structures. Our deficiencies cannot be overcome without big changes in political outlook.

If the French have a sense of living in a country where momentum is running down – demonstrations of prestige notwithstanding – they will remain without any inclination to abandon their present hankerings after perpetual income and excessive security; their hunger, in fact for privilege. If, on the other hand, they feel themselves to be engaged in achieving that great mutation of organization which is called for by the planetary age, they will find it less difficult to acquire a new outlook.

A PRE-INDUSTRIAL LOGIC

A Frenchman likes a well-made piece of work but prefers it to be in the form of craft-work, the excellence of which is gauged by the amount of sweat that went into the making of it. He is shocked by methods which get the work done without the worker seeing it emerge into being before his eyes. Indeed, he tends to regard as unreal any work-process which cannot immediately be taken in by the naked eye. The engineer himself is a peasant or craftsman in that what he admires is a well-made tool or a polished, gleaming product; commerce and finance do not speak to his heart. For many years, French industry was directed by men who took pleasure in developing fine technique rather than sales. Living in a closed circuit, they laboured under the illusion that the volume of sales depended solely on the quality of their products. Even today, there is a general feeling that work is synonymous with production.

The attitude of distrust towards intellectual work is accompanied by the hostility aroused by anything large and powerful; France has an undoubted predilection for things which are small.

For generations, industry in the eyes of the French peasant has meant the city and those mysterious characters, the international financiers whose machinations he suspected it of harbouring. Society's ills were laid at the door of 'the big men', the rich, the powerful. These same 'big' men – not so very big compared with their Anglo-Saxon counterparts – have not meanwhile done anything to make themselves, and their usefulness, familiar to the eyes of the public. They have done their best to present themselves as humbly sweating away at their jobs, instead of coming down into the market-place and proclaiming the reasons which would justify their profits.

Secretive, cooking his books, incurably down on his luck ('The weather's too good, this harvest will cause a glut. . . . The weather's bad, the harvest will be ruined. . . .'), the French employer in town or country has not been the militant champion of technical progress, but its sheepish lackey.

Among the various brakes which, in France, are slowing down the process of adapting the country to the conditions on which progress depends, attention should be focused particularly on those created by friction between classes. The wage-earners have no sense of really being part of, and taking part in, economic activity; they consequently regard finance and sales and the whole business of building for the future as a matter for *les patrons*. Meanwhile *les patrons* preach expansion and are full of lip-service for the liberalism their operations demand – provided liberalism's rules are not to be applied to *them*. Whenever change looms on the horizon they announce that it portends grave dangers for French industry. Change comes, industry goes on, and *les patrons* get a reputation for crying 'Wolf'.

Along with this there is the fact that everything industrial and technical has always raised the hackles of some of the intelligentsia, whose criticism would give one to believe that, in their eyes, France is all the greater for refusing to be contemporary. The real trouble with these people is that they are afraid of the contemporary. Those who reject technology have, in many cases, simply abdicated in face of the challenge of organization; they have run away from the job. Technology is deleterious when not under control, but there is one sure way of dominating it and that is to encase it in the appropriate structures. And this is where the shoe pinches, this is what hurts those unavowed partisans of the past whose inmost wish is to stay put, fortified behind their privileges, intellectual or material. In France, hostility to technology is mainly an attitude of those who are snugly ensconced, or ignorant.

These attitudes, which carry a good deal of weight, cause France – despite her possession of some degree of political influence and the ability to mobilize it on behalf of creative modernization – to seek a fictitious self-preservation by envisaging a Europe which would give her all the advantages of its greater size and scope, without obliging her to accept the rules inherent in these larger dimensions. She is guilty of wishful thinking. If Europe is regarded as a device to enable some nations to compensate their inadequacies at the expense of others, the continent is reduced to a talking-shop, a place for haggling in. A Europe of the nation-states would be a Europe of narrow, purely commercial negotiations, with every country trying to wring the best bargain out of the others. It would not be the Europe of creative innovation, capable of inspiring the old nations with new ambitions and of supplying the means by which those ambitions could be realized.

The French have everything to gain from a change of front, wagering their all on an 'open' future, a future of European dimensions. If a federal setting were to replace the present national one, their peculiar genius for service in the public sphere would place them in a leading position at both European and world level (Adenauer was quite clear about this, and said so). Instead of patching up obsolete doctrines and programmes, fussing over the reform of the milling industry or whatnot, not only marking time but wasting it in large quantities, they would be able to set first-class administrative brains to the task of formulating the new doctrines and programming tomorrow's world. We have no shortage of men capable of erecting the new structures and ensuring their rapid development.

Such a change of outlook is by no means inconceivable. France has had great epochs before now, such as that of the Encyclopaedists, or that in which Marie Curie came to our country (without meeting any hostility because of her Polish origin) and was twice awarded a Nobel Prize for the work she did while living among us. The French of that period had no hesitation in being proud of her; whereas they now sneer because a Nobel Prize is awarded to a German physicist domiciled in the USA! But inherent in the greatness of those epochs was the fact that people had hold of the genuine notion of independence, which is a different thing from nationalistic vanity. From now on, the terms in which we must think are those of human exchange, intercommunication. The position we occupy in the world depends on the degree in which we take part in this contact between man and man, in the movement of goods, ideas and culture. There is no healthy development without competition and selection. By accepting flux in preference to isolation we shall be selecting the fields in which the genius of the race is peculiarly gifted, and it is thus by this means that we shall once more provide ourselves with a decisive role in the affairs of the world. When one is no longer powerful enough to be present in all fields one must station oneself at the junctions and crossroads through which everybody else must pass.

France's major problems, in many cases, are identical with those of Europe. So it makes sense to seek a solution in common. But solving joint problems means going beyond the 'Europe of the nations'. Only expansion – of ideas, as well as of the economy – will render big adaptive changes possible, and only big adaptive changes will enable Europe to move forward from the difficult stage she is in now, steadily losing ground all the time. France can contribute powerfully to this forward movement provided all the qualities which have earned her her place in history can somehow be liberated from those hampering adhesions which make her cling too closely to tradition, and can be used in the service of a cause worthy of her past.

CHAPTER FOUR

GROWING PAINS: INFANTILE MALADIES AND THE CRISIS OF GROWTH IN THE PLANETARY AGE

We are reaching the point in our thoughts about the organization of the world at the dawn of the planetary age at which it is necessary to recall just what is fundamentally in question.

Never have so many books, theses, reports, editorials, discussions and radio or TV programmes been devoted to the future. Many of them are interesting, yet on the whole they overlook the real issues. They do indeed describe the changes which are going on, but fail to reduce them to a synthesis. In order to achieve mastery over the problems of today and tomorrow it is not enough to analyse these problems one by one, piece-meal; a path which often leads to some kind of abdication: the abdication of the masochists, who accumulate alarming descriptions to prove that we are on the brink of huge catastrophes; or the abdication of the *laudatores temporis acti*, who absolve themselves of their debt to the future by clinging to the lessons of the past. Both these categories of people reject innovations, or assert that they must be admitted prudently, cautiously, so that time may be able to perform its gentle work – forgetting that we are not free to maintain or discard old structures as we please, and that evolution and development have speeded up so greatly that structural reform must be carried out as soon as and as fast as possible.

The history of the world is dominated by the evolution techniques. This obvious truth is seldom recognized by historians. They attach importance to men, rightly enough, but pay too little heed to the consequences of the applications of major technical innovations. Yet these applications are invariably involved in the origins of the main stages through which mankind has passed – including the development-stages of organization, the best example of which in the ancient world was given by the Romans, whose language supplied the support for the diffusion of their system.

The irreversible character of development is due to the changes resulting from the acquisition of new knowledge, and from the ensuing practical realizations. The men who truly dominate the epoch in which they live are those who espouse it. Others may shine for a few years yet 'leave not a wrack behind'. They consolidate, temporarily, obsolescent features whose subsequent desiccation and hardening invite revolutionary outbursts as soon as it becomes imperative to make up for lost time. Such men do not appreciate fluidity and its built-in imperative which demands our being continuously capable of transforming structures.

The more technique progresses, the more frequent and numerous are the consequent changes in production and trade. New materials and tools and new modes of work-organization modify our way of life, our outlook and the time-honoured equilibria by which our lives are governed. They present us with problems of growing complexity but at the same time carry within themselves the means of resolving them, provided we are ready to adjust our institutions accordingly. It is true that our world, at the dawn of the planetary age, is a world in which mankind is in danger of committing suicide, and the individual feels pressurized by society, and hunger is still with us; equally, however, it is the world of cybernetics and communications. Their complete working-out is impossible without as radical a revolution in the relations between peoples as in technique itself. If this revolution does not occur, or occurs inadequately, we shall have, not the epoch it ought to have heralded, but one of disorder and failure for mankind. Observations like this are easy, anyone can make them, which is perhaps the reason why too little notice is taken of them;

intellectual snobbery bans them from both philosophical discussion and from political decision-making.

The people in charge, in Europe even more than elsewhere, spend most of their time consolidating arrangements which are not worth the trouble, and fussing with red tape. And these activities are pursued in a restricted framework that may have been all very well in the nineteenth century but is now completely out of date.

The adoption of a purely national, or even European, way of looking at things as a basis for the conduct of affairs causes the keynote, which is planetary, to be forgotten. Our rulers behave like the French nobles in the late eighteenth century, who were at pains to ensure the continued granting of their privileges by the king at Versailles, but averted their gaze from the developments foreshadowing the destruction of the monarchy.

Increased technical progress is causing increasingly numerous and complex links to be woven between peoples, and is tending towards planetization and practical solidarity between different countries and their inhabitants. To meet its challenges, therefore, the world vantage-point is the only suitable one for us to adopt.

Humanity's great issues, at the dawn of the planetary age, transcend individuals and nations and, like it or not, will eventually impose themselves on us all. So the best thing is to devote ourselves without further delay to the building of planetary society, accepting present-day realities as our point of departure.

To approach the question from the right angle we need to bear in mind the fundamental conditions of our epoch:

(1) The third world, the world of poverty, under-development and revolution, has entered the 'forum' of the planetary age.

(2) Humanity is capable of committing suicide. The balance of terror is an insufficient safeguard against this possibility, and peace is permanently threatened in various ways.

(3) The problems which formerly presented themselves on the scale of the city or the nation are now posed, ever more frequently, on the planetary scale.

This set of data demands a new organizational structure

between countries; the American solution, the Soviet communist solution, and American-Russian partnership, are all
inadequate in this context.

THE THIRD WORLD AND ITS PROBLEMS
ARE EVERYBODY'S BUSINESS

One of the chief effects of the Second World War was to
make millions of people conscious of their position as colonial
subjects.

Since then they have been continuously occupied in emanci-
pating themselves. Previously, they had no history; they now
have a common purpose. They have entered the process of
economic development, with all its clashes of interests, internal
conflicts and stubborn disagreement, and its cruelty. But by so
doing they have sloughed their anonymity and mean never to
have 'civilization' imposed on them by others, even if in
practice they find it impossible to avoid being affected by
outside influences.

In 1967, Tibor Mende, addressing the general assembly of
the *Centre de réflexion sur le monde non occidental* (organized by Dr
André Gros), reminded his audience that, in the present-day
world, one human being out of three remembered the experience of living under Western domination, one out of three was
living under a communist régime, one out of four was Chinese
and two out of three were underfed.

The greatest segregation of modern times is, in fact, hunger,
caused by the widening gap between population-growth and
food-production.

World population was of the order of 3 thousand million in
1960. The total is now about 3·5 thousand million; it will have
reached 4 thousand million before 1980 and 6 thousand million
about the year 2000. At the present rate of demographic
increase there would be, in the year 3000, 15 people to approximately every 1·6 square foot of dry land. In order to get at
what these facts really mean, the expression which requires to
be pondered is 'a thousand million'; it is too large for immediate
comprehension.

In order to help its customers to take in this magnitude, the
Crédit Suisse expressed itself in the following terms in 1967:

We can get a peculiarly striking picture of the bigness of a thousand million if we take the smallest unity of time in common use, the second, as our scale of comparison. A thousand million seconds corresponds, in fact, to thirty-one years eight and a half months.

If we convert the value of Switzerland's gross national product, approximately 64 thousand million francs, into seconds, we get something still more impressive: the answer is 2,034 years, which takes us back to 68 BC, when Julius Caesar, as Rome's proconsul in Spain, was still almost at the earliest stage of his political career.

In terms of people, a thousand million represents 20 times the population of present-day France and 5 times that of the United States. In 20 years, therefore, mankind will increase to the extent of 20 extra Frances or 5 USAs.

The population-explosion during the next thirty years in the under-developed countries will be much greater than in the last fifty. Whereas the advanced countries (Europe, the USSR, North America, Japan and Oceania) will increase their population from 1,050 million inhabitants (in round figures) in 1970 to 1,200 million in the year 2000, the under-developed countries (East Asia excluding Japan, *plus* Western Asia, Africa and Latin America) will increase theirs from 2,530 million to over 4,500 million in the same time.[1]

A less well known fact which is still more characteristic of development between now and the year 2000 is that the countries of the southern hemisphere (which includes Southern Asia, Latin America, Africa and Oceania) will be more highly populated than those of the northern hemisphere (Europe, the USSR, North America and the Far East). The ratio at present is 8/7; by the year 2000 it will be 7/5.

Now political and economic influences have always, or almost always, made themselves felt in a north-to-south direction. The constellations visible in the northern hemisphere bear ancient names which remind us of the dominant status that hemisphere preserved for thousands of years, because of the Greco-Roman and Chinese civilizations. The constellations of the southern hemisphere have modern names, such as those of the European travellers who discovered them, or those which have been given to them of late years in a spirit of touchy emancipation.

[1] See Maurice Guernier, *La Dernière Chance du tiers monde* (Paris: Robert Laffont).

One prosaic sign of the north's domination of the south is the fact that the hands of watches, everywhere, turn from left to right, the same way as the shadow on a sundial in the Western hemisphere.

What will happen to the white enclaves in the southern Pacific regions and South Africa when demographic pressures have increased still more? What will happen to the United States' position in Latin America when the latter's population has risen to twice the size of that of North America?

A terrific imbalance is being created. The most severely disinherited masses have acquired the power of expressing themselves. Their acquaintance with technical civilization includes the medical aspect, which is largely responsible for the population-increase, and the transistor radio, which gives them an inexpensive means of being informed about what is going on and also, without knowing it, of being exposed to the various 'psychological infections' with which the wave-lengths are poisoned. On the other hand, they are not yet blessed with the motor car (which in their eyes is a badge of individual 'liberation'), on account of its concomitants of expense, collective equipment and insurance policies. This situation is one of the pointers to the fact that fanaticism gets diffused more widely and far more quickly than prosperity. The basis of the revolt of the third world is information and propaganda, and the placing of both at the service of subversion. In the long run the industrial countries may be going to find the revolt difficult to grapple with. It is a fact that modern methods of warfare make it possible to win battles against large armies, but not to effect long-term occupation of populous territory in which there is a strong guerilla movement. In its various forms, resistance to occupation is becoming more and more vigorous. After all the other examples we have witnessed, from Algeria to Vietnam, the latest is Israel; no doubt the Israelis can beat the Arab countries once, twice or ten times if need be, but in spite of living as a nation under arms Israel cannot occupy them. In other times, the main thing was to win; occupation was an easy matter, and after collecting such booty as they had intended the victors could either go home or take possession of the losers' territory. This is no longer the case. Even if the poorer countries represented a vital threat to the West it would not be practicable to make war on them, since to occupy them for any length of time would be out of the question.

The danger for the richer countries, and particularly for Europe, is indifference, blindness and ignorance. Western Europe was afraid of Stalin because he was at the gates of Berlin and his tanks could have reached Brest in two days. The difficulties lying in wait for the world in the planetary stage are more diffuse and more permanent. The conflicts caused by de-colonization and the rise of the poorer nations keep assailing us endlessly, one after another; we do not so much see them in the form of so many events, as live with them, as a man lives with his ulcer.

The motives which ought to be impelling Europe to play a large part, and one useful to mankind, in this field, demand a much bigger stock-taking, a much sharper act of awareness, than that which helped to set on foot the movement for European unity after the Second World War.

In the under-developed countries, both food-supplies and equipment are increasing too slowly to satisfy the many extra mouths and, *a fortiori*, to cope with endemic malnutrition, despite the productive possibilities offered by modern methods. If these had been applied at least fifty years ago they might have been sufficient to cope with the problem.

Differences in productivity are such that an American farmer feeds forty-four people, a French farmer twelve, a Soviet farmer five, a third-world farmer rarely more than two and in many cases only himself. Food production has not increased as fast as population. Since 1959 (see René Dumont and Bernard Rosier, *Nous allons à la famine*, Paris: Editions du Seuil, 1966), the third world has been incapable of feeding itself, despite the improve-ments the Americans have succeeded in introducing in some sectors of Indian agriculture.

It is quite plain that, faced with problems of this order of size, present aid-programmes will be insufficient. Funds trans-ferred from the rich countries to the poor ones amounted a few years ago to 0·8 per cent of the national product of the former; the Geneva conference of 1964 predicted the figure would need to be 1 per cent; it fell to 0·6 per cent in 1967. These amounts give one some idea just how easy it is to show up the pitiful impotence of our nationally-conceived policies towards the third world. Aid makes no sense unless the programmes which are its practical embodiment are planetary in size and scope.

What is needed is a search for a form of co-operation between the developed and under-developed countries enabling the gap between their living-standards to be reduced by spreading the use of modern technology everywhere. Co-operation of this sort cannot possibly be initiated and directed by one country alone, however powerful.

An equally important task is to arrest the trend which causes the ablest minds in the poor countries to become expatriates. In a report to the United Nations in 1966, Ehsan Naraghi, director of the Institute of Social Sciences, Teheran, drew attention to this aspect of the brain-drain, an aspect almost unnoticed in Europe. There are rural areas in the third world which are totally without doctors and technicians; and in most parts of the third world the facilities for producing trained men are terribly inadequate.

The lack of equipment, too, is daunting.

AT THE DAWN OF THE PLANETARY AGE, THREE GREAT FRONTIERS: HUNGER, EDUCATION, EQUIPMENT

All these observations, which we could duplicate many times over, are intended as a reminder of the three great frontiers separating the countries of the world at the dawn of the planetary age. Their names are hunger, education and technical equipment. In order to make these frontiers less intractable there will have to be an up-dating not only of the structures of the under-developed countries, but also of those of organization at world level.

Are the problems of development in the under-privileged countries really being examined in depth? Recent studies show that there would be no big development-problems if the world had a population of 1,500 millions. Soon, however, the population of the world will be four times that figure. Someone, somewhere, has got to start thinking, in world-scale terms, about the answers.

There are not three worlds but two, the Western and the non-Western; and the non-Western, unified by its overall human situation, despite differences in economic, political, cultural and religious circumstances, constitutes a larger entity than the 'third world'.

'In matters of agriculture, trade, employment, etc., decisions taken "from below", from a national point of view and on a restricted international horizon, are bound to prove questionable and open to challenge.'[1]

Some people in the wealthy countries are tempted to answer these remarks by saying that the Western world is not called upon to embroil itself in development-problems and should go on its own way, leaving the now under-developed countries to adapt themselves to modern technological requirements as best they can. This attitude would be possible only if the 'third' world were not aware of its own poverty. But it has become aware of it; Nehru, for example, said, 'What is new in India is not poverty but the Indian people's awareness of it and determination to become free of it.' This awareness, now widespread, accounts at once for the outbreaks of violence occurring from time to time in the non-Western world, for the efforts which that world is making to become organized – in Africa and Latin America, for instance – and for the ever-greater tendency to agreement among the members of 'the trade union of the poor'. The Brazilian from Recife and the Indian from Kerala are better informed of how the rich half lives than, under Aurelian, the 'barbarians' of the Silesian plains were about the advantages of life in Rome. The attraction exerted by the capital of the Roman empire aroused feelings less intense than the jealousy, envy and anger aroused by the wealth of New York, Paris or Moscow among the peoples now entering the most difficult and painful stage in the growth of industrial society, namely the first stage. The most violent revolutions are often those fought by the poor on their coming into contact for the first time with the rich; the moment at which they can see their poverty clearly.

It could be that Chinese communism will prove capable of gaining control of this current, and turning it to its own advantage.

Russia has come to a halt on her revolutionary road. Revolution was intended to be an irreversible process, and in its way it held out undeniable hopes for betterment. It has been con-

---

[1] General assembly of the *Centre de réflexion sur le monde non occidental*, 1967.

verted into armed nationalism. Lenin wanted to get beyond the stage of nationalism and military might, but, as we know, things turned out differently.

Possibly China will follow a similar line of development, for while on the one hand she sets herself up as the guardian of world revolution and the guardian of the ferment of change, she is also tempted to mobilize on behalf of the Chinese nation – a notion she is in process of discovering for the first time – immense forces, and Asiatic pride, and – the bomb. This does not alter the fact that she is well placed to pose as the leader of the under-developed peoples.

In short, the planetary stage, at which we have now arrived, is characterized at once by the dominant position of the United States and the extraordinary potential of China and, with her, of all Asia.

The Chinese have the advantage of huge dimensions, both in territory and in numbers. Both the size of the population and its innate gifts are such that, inevitably, revolutionists and the disinherited, in considerable quantities, will turn towards them. But, as we need hardly recall, they are implacably hostile to the whites, so that the conflicts caused by development-problems will be accentuated by racial conflicts. These will be so big and formidable that the white countries should make a concerted effort to attain to the forms of organization which will enable them to avoid or canalize the great revolutionary explosions that the future probably holds in store.

At present they are busy with quite other things. But then, it is a characteristic tendency of the West to buy itself a comfortable conscience on the cheap; an attitude reminiscent of the time when a good many Catholics regarded putting something in the collection-box at High Mass on Sundays as a sufficient solution of the social problem, or at least as being enough to make them feel they were doing their duty in that connection.

The reactions of the under-privileged peoples are the premonitory signs that a large, long-term movement is under way which will shake the world all the more profoundly in that hunger is too widespread to be rapidly reduced, and that the transition from absolute under-development to an awareness of a better future will never be a smooth and comfortable thing.

UNDER-DEVELOPMENT AMONG THE 'HAVES'

Under-development exists even inside the wealthy countries, in the USA as in the USSR, in Italy as in Britain. Still more important, the feelings kindled by under-development – jealousy, destructive scrutiny of the established order, lack of faith in progress, the wish to 'drop out' – all these are rife in the wealthy countries.

In addition to the segregation caused by differences of race and living-standards there is that introduced by technology. It is true that modern life demands more and more engineers, but this does not do away with the need for labourers to pour reinforced concrete, or handle pneumatic drills on the roads.

In the United States these jobs are generally done by negroes; Europe has recourse to her poorer provinces, such as Greece or Portugal, and to North African labour.

Pockets of under-development always tend to produce the revolutionary ferment, notably in the USA. As early as 1835, Tocqueville was writing that 'the most formidable of the ills threatening the future of the United States is that arising from the presence of the blacks on its soil'. The historical forecasts of Tocqueville, unlike those of Marx, have proved accurate. Yet there is no such thing as Tocquevillism, whereas Marxism has spread widely; which clearly indicates that great political movements are not necessarily based on the most sensible ideas, and that one of the great challenges of the planetary age is to endow politics with roots in intelligence, not passion. If the United States, Europe and the USSR do not take up this challenge and embark on a genuine search for solutions on a level with the scale of the problem, some very lurid speculations about the future will become permissible.

The possibilities are various. The whites, hostilities having broken out, may fight one another by proxy, drumming up the poorer peoples to settle their quarrels and using them as agents of violence. Or, on the fringes of the empire of prosperity – in Siberia and the southern United States, but also in shanty towns more or less everywhere – there may be an insidious demographic invasion stemming from racist revolts and the various forms of attack on the practice of democracy which accompany that type of revolt. Or China may so exploit her political apparatus as to extend her sway over the under-developed peoples, in which case there would be a danger of war. But the poor nations, who constitute the marching portion of humanity, are so well supplied with manpower that they will not be deterred by the prospect of heavy losses as they advance; whereas if similar losses were to reduce the numbers of the Western peoples, the world's best producers, the influence of the West would shrink and mankind would enter upon a new Middle Ages.

Naïve optimists retort that there is no danger of any such thing; the West is too powerful. We shall content ourselves with drawing their attention to a passage in Robert Heilbroner's *The Great Ascent* (Harper Torchbooks):

We have to envisage the political outlook confronting an isolated America, or even an isolated Western world. It is not reassuring. A stronghold of privilege under siege does not tend, behind its closed doors and guarded walls, to support a wise, tolerant government in its midst. To live in fear of a developing world, to regard that world's successes as so many personal defeats and to see a threat in this un-folding of the course of history which is tending to make good life's deficiencies among the disinherited peoples in the south and the east, might well lead, in the West, to the worst political eventualities. Isolationism may be able to deliver us from the necessity of treating externally with extremist governments, but in all probability it will do so at the price of obliging us to treat with them internally.

THE BALANCE OF TERROR INADEQUATE
TO ENSURE PEACE

Perhaps the most significant fact of the planetary age is that humanity as a whole is now in a position to commit suicide. This possibility constitutes as important a threshold, in the evolution of the organic kingdom, as does the transition from the state of animal instinct, in which suicide does not occur, to that of man, who has arrogated this sombre power to himself.

Both world wars started in Europe, arising from conflicts which were intrinsically European in the first place and whose causes were clashes of interest inside the continent. Only very stupid people, such as Hitler, were capable of imagining that the rest of the world would stand aside from the events which had set the key continent on fire. The two great world conflicts led to the downfall of the old Europe.

Today everyone is aware that the future of humanity itself is at stake, which accounts for the comparatively sensible behaviour of the two great nuclear powers.

The data of the problem of peace and the possible suicide of mankind have been set out by a number of authors; one of the clearest and simplest expositions is that given by Pierre Sudreau (*L'Enchaînement*, Paris: Plon), whom it is pertinent to quote again here. He has written:

> The arsenal is ready. An order, a finger pressing a button, and the festival can begin. . . . Every period has its opportunities and its dangers. What characterizes our own period is that both have now been extended to the point of covering the whole earth. Men have often been faced in the past with a choice between all and nothing, life and death. But that was the life or death of a hero, a village, a people or a state. It is now that of all mankind.

Public opinion, often inadequately informed, is getting used to the danger. In so far as it perceives it at all, it experiences a feeling of impotence when facing the vastness of the problems posed by an atomic future and, strangely, it tends to abandon control over it into the hands of a few individuals. It sees that the two super-powers, terrified at the idea of using atomic bombs, have set up the balance of terror. But this balance is precarious; atomic power has endowed warfare with an unpredictable quality which demands other solutions than those which were used in former times to bring hostilities to an end.

Federalism – using the word to denote the biological organization of political life, a possibility thrown open by technical advances such as telecommunications and the computer – would be a more reliable means than the present balance for preventing man's accession to the planetary stage from being preceded by a world war. But this new-style federalism is slow to arrive, because the bodies working for it are low-powered.

Europe has the opportunity and task of exerting a different influence from that of the two great nuclear powers, by associating atomic equipment with a policy of neutrality which would provide federalism with its guarantee. Increasing collective awareness of the danger ought to lead to the creation of a kind of world police force, which would be all the more useful in that we have now entered upon a series of conflicts of a new kind.

The Vietnam war is not a continuation of the Second World War, but the first war to form part of the labour by which planetary federalism is being brought to birth. The Indo-Chinese war marked the end of colonialism, and its causes were comparatively simple. Those of the war in Vietnam are very different and much more complex. The war is being fought between the United States, which had military and political footholds in South Vietnam, and North Vietnam, which came to the support of revolutionaries who were operating all over South Vietnamese territory; the inhabitants of the latter no longer have a very clear idea who is ruling them, and to what end. Originally, the Americans were not aiming at a military victory. Nor has there ever been an official declaration of war. Moreover, the war would not have acquired such an extension in time if the USSR had not taken a hand, and if China's redoubtable powers of direction and control had not been added to the data governing the problem.

Further conflicts of the same type may be expected. They could well degenerate into world wars; nor, to prevent this, can we trust exclusively to the wisdom of the USSR and the USA, which, ultimately, do not possess the means of imposing their joint will (assuming that they have one) on the nations. Europe would seem to be better placed to exert a positive influence on those two powers' settlement of others' conflicts, because of her considerable moral authority, due partly to the sufferings she underwent in two world wars. But she would have to provide herself with the means of exercising such an influence on the world, an influence which would not have to be based on military power in order to prove effective.

We are not living in the days when Stalin could dismiss the power of the Vatican with the ironical query 'How many divisions has the Pope?' Since that time moral authority has acquired a certain ascendancy – Kosygin's visit to the Pope is a pointer to this. Let us make use of this ascendancy. Along this path, and no other, can Europe show her true worth.

Obviously this presupposes a true renaissance of her powers. We must make use of our past, transform it into our gift to mankind. We shall then cease to use it as a subject for nostalgic regret.

FROM TOWNSHIP AND NATION TO THE PLANETARY SCALE

The police, the organization of medicine and public health, the regulations needed to control our economic arrangements, the harmonious dovetailing of production activities, and the laws which protect the smooth running of society, all these exigencies of collective existence now clearly have their being on a wider plane than that of a city, a country or even a continent.

The gap between the development of technique and that of the organization required, both to exploit technical possibilities to the maximum and to sidestep the worst of the inconveniences they bring in their train, is one of the characteristics of this century. The ineluctable consequences of technical advance are general, and world-wide; the governmental and organizational structures of our society are still uncertain, limited and national. There are dangers which they will not enable us to face, dangers of which public opinion, obsessed by the possibility of atomic war, is too little aware, but which nevertheless insidiously permeate our society.

Mankind, in fact, is not only capable of running headlong into atomic suicide but is also at the mercy of the poisons which are being produced in laboratories, sometimes unexpectedly, as incidental by-products of the rapidly rising tide of discovery. In Nigel Calder's *Unless Peace Comes*, fourteen international experts explain that nuclear devices by no means necessarily represent man's ultimate ingenuity in finding new ways of slaughtering his fellows. Over half the advanced research now going on is aimed at military application. A Swedish microbiologist, Carl Göran Heden, points to methods of sabotage by which it would be simple to render life totally impossible in modern cities, where food and water supplies can be poisoned without difficulty. Defence against biological attack is much harder to accomplish than the attack itself. Two French experts, Marçel Fetizon and Michel Magat (of the Faculté des Sciences d'Orsay), writing about 'psychic' poisons, state that ten kilograms (about twenty-two pounds avoirdupois) of some of these would be sufficient to poison all mankind. Again, it is not beyond the bounds of imagination that someone will discover a way of eliminating the ozone from the atmosphere, thus removing our protection against ultra-violet rays. The geophysicist Gordon MacDonald, a member of President Johnson's scientific committee, has indicated the possibility of adapting meteorological and climatological research to military needs. By destroying environmental equilibrium it would be possible to render life impossible throughout a province or even a country. Mac-Donald pushes his speculations to the point of envisaging the glaciation of certain regions. These forms of warfare, to which China would seem to be peculiarly vulnerable, could be deployed without their victims' becoming fully aware of the fact. It would, for instance, be difficult to determine whether a series of droughts had been caused by human or by climatic agency. Are we to conclude that science is damned? The scientists themselves are in agreement that we are confronted with a choice: either science or war must be eliminated. Such is the magnitude of the problems which the dawn of the planetary age has forced upon mankind.

THE UNITED STATES POWERFUL BUT ALONE

None of the world's present leaders is promoting the development of the spirit of association which would enable us to meet more effectively than at present the challenges of the technical era, and to eliminate the gravest of the dangers now threatening humanity with self-destruction.

The United States, as we have pointed out, is more powerfully equipped in the technical sense than any country in the world. It endeavours to weave round itself a network of military, monetary and commercial alliances, and in spite of encountering many difficulties is meeting with some success. It has surrounded the communist world with a belt of military strongpoints. But it is insufficiently assured of the friendship of the peoples gravitating in its own orbit; and it approaches world problems from a viewpoint closer to that of the nationalisms of history than to a truly federative spirit.

The Vietnam war has caused an anti-American reaction in most countries in the world. Robert Kennedy noted this in his book, *Towards A New World*:

This war has alienated from us our closest friends in the Atlantic alliance. None of them has seen fit to help us. They go on trading both with North Vietnam and with China and some European religious organizations are giving their help to North as well as South Vietnam, an attitude which would have been unthinkable in Korea or during the Second World War. I have noticed in Europe, among men and in countries with nothing but friendly feelings to the USA, a deep disquiet and a total lack of agreement with regard to our policy; their opinion is that we are getting dangerously out of touch with reality.

We have shown that the United States, because of the weight it carries in the world and the protector's role it plays in regard to some of the non-communist countries, might well claim to exert a powerful and in many ways a beneficial attraction on a large number of peoples. However, because of differences in outlook and living-standards between these peoples, and also because of nationalistic feelings and the infusion of jealousy they contain, any action of world scope undertaken by the US will arouse accusations of attempted hegemony.

Things might be different if the US allowed its presidents to be elected by all the countries which are increasingly affected by its influence. It is doubtful whether it would agree to this; but, even if it did, how much power would a country like France have, or Italy? As much as the State of New York, or anything even approaching it? At all events, the Americans themselves do not think that United States foreign policy, in its present form, is in tune with the wishes and cares of a rapidly changing world.

George Ball states this clearly in his book, *The Discipline of Power: Essentials of a Modern World Structure*: 'We are nearing the end of our role as the world's policeman and, if we are sufficiently attentive to the new conditions of a world in flux, shall be better able to face up to our responsibilities in the future.' He also says: 'The world is too complicated for the United States alone to assume responsibility for its leadership.' And he appeals to Europe to unite and intervene more effectively in world affairs.

We go further than Ball because we show that it is not enough for Europe to unite economically, as she is trying to do. As for her political union, it is not only proving slow of achievement but would in any case fall short as an answer to the problem of world organization in the planetary age.

'Super-nation Europe' would be tempted either to liberate itself from American influence and consequently to create rivalries supplementary to those existing already, of which the world has more than enough, or to ally itself with the United States to 'build an industrial structure of the power of the northern hemisphere', as Ball wishes. But the large unit so created – if it worked – would impress the rest of the world as a threat of domination. For all its power and importance, it would not solve any problems at planetary level. Moreover it would be difficult to structure. The Americans would be unable to conceive of this being done otherwise than in accordance with their own ideas. They would therefore trigger – as they sometimes do already, without always realizing it – reflexes of defensive nationalism, and these in turn would arouse the socialism of fear.

This alliance with the United States would, in addition, involve Europe in the risk of being permanently cut in two. The communist countries, which are tempted by a certain species of liberalization, would in fact be reluctant to engage in closer co-operation with the West except along lines transcending classical political relationships.

COMMUNISM, THE ENZYME OF DIVISION

As for the USSR, it has long since shown that it was relapsing into nationalism.[1] Writing in *Le Figaro*, 20 December 1967, André Brincourt remarked of Soviet television that its greatest deficiency was its lack of interest in the outside world, and that it was chiefly preoccupied with the greater glory of Russia. All the Soviet structures are in fact aligned towards the same end. It cannot be said that the universality of the communist

---

[1] The course of events since August 1968 in Prague and elsewhere in the Soviet world simply confirms, and more than confirms, our conclusion that the communist system has no satisfactory solution to the problems of association between countries; moreover, many observers have underlined the 'rift' on the plane of information which exists between the USSR and other countries, 'the sclerotic mentality of some of Russia's leaders' (Henri Pierre, writing in *Le Monde*) and, of course, the helplessness of Europeans in a matter of direct concern to them.

doctrine emerges any more strongly for this, or that the USSR is conducting itself as a great federative power.

The Internationale was originally a revolutionary trump card, to be produced as occasion demanded, but is now used in Russia exactly like the national anthem, notably at the funerals of Soviet heroes: it was heard at that of Gagarin, although he was quite as much a figure of planetary as of Russian significance. Communism, with its one-party dogma, is now obliged to take account of nationalist trends and 'liberal' aspirations.

To the leaders in Moscow, Soviet foreign policy is now of greater importance than the task of furthering a world party with a world philosophy. And it is in any case inadequate, in seeking to initiate a planetary-type organization, to set about uniting only the 'proletarians'. There are economies in which the number of those who can be regarded as proletarians is becoming smaller every day.

Whereas in the eyes of the rich countries the USSR is, as it were, an enzyme stimulating division, in the eyes of the poor countries it has entered the camp of the rich. Which, incidentally, is one of the reasons for the break between the USSR and China, the others being caused simply by differences of race and living-standards and a clash of interests along the frontier.

Just as the Americans' particular conception of the organization of the West has brought about a recrudescence of nationalism in France and may do the same in some other countries, so the Russians' particular conception of the organization of the Soviet zone of influence has caused autonomist reactions in countries which had been regarded as 'satellites', and against which the USSR has latterly been compelled to use force in order to keep them correctly in orbit.

A structure of relations between societies which is based solely on superior power inevitably prompts the weaker partners to stress whatever differentiates them from the stronger, instead of concentrating on the features which bring them closer together. Everything achieved by domination sooner or later stimulates the will to resist. This is not how planetary problems will be solved.

Even to make communist countries co-exist, it is essential to devise a federal type of organization within which the spirit of association is stronger than the spirit of domination.

BI-POLARITY POSSIBLE BUT STERILE

There remains another hypothetical method of organizing the world, an *entente* of the USSR and the USA. But can anyone really see this happening in the near future? It is true they have succeeded in reconciling their views on nuclear non-proliferation, but this does not stop them out-bidding one another in other things. They have a similar attitude, inspired by fear, towards atom war and towards China, but this has not engendered a will to work together or even to start thinking together. Supposing an alliance was in operation between them, would it not, however imposing its character, come up against the same reactions on the part of other peoples as does the Atlantic alliance, which is at least a *de facto* phenomenon?

George Ball, in the book already quoted, indicates that the maintenance of a bi-polar world is capable of arousing dangerous opposition in various quarters; his observations tally with ours. What type of organization can one in fact see emerging from an alliance of two military powers? In order to make progress in the search for structures better suited to the planetary age, a process of change and adaptation must be set in motion whose source can lie only in constructive thinking. But the bi-polar, bi-partisan idea is exclusively negative, being composed wholly of a mutual division of influence and a common stock of prudential reflexes.

It is a totally different matter to build peace by forging closer relations, making indispensable use of economic, technical and commercial co-operation to provide a new and more hopeful framework. The increasing interdependence between the peoples can be made to serve the cause of their mutual comprehension, but only if there is a political will to that effect; and this will needs a support. This is where Europe, in the present state of the world, both must and can play a part. Only she is capable of mobilizing this will, which, ideological and material differences notwithstanding, is already present in millions of men and women.

But, we repeat, Europe will not succeed in doing this unless she executes a veritable mutation.

FEDERATION, EUROPEAN-STYLE

Europe, divided physically and politically, is myopic, groping about in the closed chamber of her own economic problems; the ostrich seems to be her only model in her struggles to escape from the dangers threatening her; she wanders in a maze of absurd disputes, after the manner of factions in Byzantium. She is involved in the contest of influence between the USA and the USSR, both as a participant and as one of the trophies at stake. Unless she changes her mood and her methods she will be incapable of spreading and promoting a philosophy of action worthy of the planetary age, a philosophy whose absence is making itself acutely felt at the present time.

The industrialized portion of the world, with its white majority, is psychologically split by schisms running in various directions. Some of the peoples still have a religion or religions, others have not, so that the unifying power which religion might exert, transcending frontiers, is crumbling and vanishing.

Moreover religion, though it has been capable of prompting new developments in the past and paving the way for them, is incapable of furnishing solutions to the problems of political organization in the planetary age. Catholicism – for centuries the pillar of the West – is aware of this and has given up its world-wide evangelical mission; and perhaps, in so doing, it was hinting to statesmen that the time had passed for converting, just as it had for conquering, *all* the peoples of the world, and that the apposite thing was rather to work for a single ecumenical movement that would gather and unite all the common elements in the divergent outlooks and attitudes of the sons of men.

A new form of constructive thought is needed. It is quite possibly being fostered by the non-materialistic thinking which has been gaining ground for some time; it may, for example, possess powerful roots in the cogitations of such men as Lecomte de Noüy and Teilhard de Chardin. But the political forms embodying and expressing these roots have still to be found.

The dawn of the planetary age must be provided with its manifesto.

The first article in such a declaration would have to be devoted to the necessity of averting war. If that calamity took place, and if part of mankind survived, the poor nations, probably including China, would be the ones to get the world in their grip and the result would be a terrifying period of regression.

To have a good chance of avoiding war the only thing, as was pointed out by Antoine de Saint-Exupéry, is to give the peoples something to build together. They must find common solutions to their common problems, in defiance of their differences of language, structures and standards of life.

As long as no such centre of federative effort exists, it will be possible to set up the appropriate structures only in so far as one community sets the example. It is most unlikely that the USA and USSR – unlikely both because of their power and in spite of their apprehensions – will feel the need to switch their own policies in that direction.

So there remains only Europe.

OUR PROPOSAL: A NEW EUROPE, THE PILOT PROJECT OF THE PLANETARY CENTURY

In proposing that Europe enter upon a new path, different in kind from those she has followed until now, leading to associative structures above and beyond those of states, in other words to a federal construction, we are engaging on a Pascalian wager.[1]

No other road is possible if our continent has any desire to play the role called for by the circumstances. Even should it fail in the attempt, its efforts will have harmed neither itself nor the rest of the world.

Europe, by reason of her history, her sufferings and her human resources, holds the germ of the formulae which can provide the design for the world's future, but that germ has not yet been fertilized.

The fact that the United States and the Soviet Union – whose chosen names proclaim the *leit-motiv* of union – have, by a

[1] See p. 241. (*Tr.*)

glaring paradox, gone over to nationalism, automatically gives Europe the responsibility of fostering the ecumenical spirit and promoting federalism.

She will not get there by a mere process of addition, successively piling reform on reform, but only by practising a genuine long-term strategy – ambitious, global, conceived as a synthesis. The issue is not one of removing customs barriers or even creating a Europe of the Six, or the Seven, or the Nine, but of setting in train the organization of the world at the dawn of the planetary age in terms of the most widely distributed of this age's resources – modern techniques.

CHAPTER FIVE

PROPOSALS FOR EUROPE

More and more, and faster and faster, people, goods, ideas and industrial and commercial structures are crossing frontiers. Currencies are interlinked. Collectivities are becoming more and more interdependent, but political institutions have not kept up. The problems presented by relations between countries and between the social groups within them are not being faced on the level to which, in cold fact, they belong. Technique causes them to be presented in world terms, whereas our institutions are still conceived, and still function, in a national or at best a continental frame. It is becoming urgently necessary to leave this stage behind and resituate politics in a new dimensional frame, the planetary dimension. It will not be a question of creating a government comparable to those of nation-states but of setting up new entities, new forms of organization, which must be designed to accommodate the accelerated evolution of our technical ways and means. These new political organisms constitute our only hope of averting the grave dangers by which humanity is threatened. For the national approach to the problems of industrial society leads, in fact, and will continue to lead, either to breakdown, when practised by medium-sized countries (as is shown by the recent disturbances in France, after ten years of apparent stability), or, when practised by great powers, to tension and crises on a wider scale (as is shown by American and Russian policies and their effects).

This is a field in which Europe is capable of real innovation. And it is in her own interest and that of other peoples that she should set about it.

FEDERALISM *A LA CARTE* AND PROGRESSIVE FEDERALISATION

Federalism, as we shall see, has become imperative for reasons which have always militated in its favour, namely the fact that it seeks to reconcile the needs of collective life with the freedom of the individual, and with the diversity of the various social groups within the collectivity.

It is also imperative because, thanks to cybernetics – the tool it has previously lacked – it is the mode of organization which makes it possible at once to cope with the interdependence of people and peoples, and to conquer the difficulties produced by the growing complexity of social life.

FEDERALISM DEFINED

We asked Denis de Rougemont, who has certainly thought more about federalism and done more to get it put into action than most people have, to summarize its content and significance:[1]

I propose to use the term *federalist problem* to denote a situation in which two antinomial human realities, each equally valid and vital, are juxtaposed in such a way that the solution can be attained neither by reduction of one of the terms nor by subordinating either to the other, but only in a wider creation which embraces, satisfies and transcends the requirements of both.

I shall therefore use the name *federalist solution* for any solution which, making it a condition to respect both terms of the antinomy, sets out to compose their relations in such a way that the resultant of the tension between them shall be positive. In the language of the games theory of von Neumann and Morgenstern, we should say the question was one of determining the optimum which harmonizes

---

[1] The passage contributed here by Denis de Rougemont forms the thesis of his book, *Théorie générale du fédéralisme*.

two contradictory maxima – as supply and demand are harmonized in the form of a price.

The whole set of problems and solutions, thus defined, constitutes what I shall call the federalist policy and federalist politics, in the widest sense these words can bear.

Before asking ourselves what sort of human being corresponds to such a policy, and what sort of human being it will intend to call forth, let us note that it is the translation of a schema of thought, a bi-polar relational structure, the model for which is already known to us: namely the pattern elaborated by the founders of Western philosophy in the dialogue in which the contending parties were the Ionian thinkers and those of Elea – Heraclitus *versus* Parmenides – and whose subject was the fundamental antithesis of the One and the Many. A parallel process, connected with this one by a synchronistic if not a cause-and-effect relationship, produced the earliest definitions of man as an individual, distinct and free yet involved in his city; and of the city or autonomy (which means, literally, 'self-regulation') as the cell-unit or basis of leagues and federations.

All this is specifically Western. In the face of this same problem of the One and the Many, the various Eastern metaphysics choose to reduce the conflict by suppressing one of the terms – the Many – by means of a lengthy and severe course of asceticism whose purpose is to efface distinctness, including the individual, by merging everything into the One, which is beyond distinction. But the West, from the beginnings of Greece as a great civilization, has sought to retain both terms, keeping them not in neutral equilibrium but in creative tension, and the success of this ever-renewed and ever-threatened endeavour is what denotes the health of European thinking, its accuracy and rightness, the degree in which it extracts order from the chaos of indistinctness and from the anarchy of individuals existing in isolation; an order-seeking which applies equally to matters physical and metaphysical, aesthetic and political. *Opposition is co-operation, and the clash of opposites engenders the most beautiful harmony*, says a celebrated fragment of Heraclitus.[1]

The art, science and technique of setting up this creative tension between opposed but equally valid realities are what constitutes and defines the specific and original contribution of Western thought; and this definition holds good for federalism as it did for the great

---

[1] *Note by the authors:* It is well known how widely this duality occurs in nature, from the constitution of matter to the sexes. The regulation of every process in the organic realm is conducted in terms of antagonism. Our heart-beats, for example, are governed by an equilibrium between the tendency of the sympathetic nervous system to accelerate them and of the parasympathetic to slow them down.

age of Greece, with its dialectic of the individual and the city: a dialectic resolved by the notion of the citizen, and rendered creative by virtue of his actions.

Pierre Duclos and Henri Brugmans were saying the same thing in their *Fédéralisme contemporain* (1962):

Federalism implies that the particular elements composing the federation remain distinct, recognizable and valid in relation to the power of the federation as a whole. Federalism is a symbiosis without confusion and without the disappearance of the specific.

All Western thinkers with a respect for reality and for the conditions of life – which latter consist of antinomies, oppositions, conflict of contraries – have aimed their investigations in this direction; a tendency which begins with thinkers inspired by Christianity and notably by the great Councils from the fourth to the seventh century.

Later figures who come to mind in this connection are not only such dialectical minds as Pascal, Kierkegaard and Nietzsche and political thinkers like Rousseau, Tocqueville and Proudhon, but also the physicists and logicians of recent years.

Stressing the underlying nature of federalism, which considers the human person under the dual aspects of the individual and of the citizen who is part of his society, Denis de Rougemont adds:

The federalist analysis of a situation starts from the concrete, in the sense of beginning by examining the nature of a task or particular function which is recognized as necessary, or as promising interest or pleasure. In the second stage, it evaluates the optimal dimensions of the required area of execution, a judgment executed as a function of the following three factors: possibility of participation (civic, intellectual, economic); efficiency or productiveness; economy of means. Finally, in the third stage, after determining these dimensions and the corresponding unit (communal, regional, national, continental, world-size, or any of the various combinations of these geographical and political magnitudes), it remains only to designate the level of responsibility at which decisions relating to the task under consideration are to be taken. It may well be, of course, that decision-making will have to go on at several levels, hierarchically related. And the area of operations both can and should vary in different tasks, according to whether these involve everyone in all regions, or everyone in a few regions or in a single region.

The number of combinations that the federal method may

well throw up for consideration is undoubtedly likely to arouse alarm and despondency in officials of the old type, accustomed to taking things one at a time, in convenient round terms. But at this point in his exposition Denis de Rougemont, like ourselves, stresses the contribution made by cybernetics to the tasks of organization. Recourse to cybernetics makes it easy to do the following things, provided we want to do them and are willing to change and adapt the classical structures:

Change from a smaller scale to a larger one, refusing to remain imprisoned by nation-scale criteria; and to:

Take into account the numerous factors resulting from the interdependence between individuals and groups; and ensure that the administrative services are highly supple and responsive.

'Federalism,' writes Denis de Rougemont, 'is autonomy (of regional groups, and of enterprises) *plus* computers: that is to say, respect for the infinite complexity of things as they actually are – a respect now rendered practicable by modern technical possibilities.'

This being so, there is no longer any valid reason to oppose a gradual, piecemeal adoption of federalism (see the review *Réalités*, September 1965, for a sketch of this); we shall enlarge on the subject later.

In this connection Denis de Rougemont cites two examples: housing, and the university:

Urban elephantiasis, the population explosion, and the factory-farming conditions under which human beings are crammed into tall blocks designed for making money, not for being useful or pleasant, have produced a crisis situation whose acuteness is indicated by various symptoms, one of which is the high suicide-rate. The human being living in cheap housing, overcrowded inside his home and anxious for a little solitude, goes out into the street and merges in the anonymous crowd; but what he gets there is a bad kind of solitude, mere non-communication with others, among whom he moves as if they were not there. The solution would be to re-create the conditions of community life, starting with certain architectural dimensions and structures: housing units with from 5,000 to 25,000 inhabitants, provided not only with green spaces but with streets reserved for pedestrians and with a public square serving the purpose of an agora or forum, complete with church, town hall, markets, cafes – a place made for gossip, assignations, intrigue, and the shouts of newspaper sellers. Participation in community life depends on these material arrangements, which must be made strictly with such participation in mind.

Dimensions, however, may be numerical just as well as architectural. The present unrest in universities everywhere is caused, fundamentally, by the contradiction between general culture in the traditional, accepted sense and the acquisition of professional qualifications, whose market value is in direct proportion to their degree of specialization. But the rather aimless revolt of the students at the present time, a kind of vortex of bewilderment, is an almost automatic consequence of the increase in the student population. If you multiplied all the dimensions of a staircase by ten it would be unusable. Similarly, the tenfold increase in the student population has made a nonsense, an impossible acrobatic feat, out of any attempt at real, fruitful participation in seminars, research and even the ordinary lecture courses, so that it becomes doubtful whether the university is any use as a teaching institution and, therefore, whether it is worth the money spent on it. The federalist remedy is: recalculate the optimal dimensions of a university worthy of the name – that is to say a university which makes room for inter-disciplinary research and seminar methods, on the basis of from twelve to eighteen students under one, or perhaps two, professors, as the right size for a seminar; and adopt as the fundamental unit not the conventional Faculty, but the department of combined research; and organize and run it like a college.

In short, 'a federation of small units', to quote the solution urged by Professors Jacques Monod and Lichnerowicz at the conference held at Caen in 1966.

All civic life, from the Greek *polis* onwards, has been essentially communal. It is to the civic or political[1] level that we must refer in order to review the problem of federalism in its classical form, the only one to be found in textbooks and encyclopaedias. The problem can be enunciated as follows: how is cohesion to be ensured in a whole which is large enough to undertake common tasks such as defence, foreign affairs and economic policy, without prejudice to the autonomy and essential rights of the fundamental units of which the whole is composed? How can the whole become big enough to be strong, yet remain small enough to be free?

Here again, merely voting a constitution of federal type (however skilfully thought out), will not suffice to resolve once and for all this permanent conflict, this Protean antinomy which is for ever being

---

[1] The word is derived from *polis*, a town or city; in Latin *civitas*, whence our words civic and civics.

reborn in a different shape. A vital, living method is needed: the dimensions of the tasks to be undertaken must constantly be estimated afresh, authority for decision-making must be continually redistributed, concentrations of force must always be commensurate with the power required to be obtained (economy of means), and, at the same time, the smaller fundamental units must be made more numerous so as to maintain or augment the chances of participation, intellectual, political or affective.

Under our eyes we can already see this two-fold dynamism creating, on the one hand, broader and broader unions, corresponding to new tasks which demand continental means for their execution, and, on the other, smaller communities corresponding to local needs, the demands of education and the exercise of citizenship; and from this dynamism, this concrete dialectic unfolding itself in the two dozen or so countries of our continent, there are emerging more than a hundred regions, each with its own metropolis, which are destined to become the fundamental units of the future European Federation that will replace the nation-states fashioned in the course of the nineteenth century.

We can thus see that political federalism in or between states, the only kind discussed by the accepted writers on federalism, was in fact only a special case, a limited application of a much wider conception of human relations within the city and indeed of public relations in general. The late and much lamented Pierre Duclos showed how clearly he appreciated this discrepancy when he wrote that 'life under federalism is such that the institutional form known as the state, so far from giving it a complete outlet, hardly begins to express it at all'.

And he went on:

Federalism is something other than a mere juridical or political recipe: it is one of the major types of the integration of the political relationship and, as perhaps we may say even more truly, one of the great life-styles and civilization-styles, on a level with liberalism, socialism and democracy in its ability to nourish and strengthen the thought-life of societies and to dictate to men those 'behavioural images' whose historical importance has been so rightly emphasized by Bertrand de Jouvenel.

A EUROPE WITH OPEN DOORS

Europe indisputably needs federalism, in the sense defined in the foregoing note by Denis de Rougemont. At the same time it is hard to see what would be the guiding principle for the construction of a supranational state, with member-states obeying a growing system of laws common to them all, and progressively co-ordinating their policies in all fields: foreign affairs, defence, trade and agriculture. These states have different pasts and particular affinities. If some of them are capable of amalgamating, by all means let us help them to do so. But if, as experience shows, the path to such amalgamations is strewn with obstacles, let us not wait for them to take place but let us rather push on meanwhile with the task of promoting the European idea. Proceeding somewhat differently, let us not wait for a hypothetical unification but, rather, conclude a series of agreements under which groups of collectivities, conscious of their identities and responsibilities, will actively set about the common tasks imposed by evolution.

Let us make a start in the sectors where the weight of the past and of particularism makes itself felt the least heavily. There are many of these sectors and there are going to be more and more, because a whole string of activities, from tourism to advanced chemical laboratories, is acquiring an international character. By this means we shall see the development of federalism *à la carte*: that is to say, a network of agreements under which certain nations and collectivities will decide to co-operate on one plane or another, this plane being always clearly delimited in scope and the number of participants varying according to the aim in view. Suppose, for example, that at some future time Switzerland, or Sweden, or one of the East European countries for that matter, should sign a convention with France and other nations for the establishment of an international university; would this in any way justify France in demanding that her co-signatories also bear a hand in French military defence problems? The diversity of the interests and aims at work in a given situation must always be considered and catered for. Over-institutionalization, which overlooks the biological nature of society, is a danger to be avoided.

Federalism *à la carte* would make it possible to transcend the Europe of the Six, a setting which in many fields is proving too narrow and which must be regarded merely as a nucleus, a beginning. As an example, consider the mobility of labour, in which a certain amount of progress was recorded in 1968 but which remains only limitedly successful as yet. Switzerland, which does not belong to the Common Market, made an agreement with Spain, another non-member country, followed by an agreement with Italy, one of the signatories of the Treaty of Rome; after which France, a member of the Six, also made an agreement with Spain. Are these bilateral arrangements really contemporary, or are they a bit old-fashioned? Would it not be better to draw up some kind of multilateral agreement on a wider basis than that of the Europe of the Six? Transport is another case: does it make sense to tackle problems of transport within the frontiers of the 'Common Market' when, in the nature of things, much European traffic passes through Switzerland and could not rationally be made to do otherwise?

It will be necessary, however, to ensure that the admission of any country or organization to a European association is not in conflict with its refusal to participate in whatever other arrangements are complementary to such an association. All situations have their dependent contingencies; the notion of sets and sub-sets (to borrow a term from mathematics) must be borne in mind here.

Though our federalism *à la carte* cuts out any idea of making any institution permanent, like 'the law of the Medes and Persians which altereth not', and disclaims any ambition of founding a new state – an ambition which it automatically supersedes –, it nevertheless demands a certain adventurous spirit of resolution from all those wishing to take part in it. After all, if you want a good meal you do have to go into a restaurant, sit down and look at the menu.

Federalism *à la carte* is based on the need to build human relations organically, from the ground upwards, instead of imposing them from the top downwards. Politics should respect and mirror the ramifications of life; but we would be wrong if we tried to structure interdependence-relationships based otherwise than on the sane use and development of techniques and minds.

The men entrusted with the welfare of the nascent Europe of the Six are orientated, both by their background and by the terms of reference of their appointments, towards defending interests which are national and in many cases immediate. It is no part of their vocation to visualize a federal future, whether they be national officials serving on committees of experts, or foreign ministers with a tradition rather of scoring points in negotiation by taking advantage of situations inherited from the past, than of collaborating with an eye to the future, constructively. Every one of them, on returning to his country's capital, is more concerned to show his government that he has duly defended the interests for which he is responsible than to estimate the prospects of forward-looking undertakings elaborated in concert with other countries' representatives. No country has the power within itself to refashion its own conduct; an observation applicable to everything which is out of touch with its environment, including French universities, whose failure to achieve their own mutation internally erupted externally, not long ago, with full publicity.

Federalism is a stimulus to adaptation, whereas national pride blocks development and causes crises of readjustment of the kind experienced in France in 1968.

As for the European executive officials, whose services are too well known by now to require praise, they are tending perforce to become more and more like civil servants and are consequently losing something of their inventiveness, which was in any case severely limited from the outset by the terms of the treaties under which they were appointed.

LANDINGS ON THE MOON OR CO-OPERATION ON THE EARTH?

Before the emergence of all the technical means now at our disposal for bringing people in all the continents closer together, world federalism was a Utopian idea; but those means have made the world a smaller place now. There are Utopias which remain Utopian, and others which eventually enter the sphere of possibility. To put men on the moon was one of the latter: the Americans have done it before our eyes. Why should not Europe, for her part, throw herself into the realization of another ancient dream, that of teaching the inhabitants of the whole world the value of human fellowship; and why should she not achieve this by being the first to set the example – which would not be an expensive achievement, like space travel, but, on the contrary, a source of enlightenment?

THE LOGIC OF FEDERALISM, WHICH IS OF THE SAME FAMILY AS THE LOGIC OF BUSINESS AND INDUSTRY

Modern federalism, if it is to function well, presupposes the application of liberal principles, notably in the economic sphere. Here we must take care not to let our minds be shackled by the traditional meanings of words: liberal principles are those applied in societies where the organization of activities does not depend exclusively on the state but mainly on firms, groups, associations, trades unions and so on.

Today, the enterprise or firm is the cell, the basic constituent, of the social tissue of all modern societies, and the type of structure most highly adapted to our century and its conditions. Whatever may be going on in the way of ideologies and political doctrines, no society can be built without enterprises. If we choose cells and cell-tissues as our metaphor, the reason is that the appearance of such biological cross-references is what has indicated the beginnings of an understanding of social problems, and that the development of a society composed of enterprises presents a powerful analogy to the development of an organ composed of cells. The principal functions contributing to biological evolution are in fact realized in the enterprise. The fundamental characteristic of an enterprise is self-regulation, the function which characterizes the various levels of biological organization.

The enterprise needs to be capable of self-regulation in various ways. It is subject first of all to the vital necessity of sustaining a dialogue with its own personnel. Then it must do the same with its customers, without whom there would be no point in producing anything. The Americans have understood this so clearly that they regard it as being of prime importance; and while they do perhaps go too far in this direction the fact remains that this quest for customers is an essential part of self-regulation. Another part, equally important, is that governing the enterprise's position in relation to progress, which must be followed neither too fast and closely nor too slowly and remotely. The slightest lapse, putting the enterprise chronologically out of step with progress, may be fatal, which is why delays and bottlenecks are of such crucial interest to every enterprise.

In societies where the role and mechanisms of enterprises are either unknown to large numbers of 'intellectuals' or, which is scarcely better, are known but not respected, general development is frail and precarious. Only in so far as a society agrees to allow free play to the self-regulation mechanisms of enterprises (and hence to its own adaptation to the environment) is there any prospect of harmonious evolution. Any mechanisms, whatever their origin or purpose, which inhibit the self-regulation of an enterprise are dangerous. Remember what happened to Simpson, who met his end when competing in the Tour de France: his self-regulation was cut off by the administration of a drug to block the incoming messages of fatigue in his nervous system, and the result was death. Everything in this world has its own level of regulation, and tampering with the circuits merely introduces complications.

If an enterprise happens to be national there arises a vexatious species of interference between it and government, entailing the intervention of political factors which distort natural mechanisms. This has been taken into account even in the USSR, where there has been a remarkable swing back towards the idea of an enterprise being allowed to respond freely to the natural forces of regulation, including profit; an idea which was formerly anathema.

It is beginning to be understood that the technical world functions according to laws which ideology must take into account. So, if Europe means to be competitive, it is highly important that she encourage and develop the natural functioning of enterprises; it being admitted, of course, that this functioning both can and must be improved.

Business methods, and the business approach to problems of association, are of proven flexibility, diversity and efficiency.

Our giving priority to the enterprise, and to a certain form of market economy, springs not from some arbitrary principle but simply from observing facts. The efficiency of a competitive economic system has already been demonstrated by Claude Bruclain, in his book *Le Socialisme et l'Europe* (Editions du Seuil). According to him, the market is nothing but the materialization of a set of tensions between the supplier and users of a given product or service. To eliminate the market would not eliminate the tensions.

The expression of these tensions in the form of a price plays a decisive part in orientating the behaviour of the suppliers and that of the users. Abolition of the market immediately compels recourse to some other system in order to determine that behaviour. Any other solution than the market must necessarily be based on the use of authority, in other words of compulsion involving procedures more complex, and in many cases more cumbersome, than those the market provides.

EUROPE AND THE SPIRIT OF COMPETITION

To observe that, in the national setting, the results of the market economy are not always satisfying does not justify damning the mechanism out of hand; and in any case it would be necessary to suggest something more appropriate in its place. In general, and provided the market is made use of as a technique of adjustment, it provides means which are more flexible and effective, and more susceptible of being kept in control, than any systematically authoritarian method of allocation and distribution. Those means have in fact proved their worth both in the United States and in Europe.

If then, at state level, administrative control from the top leads to results which are no better – on the contrary are even worse – than merely keeping a hand on the play of market forces, there is no reason for recommending the adoption of such control at European level.

To try to set up a kind of super-administration with centralizing departments, an apparatus in which each national authority would seek to gain the preponderant influence, would amount to paving the way for a new 'country', a neo-country consisting of the administrative power. Such a course, if aimed at serving a super-nation, would stand little chance of success, for the simple reason that the administration 'rigidifies' whereas enterprise 'adapts', with the result that we should move not towards efficiency but away from it.

Earlier, in Chapter Three, we pointed to another reason why the liberal spirit must necessarily accompany federal organization and action. We make no apology for returning to the theme here; it cannot be too strongly emphasized that the rules of *dirigisme* (overall government from the top) – rationing and other such contingency-measures, organized by the administration – are a legacy from times of shortage, caused either by war or by the economic difficulties of states in the earliest stages of their development.

To claim that *dirigisme*, born of penury, could ever lead to abundance – which is regulated by competition and the whole set of market factors, including such incentives to spending as advertising and credit – is one of the most absurd illusions of our time, and it is irritating to see that there are still Europeans capable of being taken in by it, whereas the most alert economists in the socialist countries are now disowning it. They have come to understand that obtaining good results from production gives a better chance of achieving some measure of fairness in distribution.

The example of Sweden is highly convincing in this respect, and the socialists are paying more and more attention to it.

The people who look towards *dirigisme* for far more than it is inherently capable of providing are reminiscent of Ugolino, who wanted to reduce everyone to poverty in the cause of equality.

It is true that for some of these people the rejection of the market and its rules is attractive as a way of averting a united Europe and rebutting federalism as at present expounded. It is, in fact, difficult to be simultaneously dirigistic internally and liberal externally, since the rules of the market, like any other rules, impose a discipline of their own; they imply a commercial vocation, a mind that turns naturally towards trade; and trade is beneficial only in so far as it develops in a competitive economy.

These considerations should be enough to spur countries like France or Britain to shun any temptation to adopt *dirigisme* as a national policy. Can we, indeed, dignify with the term 'policy' or 'programme' a deliberate choice to remain poorer than other people for the mere satisfaction of being more regimented than they?

FREEDOM OF CHOICE

The liberal doctrine is connected not only with the idea of efficiency, but also with increasing the number of options and with promoting initiative. If all the nations of our continent had this outlook they would be more inclined to work together towards a federal Europe.

One of the chief reasons for choosing the enterprise (the firm) as the fundamental social cell is that freedom of enterprise offers both to the individual and the group of individuals the greatest chance of development and self-development.

Vigorous advocacy is needed on behalf of initiative, the factor without which the number of enterprises would remain static. It is essential to protect and promote the vitality of little firms, which is quite as important as the spirit of enterprise in the big industrial combines.

Marc Saporta and Georges Soria, comparing the USA and the USSR in their book *Le Grand Défi* ('*The Great Challenge*'), noted that whereas the USSR had more industrial undertakings with over 500 employees than the US (7,400 as against 4,800), the US had a larger number of medium-sized undertakings, with from 100 to 500 employees (24,000 to the Soviet Union's 19,000), and a much larger number of small ones.

It is intriguing to observe that, faced with the need to increase productivity, the Russians have concentrated on increasing the number of small undertakings. Lack of these forced the big ones to try to do every aspect of the job themselves, including spare parts and repair work, regardless of whether it paid or not.

The present trend in Russia is thus an argument in favour of the small firm; one argument out of several.

The small firm (100 employees or less) and the medium firm (500 employees or less) are flexible. They are good at adapting themselves to market developments. They can launch a new product more quickly than any large firm. The board of a giant enterprise sometimes takes three years to decide on a new operation; that of a medium-sized one, consisting of a few people or possibly only one, can reach a decision in a few days.

Contrary to what is commonly believed at the present time, many inventions first see the light in small firms. Anything whose construction requires only a few people is, in practice, usually constructed for the first time in a small workshop. Of course there is an increasing tendency for the crucial discoveries to be made in big firms, but if these organizations had not the means to buy up the little ones' patents – whenever they do not buy up the little firm itself – they would not be able to advance, technologically speaking, as fast as they do.

WHAT EUROPE NEEDS: THE COMBINATION OF TRANSNATIONAL GROUPS AND A LARGE NUMBER OF SMALL FIRMS

The need to encourage small firms in no way excludes the need to encourage the creation and rapid development of intra-European, multinational enterprises. Such undertakings are a prefiguration of planetary organization in the future, since their activities are conceived on the planetary scale and the type of organization they are working towards is one corresponding to that dimension.

Present figures show that two out of every three transnational concerns have their headquarters in the United States. Even without sharing the whole range of contemporary anxieties and the anti-Americanism resulting from them (our own attitude to this question has been stated in the chapter on the United States), we feel bound to point out that it is unnatural for a firm to exercise a big influence in territories beyond its own home ground without their inhabitants having the faintest chance, even if they are shareholders, of influencing its policy and actions.

In 1967 the weekly magazine *Entreprise* organized a conference which was attended by leading members of fifty world-wide firms. The purpose of the gathering was to work out a few lines of thought concerning the form which transnational enterprises ought to take, so that they should be seen to be bound up not with the political advantage of a single country but with the interests of the whole set of countries in which they operated. One of the solutions put forward was to make it possible for people of all nationalities to rise to high appointments in transnational groups, provided of course that they had shown the necessary ability. Another proposal was that the findings of research departments should be pooled, as is already done by IBM; another, that there should be multinational associations of shareholders. Obviously all this constituted no more than a preliminary approach to a very big problem. But the same approach will also be the correct one for European federalism.

The International Chamber of Commerce is keenly interested in the problem, and it may well be able to help European companies which have reached the necessary size to enter the ranks of these transnational undertakings.

The creation and development of transnational enterprises would make Europe into a more coherent entity than it is at present. But the foundation statute for European society, awaited impatiently for years past by intelligent people, has not yet been hammered out. So the appropriate move is to turn this delay to account by drawing up the statute for a Europe conceived on broader lines, a Europe which would lead the way for the rest of the world.

It is high time for action. European-based transnational firms have got to be founded, and they have got to function well: because they are the indispensable condition for the European challenge – necessary in order to provide it with its economic and technical basis in world dimensions, and to surmount the very serious gap between European and American management; the latter is so far ahead.

For in fact the only apprenticeship, the only real training for steering the modern world and for understanding and fashioning the highly complex organization it demands, is that obtained by working in a very big firm. Experience in running an enterprise on that scale would be an excellent preparation for governing collectivities. We have already pointed out what a pity it is that the Americans, who are so good at running their firms, do not make more use of their skill in that sphere by transferring it to the conduct of political affairs. Europe owes it to herself – at least if it is her ambition to perform a planetary role – to take hold of the experience embodied in the transnational firm, make it her own and thereafter transpose it to the political plane. It is perfectly possible to imagine this being done, but no one has ever really tried it.

In general, development should be such that, as regards the part they play on the economic side, governments will continually and increasingly take their cue from business methods, and not the opposite – that is, they must not impose civil service methods on business.

Organization, here and now, on the threshold of the planetary phase of history depends on structures of the business type
more than on administrative structures. If Europe possesses
none of the large-scale groups which, directly or indirectly, are
going to generate new forms of organization (not only in the
economic realm, be it noted), then the project for a new Europe
will remain 'cribbed, cabined and confined' by the narrow
limits within which it has so far been conceived.

FEDERALISM, PROFIT AND EFFICIENCY

It is obvious that, in the business field, progress is inconceivable
without profit, a return on capital invested. There are many
good-hearted people who obdurately refuse to admit the truth
of this; they regard profit as a means for the powerful to oppress
the poor. But profit today no longer bears this aspect, if indeed
it ever did. Rezcol Nyers, secretary of the Central Committee
of the Hungarian Workers' Party, declared in 1968, during the
debate on the budget in the National Assembly in Budapest:
'Profit is the true index, and the only one, to the economic
soundness of an enterprise.'

Real profit provides the means for preparing for the future
by continual reinvestment. One of the deep-seated reasons for
the European countries' fear of the United States proceeds,
surely, from the observable difference between the capacity of
American and European firms to accumulate a margin for
development – or, in one word, profit. Comparison of the fifty
leading European and American firms in an average year
shows that, for the same number of employees (4·7 million in
Europe, 4·6 in the United States), turnover in America is more
than double that in Europe (an index of 210 in America as
against 100 in Europe) and that American net profits are nearly
four times as great as European (380 as against 100). So we
need not be surprised if the potential for adaptation to the new
possibilities born of technical advance is much greater in the
United States than in Europe.

Profit, of its nature, involves risk. Every profit extracted by
means of a monopoly, or from some arrangement between a
firm and the state, presents a somewhat debatable character.
In this respect, the European federation should emulate the

competitive spirit which, with good results, animates the Common Market experiment.

To accept these findings means puncturing certain myths still far too current in Left-wing circles. The Left should be the active wing of humanity, humanity on the march, not a refuge for antediluvianism. 'From what the past has to offer, let us keep the flame and not the ashes,' was a saying of that great socialist Jean Jaurès, more than seventy years ago. Can the Left go on rejecting the principle of lending money at interest, for example, in view of the fact that, on the one hand, money is continuously depreciating so that hoarding makes no sense, and, on the other, that despite residual inequalities the rise of prosperity is general and classless? The Rumanians and the Russians have begun lending money to the state at four per cent per annum. Which is to say that the principle of putting out your money at interest has recrudesced even in countries where it was formerly proscribed.

It is vital that public opinion should rid itself of its all too prevalent prejudice against anything which greases the wheels of a system based on business enterprise. The whole bag of ideas relating to the role of the state, nationalization and, at the other end of the spectrum, the effects of initiative, would repay careful review.

Experience is tending to show that nationalized enterprise is by no means ideal, even in the eyes of its proponents and initiators.

It may fairly be conceded that certain public services ought to be run under direct state auspices. Even there, however, room must be found for the business spirit; activities which are normally regulated by the rules of the market must not be subjugated to rules emanating from the administration.

THE STATE AS COMPANY CHAIRMAN: DIFFICULTY OF NOT PUTTING THE BRAKE ON THE DEVELOPMENT OF STRUCTURES

The state-as-board-of-directors does not, on the whole, turn out to be a '*structure d'équilibre*', a structure with the built-in property of tending to maintain its own equilibrium and therefore, to some extent, that of those surrounding it. Here again,

France in 1968 supplies the illustration: it was in the nationalized undertakings that social problems, with only a few exceptions, were most intractable, and that the anti-economic attitude of some of the wage-earners manifested itself with the greatest virulence.

Liberal conditions require that the citizen should feel at his ease in the organization for which he works, which implies among other things that he should be able to change his job – move to another firm – if he wants to; and also that the organization's leaders and cadres should be real human beings – not the more or less responsible, or even irresponsible, representatives of a state which is multi-faced or virtually faceless.

Other necessary stimuli to economic activity are an interest in results and real participation in decision-making; the complement to which is personal identification with the objectives, the responsibilities and, in short, with the whole being of the system.

Over-intrusion by the state in business and industrial undertakings reduces the prospects for progress, both individual and collective; it also has the drawback of impeding the development of agreements of the federal type.

It is moreover, observable that, confronted with the development of multinational companies, some governments set up national enterprises whose essential purpose is to resist the growth and influence of structures outreaching those to which governments of the conventional stamp, and their administrations, are accustomed. This species of intervention should be curbed; to the existing frontiers it adds new ones, industrial frontiers, which are harder to efface.

On the other hand, there is nothing against the state promotion of moves aimed at launching new industries, or at helping innovators to whom the bankers would refuse the requisite backing.

Industrial Europe, without whose existence the quest for a new type of political structure based on federalism would be wasted, must be re-considered in the light both of the last twenty years of development and of the narrowing gap between different points of view on the functioning of an economy. Socialists like the Swedes, who reconcile their socialism with freedom, and certain of the French socialists, who hold that the society of their choice can only come into being on a basis of higher productivity, and the Germans, who talk of a type of planning aimed at strengthening, not restricting, free enterprise, and non-socialists like the Dutch, who practise industrial programming, are in a position to come together with a view to conceiving an economic system which would give business its full place and scope and at the same time respect the freedom of those whose lives are immediately or remotely involved in it.

It is in connection with enterprises endowed with a genuine personality, or of organizations conceived in the image of those enterprises, that the peoples of the world will be able to come into closer understanding; and this is the reason why federalism must be liberal in its approach. Moreover, federalism is meaningless unless its validity is general, not local and particular; and how can this be so unless the spirit guiding federalism is liberal?

ENSURING THAT THE FEDERAL EUROPEAN EXPERIMENT SHALL BE 'GENERALIZABLE'

In the process of conceiving new structures for Europe, care must be taken to ensure that they are applicable not only to the countries and collectivities which can be counted on to join in at once, but that they will be both appropriate and free of access to all those who may wish to come in later on.

It must be borne constantly in mind that the chief purpose is progressively to reduce the gulf which has developed between, on the one hand, the organization of relations between peoples, and, on the other, the new conditions imposed by technique since our entry into the planetary age. The purpose is not to create a super-nation as an addition to the existing nations and empires.

There is a tendency, current to some extent in France, to regard Europe as a mere extension of the nation and the national concept. Some of the British also adopt this view: 'The Commonwealth is dead, so let's put the United Kingdom in command of Europe.' Plans of this kind are foredoomed to failure for the simple reason that their proponents content themselves with transposing old recipes into the setting of a radically changed society.

The structures which Europe needs for herself, and which she must also propose to the world, are not confined to the governmental plane. The structures comprising modern society are structures of enterprise (industry, business), of education, culture, leisure, medicine and public health, etc., which go far beyond the classical concept of the state and permit forms of association transcending state structures.

Links of various kinds – economic, intellectual, cultural – must be woven between the different national collectivities, alongside whatever governments may be able to achieve in the same line, but their development in both size and quality must be carefully watched to ensure that they are in harmony with the political 'grand designs' proper to our epoch.

Taking these general observations as accepted, how are we to proceed in order to make Europe the starting-point for applying the methods of practical federalism, our federalism *à la carte*?

Three action-programmes, which can be carried on simultaneously, suggest themselves; thus:

1. Setting up economic Initiative Centres (*Organismes d'incitation économiques*), or, where comparable bodies are already in existence, stimulating and broadening them.

2. Creating European Centres for realizing common (international) projects in new sectors where practically everything has to be done from scratch, in whatever country.

3. Building up 'Thought Committees' (*Comités de Réflexion*) – 'intelligence pools', on the analogy of the great American Foundations; the studies carried out by these 'intelligence pools' to be co-ordinated by a Federal Chamber of Synthetic Study.

In the following pages we shall attempt to outline, broadly at least, the nature of these undertakings and to give a few characteristic examples. It will of course be understood that in many cases the work of such organizations would dovetail; they will be complementary to one another. And, naturally, we do not claim to be presenting anything more than a first try, a sketch.

THE DEVELOPMENT OF
FEDERALISM À LA CARTE

(i) *Initiative Centres*

The first thing for the Initiative Centres to do, in their function of steering economic policy in a European direction, is to abolish customs duties. What has already been accomplished in this respect is of great importance.

History will record that countries like France and Britain (which will follow not long after) were rescued by the Common Market from their tendency to isolation and their refusal to adapt themselves from the new conditions of competition. Autarchy – an idea which France is not the only country to have entertained, Germany having elevated it to that dangerous pitch, with results we remember too well, and having been converted to free trade after her defeat – is associated with an early, over-simple conception of independence, dating from times when nutritional needs were relatively primitive. 'The state, as Fichte thought of it, required to be economically self-supporting because it was insufficiently developed and still unready to chance its arm in the hazards of external trade,' as Pierre Clair has rightly said in his book *L'Indépendence pétrolière de la France* (Paris: Cujas).

A nation gets its income from making a comparatively small number of products, which, moreover, are all fairly similar in nature. Nations survive, generally speaking, by means of imports, or, more precisely, by importing a few strategic products. The five leading items in the total volume of goods and materials imported by each country constitute a significant pointer in this respect. It would seem that all the nations are, of their very nature, economically inter-dependent.

The degree to which a country participates in the flow of trade, and the nature of the products or ideas it has to offer to others, are of greater account, in terms of its real importance, than its efforts to appear independent.

EXTENDING THE CUSTOMS UNION BEYOND THE SIX

The development of the European economy is therefore leading, today more than ever, into the world market; it is promoting trade.

In ten years, trade between the six Common Market countries has increased more than three times over. The interpenetration of the economies of the European countries has become greater. But the wider market, wider than Europe's, is building up at the same time. It is not a fact of nature, any more than is the competitive economy; on the latter, cf. the accurate observations of Octave Gélinier.[1]

Practical moves towards the creation of the big market, the market we need – which is far from having come to pass in Europe as yet, despite recent progress – can take either a negative form, such as the differences between standards, design, etc., which still exist from one country to another and stultify competition, or a positive form, such as setting up a general tariff framework. These measures must be such as to encourage competition right down to consumer level. At present, competition takes place at producer level, but the protection afforded, variously, by transport arrangements and trading channels results in favouring certain producers and certain distributors but *not* the individual purchaser. When, for example, German manufacturers of cameras or electrical appliances sell their goods on the French market at prices about equal to those current in France, whereas in fact they could charge thirty per cent less – at least to judge from the prices of the same articles on the German market – it cannot be said that the public is receiving from competition the benefit it has a right to expect. Another essential point is that future quasi-governmental bodies, and the Commission of European Communities, must encourage competition between different distribution networks just as actively as that between manufacturers. In this connection, mail-order business, which affects direct contact with the purchaser, is a good example of the sort of feature which deserves encouragement.

A presupposition of the big market is that men shall be free to move about and settle to work anywhere. This freedom is mutilated at present by lack of agreement about degrees and technical qualifications; some are accepted in all countries,

[1] Notably in his two fundamental works, *Morale de l'Entreprise et destin de la Nation* (Paris: Plon) and *Le Secret des structures compétitives* (Paris: Hommes et Techniques).

others not, and these extra 'frontiers' are taking too long to disappear.

TOWARDS A COMMON CURRENCY

Europe very nearly achieved a single currency through the agency of the European Payments Union, in which the various countries' accounts with one another were recorded in a common accounting currency and were paid automatically, except in cases of unusually large indebtedness. Curiously, just when the Common Market was in process of being set up the European Payments Union was fading out. Now, as we pointed out in Chapter Two – and the fact is too important not to be reiterated here – it was *railroads + the dollar* which enabled the Americans to create their own big market.

A common currency will therefore be a decisive factor in the development of the GCM, the 'greater common market'. This currency should not be thought of as a mere successor to the currencies of earlier periods, but as an innovation in relation both to existing currencies and to the concepts still adhered to in many financial circles.

Nor is this all. Since developments in Europe must not be pursued without thought of the planetary dimension, Europe, in devising her currency, must also think ahead to the contributions she can make to the solution of world monetary problems.

In this connection it would be an excellent thing to cease tying international settlements to a national currency, however strong and prestigious, and to gold-output – an uncertain process and a highly political one at that. World expansion and the demands of trade, notably with the emergent countries, are such that it is quite possible for a nation to need more cash – liquid assets, as the experts call them – than gold stocks allow. Europe has it in her power to rescue the world from the grip of the present monetary system, which originated with the Lombard bankers, by creating at once, for her own use and as an example for others, a monetary system utilizing the resources of cybernetics. It would be easily within the bounds of possibility periodically to define the values of the various currencies in relation to one another by assembling the parameters (about forty in number, at most) which give the most accurate picture of the situation obtaining between the nations' economies. The value of a currency would be measured directly by the value of the economy it represented. Obviously it would soon become necessary to start thinking of a monetary unit common to all Europe, but this would in no way preclude internal balancing operations (an example of sets and sub-sets – which are something we ought to bear in mind at all times).

By using cybernetics in organizing our monetary arrangements we would be able to carry out international settlements much more simply and increase and improve our supply of economic information. Gauging one currency against another requires, in fact, that we have really trustworthy figures to work on. And let no one say that the necessary data are impossible to collect. Here, we are in the presence of something like astronautics, whose demands have had the effect, among other things, of improving the refinement of metals and raising mechanical reliability to a higher pitch than ever before. The demands of a monetary system, computer-based and capable of keeping the relative values of currencies continuously in view, would bring considerable advances in the power of our statistical tools.

It is worth pointing out that numerous statesmen, of all political denominations, have demanded the establishment of a monetary system better fitted to meet the needs of our time (and, as we would add, making use of contemporary technical possibilities). It should also be noted that the Institut Battelle has suggested studying a mathematical model which would enable an approach to be made to solving the problems by means of simulation. It is for Europe to lead the way in this field; the United States, after all, may well feel it has a vested interest in the existing state of affairs, and in any case suffers less from its drawbacks.

Along with these major, far-reaching undertakings there are other much more modest ones of which the psychological impact on the public might be considerable: for example the creation of coins which would be legal tender in several countries (rather like some railway tickets); something on the scale of a one-franc or ten-franc piece would make every day transactions much easier. In designing our major measures for getting Europe on the move we must take care of all the minor aspects too, beginning with the removal of customs officers by adjacent countries which have decided they no longer need a frontier between them.

A EUROPEAN PATENTS UNION

There is no need to multiply examples of the things our Initiative Centres may have to undertake. One such, however, demands special mention: the question of patents and standards, which, like monetary reorganization, is an outstanding problem of such significance that one wonders why it has been left so long unresolved.

A European patents union would be in existence already if, fifteen years ago, sensible structures had been adopted for patents – most of which run out after that length of time anyway. Much time and money would have been saved, and a number of conferences, caused by the jumble of different national laws, would not have had to be held. Europe would be better armed to face her biggest competitors and would moreover have been able to propose solutions of more than European scope. Instead, lacking the will to reach a genuinely federal solution, we have been marking time on the spot.

It is the same with standards. Undoubtedly the efforts of such a world organization as the International Standards Office are worthy of encouragement, but an approach at European level would be able to get concrete results much more quickly. Standardization of most tools and mechanical products would moreover stimulate healthy competition and raise productivity. The repair of non-standardized articles always creates problems and pushes up their cost ex-works; if an article is standardized, repairs are standardized too, a practical barrier to trade is removed, and lower prices attract higher sales. Not long ago, Norway requested Britain, France and Germany to get together and draw up standardization agreements. This was one sign among many of an evident need which the growing volume of trade is bound increasingly to confirm.

Consequently our initiative-organizations must produce practical results in this field and produce them quickly: otherwise the Americans will impose their standards, as they have already imposed their language, more or less everywhere, and will thus strengthen their preponderance.

All we are doing here is to give a string of examples of what can be done to endow Europe with federal structures which can also be set up over a much wider area.

These structures must be designed and resolved upon without further hesitation. Europe has not got eternity before her, with plenty of time to accustom herself gently to change. The great challenges we are up against will not await our pleasure. Before the end of the century China will be singularly more dangerous than she is today. The United States is augmenting its economic potential by an amount equal to that of France once in every eighteen months. In less than thirty years Japan will be more powerful than the Common Market. Every year the USSR is taking a more decisive part in planetary affairs.

The earth goes on turning and Europe has survived so far. But time is against her.

(ii) Commissions of Common Creation

Thought should be given in advance to the establishment, after the organizations designed to create a real Common Market have performed their several tasks, of special commissions whose concern it will be to promote European operations in new sectors of economic activity.

The need for them is making itself felt in the conquest and use of space as well as in information science, transport, oceanography and, of course, research. This list is not intended to be complete, and can be extended as new branches of knowledge and technique make their appearance.

To throw our proposals into sharper focus, let us cite as examples three fields in which a European commission is an undeniable necessity: atomic industry, pollution of the environment, and water.

EXAMPLE: THE ATOM

The realization of just such an 'office' or commission as we have in mind is illustrated by Euratom – or could have been.

All the conditions were present for success. Europe had been granted American aid (a sort of Marshall Plan on the technical side) to enable her to catch up on the time lost through war; after the war she had to rebuild from nothing. With this aid, she was in a position to develop a co-operative association and to set up, by common endeavour, a great inter-European atomic industry, including the production of atomic energy.[1]

But the attempt failed. Instead of banking on Europe as the relevant thing, a future 'personality' as it were in the atomic field, every country tried to keep to itself the knowledge and techniques in which it placed the highest hopes, with intent to beat its neighbours in the race. This tendency to hoard essential research, keeping it protected behind the ring-wall of nationality, is common; it is also misguided.

Another error to which Euratom fell a victim was to underestimate the importance of technology and overestimate that of science. This error is very frequently encountered, especially in France. In atomic matters (on the classical, mainstream side, that is), the hardest thing to get hold of is not the pure knowledge but the applied, the technical ability to construct atomic power stations at once efficient and competitive.

Unless we make a return to the road represented by Euratom, it is to be feared that Europe's atomic affairs will be centred round two main types of reactor, one from Westinghouse and the other from General Electric, both of course American. It is time, and there is only just time, to save the situation by launching transnational companies with resources sufficient to develop a European atomic technology.

Most people are quite indifferent to problems like that of Euratom, and yet – to take the example which, to a Frenchman, is nearest home – the megawatt produced by French power stations costs over twice as much as that produced by American stations. And be it noted that Europe is where atomic power stations ought to have been built sooner, because the cost of conventionally produced electricity (from coal or oil) is higher in Europe than in the States. Because atomically produced electricity ought to have cost the same in Europe as in the States (or less, because labour costs are lower here) it ought to have been developed with all speed.

The European time-lag is being piled up in other ways too:

[1] Cf. Serge and Merry Bromberger, *Les Coulisses de l'Europe* (Paris: Presses de la Cité, 1968).

for example in the use of atomic explosives in mineral prospecting and major building operations. A considerable number of underground atomic blasts have been carried out in the United States. Europe has produced only one, in the Sahara, as part of the research towards making a rather small A-bomb.

As a final illogicality, the Europeans have gone to the length of creating their own competitor to Euratom in the shape of the Nuclear Agency of the OECD.

What we should do now is to re-initiate, on a new footing, an experiment which failed because, for one thing, the European spirit simply was not in it, and, for another, the relevant problems of association had not been anything like well enough understood. Combined effort in atomic energy development should have been, and should now be, concentrated less on research than on technological initiative and effort aimed at creating intra-European enterprises or encouraging intra-European agreements. The enterprises should have the added facility of being able to place orders with government departments. Official help from the states involved should be given only to firms with a record of encouraging association – combined effort between themselves and other firms and organizations – in every suitable way, according to the occasion. We shall get results capable of putting her on an equal footing with her great competitors only in so far as we abandon the policy of 'the Community of the Waste Bin', which consists of treating international joint-action programmes as a kind of disposal plant for projects which do not look much like succeeding.

The thinking which should have been done, and will have to be done, runs rather differently; something on the lines of the Swiss Atomic Energy Commission, which recently crystallized its programme in the following terms:

To participate, with any acceptable partners, and under any circumstances which may offer, in the existing possibilities of building nuclear factories utilizing 'light' water;

To specialize in the development of special components, within the reach of our technical capacity;

To participate in the development of a high-temperature station, if an advantageous agreement on a European scale can be reached;

To seek association with some outstandingly powerful group

with a view to developing reactors of the super-regenerator type.

The Commission has formulated the following recommendations for the future of the Swiss Reactor Research Institute at Würenlingen:

To develop the theoretical knowledge, and thence, if possible, the technological foundations, required for fast super-regenerator systems;

To develop the technology of plutonium for use in fast super-regenerator reactors;

To assist industry by placing accounts of experimental results at its disposal for the development of reactors.

To assist electrically-powered factories with any problems arising when nuclear power stations are brought into operation.

EXAMPLE: ENVIRONMENTAL POLLUTION

Compared with the other kinds of commission to be set up, that concerned with the various species of pollution caused by industry will have a problem of at least equal urgency to deal with. Pollution studies, as the reader is aware, are intended to reduce the pollution of air and water, and the frequency and intensity of noise. In France a new department of the Ministry of Industry has recently been created for this purpose; which is a matter for congratulation, certainly, but can these things really be adequately handled within a limited, national setting? Is anyone quite clear, for instance, how the pollution of the French Rhine is to be separated from that of the German Rhine; or why it should be logical to treat the smoke of the Ruhr and that of Britain as isolated problems when both are in danger of reaching Scandinavia? Regulations governing the use of factory equipment ought to be the same, irrespective of whether it was manufactured in Mons or Rheims. Uniform European standards would have the further advantage of necessitating uniform apparatus for measuring pollution; which, incidentally, would make the apparatus less expensive.

Since human beings and toxic levels are the same everywhere, are there any rational grounds for preferring national systems of surveillance to a European one?

Although studies have been made to this end – often on private initiative – and the Council of Europe is giving attention to the problem, decisions and regulations are still only national. No decision has yet been made to apply a single type of regulation in Europe, even as regards radio-activity. To give one instance: not long ago, atomic establishments in Belgium were governed by different regulations from those in Holland, a little over sixty miles away; though both, in principle at least, were under the jurisdiction of Euratom.

EXAMPLE: WATER

A serious threat is hanging over Europe: shortage of water. The more populous and industrial a country becomes the greater the danger it runs in this respect. Over 20 cubic metres [706 cubic feet] are required for the manufacture of a ton of paraffin or sugar, 150 cubic metres [5,397 cubic feet] for a ton of steel. Water requirements per individual inhabitant have increased by from thirty to fifty times in the last fifty years. Before 1914, individual consumption was between 10 and 12 litres [2·2 and 2·64 British gallons, or 2·6 and 3·2 US gallons] per annum. The figure will soon be forty or fifty times larger. And Europe is thickly populated and highly industrialized.

We all think about water in miniature terms, 'you in your small corner, I in mine'. But rivers cross frontiers. Is it beyond the wit of man to visualize the possibility of a European water supply network? At present we content ourselves with national or even local arrangements. A brook rising in French Savoy changes its nationality on joining the Arve at Geneva; a situation which might have come out of that gay satirical novel *Cloche-merle*, by Gabriel Chevalier.

Close European co-operation is essential for the planning, construction, finance and utilization of the great inter-regional water supply systems which will have to be set up in the not too distant future. Various large projects do in fact already exist, on paper, calling for continental-scale use of water resources. One of these is a plan for turning Lake Constance into Europe's biggest reservoir, with huge mains leading to Stuttgart, the Ruhr basin, Belgium and Holland. Another scheme, the work of a Swiss engineering firm, envisages supplying the Ruhr and

Belgium with water from the Lake of the Four Cantons (Lake Lucerne). The Alps, indeed, constitute the great natural well-spring not only for northern Germany and Holland but also, even more obviously, for south-eastern France and northern Italy. In Scandinavia there has been a proposal for a drinking-water main from Norway to Belgium, passing through southern Sweden, Denmark and northern Germany and supplying Copenhagen, Hamburg, the Ruhr basin and Holland on its way. To realize this plan – a water-main some 950 miles long – would however entail building two bridges, one from Sweden to the Danish island of Zealand and another from Zealand to Funen and the mainland. The cost of laying the main could be reduced by twinning the latter with a pipeline taking natural gas in the opposite direction, to Scandinavia from Groningen.

The primary problem in all these projects, as also in that of discharging used water from the industrial Ruhr through a system of drains to the North Sea, is that of finance. The cost of the civil engineering involved will raise the cost of water to industrial and domestic users, and it will certainly be impossible to go on supplying water at the prices in force at present. The only way to keep investment costs down will be to design and finance operations on a European scale.[1]

The European Water Commission, whose establishment is greatly to be desired, would not even have to execute costly studies before getting down to the actual work; the studies have been made already. Even so, there is no time to be lost; the sooner such a commission can be on the job, the sooner we should be able to cope with a situation which is certain to get worse as long as merely partial solutions continue to be applied. To persist in dealing with the problem on the national scale will merely aggravate the difficulties which sooner or later, and for one reason or another, will compel its being thought out afresh on the European scale.

(iii) *Thought Committees*

Society in the various European countries, their respective levels of development being all similar, is going to experience

---

[1] Cf. the article by Casimir Kat in *Communautés européennes* for May 1967, from which we obtained the facts on which this passage is based.

without exception the impact of modern techniques and will have to accept enormous changes. Instead of leaving these changes to chance and merely letting them happen, we must see them coming and prepare people's minds for them beforehand.

Because change is forcing itself on the whole of Europe, the rational thing is to look at it from a common European viewpoint, and this should consist of respect for the individual and a desire for his wellbeing and progress.

The Russians accuse present-day China of regarding human beings as so many nuts and bolts (a far more technological comparison than the old idea, man as robot). Plainly, Europe's efforts must be directed towards averting this nuts-and-bolts version of the human condition. It is therefore essential to ensure at once the health and productivity of society and the free development of the individual.

A fact we shall never tire of repeating is that we have now reached the stage at which the computer can be used *either* in order to apply planning to everything, including the individual, *or* in order to extend the wave-band of possibilities, both for the individual and for enterprises. It is therefore more necessary than ever to cultivate the sense of freely-accepted discipline. Technical advance is accompanied by a socializing movement; road-planning and traffic-control are a good example of this. Modern technology, if its results are to be beneficial, presupposes general adherence to certain rules of organization, rules devised not in order to enslave the individual but to allow social life to function without exerting murderous collective pressures on him.

However, the imminent changes which are bound to affect both social organization and individual behaviour are going to shatter numerous structures irrevocably. To answer the challenges of our century (and it is these, far more than the American challenge, which are the point), we need a forward-looking sociology; we must become the architects of our own future. That future must in the first place be European, with the prospect of acquiring a still wider character. The nature of the problems posed is identical in a considerable number of countries. The chance of finding the correct solutions is much better in a single, federal setting than in a plurality of national ones.

What is more, joint study of the problems would help to pave the way for a community of outlook – which is a larger conception altogether.

THE METHOD OF THE ENCYCLOPAEDISTS SHOULD BE APPLIED TO THE TWENTIETH CENTURY

The pooling of research and intellectual inquiry is one of the conditions which must be fulfilled if Europe is to raise herself once more to world level.

If we take two countries with the same level of educational development, one of which has twice the population of the other, the statistical chances that the first will win twice as many Nobel Prizes as the second (the Nobel Prize being taken as a pointer to intellectual and scientific influence) are high. The number of students therefore who will be taught by a Nobel Prize winner will be four times greater in the country with twice as many inhabitants; in other words, selection will correspond directly to the square of the population-size. Roughly speaking, if we assume that Europe has a university population (about which we shall have something more to say later) three or four times as great as that of any single European country, the efficiency with which the services of men of outstanding ability are used will correspond to the square of this ratio; that is, say, ten times greater. Remember that that represents an increase from 1 to 10.

This is a phenomenon which sould be kept in mind when talking about efficiency and arguing whether or no a genuine pooling of European resources is worth while.

The question has, moreover, been answered in the affirmative on more than one occasion. Grants from the Rockefeller Foundation enabled Niels Bohr, studying the atomic nucleus, to create in Copenhagen a truly universal school of physics whose team of research scholars were German, French, American and British.

The progress made by this team ranks as one of the highest scientific achievements of the twentieth century. It proves that the pooling of intellectual resources brings results. The question therefore is: how is this procedure to become common practice?

The best means to this effect will be to apply new working

methods, derived from those used in another age by the Encyclopaedists. The approach must be to convoke universalists – men who in addition to having their own special fields have never lost the sense of synthesis, an ability to see the wood as well as the trees. It would be unthinkable to go on letting contact between them depend on chance encounters at conferences. Those whom we must set working together are too numerous, and the problems they have to solve too complex, for us not to foresee a working structure in the form of a huge *ensemble* of institutes of prospective sociology, whose branches would be many and various but which would always provide opportunities for inter-disciplinary get-togethers and would also possess a central nucleus for synthesizing results and implications.

The purpose of having recourse to European consultants would be to gain deeper insight into the nature of major problems, both on the part of politicians, who have to make decisions, and on that of the informed public generally, who would have a better idea of what was at stake in a given political issue.

The public gets plenty of information about novelties, but too little about the alterations in structures and outlook which our age demands. Writers and speakers on this subject like to gloss it over pleasantly and doll it up with anecdotal detail. Though they sometimes come out with diagnoses they take care not to suggest remedies – except when experts, anxious to make a show, break out into polemics, the only result of which is to dazzle the non-expert and leave the issues nicely confused. Altogether, the situation hardly favours knowledge. The men who, today, ought to be making thought serve action (those who, in the eighteenth century, would have been called philosophers) have proportionately less authority than in the past; a natural consequence of the fact that literacy and articulateness have greatly increased, that the dissemination of information is vastly greater, and, finally, that a much wider variety of ideas is expressed.

All this does nothing to diminish the necessity, in this time of exuberant development, when reforms suitable for application throughout Europe must be worked out, of conferring authority on a limited number of universalists by combining their activities and setting up bodies which will enable their conclusions and proposals about our major contemporary problems to be as widely diffused as possible.

Such an undertaking presupposes that relief from the pressures of ordinary life shall have been afforded to the individuals in question during the periods (short periods, as will be seen) which they will devote to studies in depth carried out through teamwork. Today, just when thinking of this kind ought to be more concentrated and intensive than ever before, it is unusual for men of high intellectual stature to be 'at disposal'. This is observable even at the level of theoretical thinking; but later, at the level of practical politics, things are even worse; electoral contingencies compel political leaders to give up most of their time to lesser tasks, and, in all too many cases, destroy their ability to appreciate the hierarchy of problems and distinguish the essential from the inessential.

The complaint is often heard that technical advances are inadequately utilized and that development is left to take place haphazardly. But what has been done to avoid this? The committees whose creation we are suggesting would supply the remedy. They would be forward-thinking groups, assessors of the future – selected, moreover, partly from men at the height of their careers and partly from their juniors, still full of the zest and 'attack' of youth – and they would make it their aim and ambition to compare the facts of experience with those of experiment and draw the right conclusions.

One must continue to emphasize the federal character of the thinking required today. Just as the water-tight compartmentation of knowledge must be broken down, and interdisciplinary communication is indispensable to the growth of the principles of modern social architectonics, so also must we broaden our forms of association, raising them to the European and trans-national plane.

At other moments in history, tasks of this kind have been entrusted to academics. This is still a sound procedure, provided it is re-designed both theoretically and practically. Already the USSR, with its Academy of Sciences, has succeeded in giving a big impetus to science and, partially at least, controlling it in the interests of efficiency. In the United States, the Foundations have been developing massively (the Ford Foundation's resources are in the neighbourhood of a thousand million dollars). Examples like these can show us how to build up an anticipatory sociology bearing on every branch of the human sciences, and yielding the most effective pointers for arriving at intelligent political orientations.

It would be an odd thing indeed if Europe, the original nursery of this kind of forward thinking, which was subsequently applied so rapidly and on so big a scale in the United States, should prove incapable of setting up the equivalent of a Rand Corporation.

The Rand Corporation, a private, non-profit-making body, was set up on profits from Air Force contracts. Its staff of 400 are specialists of various kinds (economists, mathematicians, sociologists, etc.) who are allowed to spend half their time on their own research. It is particularly concerned with studies relating to the future, with a view to anticipating crucial thresholds and forecasting as accurately as possible the times at which they will occur.

'Europe's Rand Corporation' would not be the only European Thought Centre, but would make it possible to place the work of the institutes responsible for studying major problems on up-to-date methodological foundations.

It would keep an eye on the probable future development of techniques with a view to ensuring their being used in the best possible way, namely to foster the values defined by the 'generalists' responsible for cultural preoccupations. Productivity must, in fact, be placed at the service of a 'development society', not a consumer society merely, and basely, concerned with getting and spending.

Towards the 'European Rand Corporation' would gravitate the countless studies carried out by committees, conferences and learned societies which, all over Europe, are devoting themselves to contemporary problems but which are short of the means required to carry out their investigations, and are working on too small a scale to act as pilot-plants for our century and for the world.

MATCHING AMERICA'S FOUNDATIONS

Europe must get herself organized to make the best use of the outstanding minds which, in every country, appear capable of interesting themselves in the questions posed by the transformation of society, and laying down modern directives for the benefit of governments and politicians. These studies would enable real reforms to be set in motion; whereas what frequently happens at present is that the best men holding political office or other positions of responsibility fritter away their talents on minor reforms at once disenchanting the public and giving diehards an alibi for damning all change as futile.

Later, we shall underline the methodology permitting Thought Centres to be transformed from dream into fact. Let us meanwhile note that these committees or Institutes (Foundations would be the word for them if suitable financial legislation were introduced and contributions were levied both from individuals and from firms and states with an interest in the results[1]), would be composed of men selected on individual merit alone: in the gamut of European organizations, the presence of government representatives is logical where decisions on immediate practical measures have to be taken, but would be paralysing where general propositions are discussed and new constructions prepared.

Already a host of organizations, under private auspices and financed in some cases by generous individual Europeans, are working in the direction of European cohesion. But they are doing it dispersedly, and are winning too little support to have any political effect.

---

[1] Cf. the observations of Michel Pomey (*Le Figaro*, 13–14 July 1968), their herald and champion in France: 'As social progress is a continuous creation of needs and solutions of which government departments and public services reflect merely the transient image, it is pertinent to envisage, on the fringes of the public sector, a whole zone of ideas, discussion, experiment and innovation, in which the leading role will have to be played, voluntarily, by private citizens, through the instrumentality of organizations – such as the Foundations – half-way between professional associations and public departments, under private management but with all proper safeguards.

'The Foundations are private, independently established, disinterested in their aims, financed (except in special cases) by the initiative of private individuals, and governed – since they have no members and therefore no general meetings at which to elect directors – by an administrative council set up under permanent articles.

'Abroad, notably in the United States, the Foundations play a leading part as catalysts of human progress towards liberty.'

Americans and certain Asians could of course be admitted to our committees. It is always good to hear the views of external observers when setting out to replace old structures with new.

THE ROLE OF THE STUDY COMMITTEES

Not catalysts, called in temporarily to effect a transition, but organisms adapted specifically to fulfil the imperatives of the age of fluidity (*mouvance*): such would be these committees. In order to tackle, with good hopes of success, the increasing volume and complexity of the problems of our time, they will need to be interactive, complementary and well balanced.

The studies they produce may serve as a basis for the main lines of thought from which political and governmental activity draws its sustenance. If anyone points out that studies of this nature are already being made inside the existing status, our reply is a reminder of the fact that no country can re-shape its own life at all quickly from inside, on its own resources alone, and without revolution. Tradition and habit weigh too heavy and adaptiveness is crippled. Federalism, with its breadth of outlook, can provide a healthy curb to these adverse tendencies, and gives reason to hope that the expected mutation will be effected.

There is no reason why these study committees, applying themselves to the really big problems, should not be numerous, provided they are properly co-ordinated. So many subjects spring forcibly to mind: the problems raised by the prolongation of human life; the right aims for town planning; language teaching (including, if possible, the wide adoption of 'passive linguism' – speaking your own language but understanding the other man's, who also understands yours); new forms of transport and new directions in its organization; the development of information and information-science; the organization of leisure; how to increase tourism; and so on.

By way of example, and to show more clearly in what spirit it is desirable to approach the problems which are common to all Europe, we shall now make a quick examination of two very different fields, chosen deliberately for that reason: youth, and medicine.

COMMITTEE FOR YOUTH PROBLEMS

There is no need to insist at length on the massiveness of the problem of youth in all industrialized countries. In most of them, the under-twenty-fives represent, or soon will represent, between forty and fifty per cent of the population (forty-four per cent in France, nearly forty-six per cent in the USA, forty-five in Japan and thirty-six in West Germany). The commotions we have been witnessing for some years now, starting with beatniks on British beaches, continued in a more violent form by Holland's *provos* and by the protesters at Berkeley (California), culminating in the explosive events of Spring 1968 in Germany, Italy, Spain and France and also in Eastern Europe, abundantly illustrate the forcefulness with which youth is expressing at once its rejections, angers, dreams, ambitions, despairs and inconsistencies. Previously, youth was both formed and informed by the environment, usually rural, of its birth, and by its teachers, in the widest sense. But now, both formation and information come from such a multiplicity of sources that youth can work out its own ideas for itself. Today's young not infrequently know more, or at least possess greater curiosity, than their appointed teachers.

They are also growing up into a world which, though materially strong, is ideologically weakened. They are more and more reluctant to submit to collective disciplines imposed in a national setting, in the name of principles in which they no longer believe. They have an urge to discover the aims of the society they are growing up in, but the discovery is rendered harder by the fact that many adults have a guilt complex about the nature of society today.

Not all young people are students, far from it, but it is certainly at student level that the shocks and tremors show the greatest amplitude. Augmentation of the student mass has created a special class of citizen, a very special one since, by definition, it is always being renewed. But despite this continuous flow, childhood and adolescence (sometimes rather prolonged) has acquired a social 'personality' on a par with that of the peasants or the industrial workers. Why? Because today the adolescent, whether a student or not, goes about almost exclusively with other adolescents. The views of his peers take precedence increasingly over those of parents and teachers, who in his eyes represent authority.

This phenomenon is going to increase.

There is the important additional fact that those who have obtained educational qualifications find that the abundant hopes they cherished while doing so are by no means justified by their subsequent experiences. A degree is usually regarded as the key, and the right, to a quality job. But the commoner degrees become, the more banal do the corresponding professions also become. The consequent disappointments are aggravated by the fact that no ambitious project or vision is held out before young people, through which they might satisfy their thirst for action.

The creation of a federal Europe would fill the gap. It would involve extending the technical experience which is part of many educational courses to include a period in one of the emergent countries, thus building up a form of citizen service. The young must be made interested in Europe, not so much because Europe's future promises a certain sort of prosperity as because the Europe we envisage is the only way of affording an ideal which transcends material betterment and gives youth an outlet for self-dedication.

The initiatives already set on foot in this sphere are a matter for congratulation. There is, for example, the project for building a European Youth Centre, as decided on by the eighteen member countries of the Council of Europe; the Centre's aim will be to use every effective means of training youth leaders with a European spirit and outlook. The Vatican and Spain are both going to take part, in principle, in this work, a feature which is in thorough conformity with the principle of federalism *à la carte*.

The group of universalists of the 'social human sciences' type, who in our scheme of things would serve the various governments as advisers, integrators on the subject of youth problems, will have to put on their thinking caps to find the best ways of developing the citizen spirit to a point beyond the ends it served formerly, among today's youth, who speak of freedom as nations speak of independence, and who are veering into anarchy just when human and social evolution are imposing the disciplines of socialization. A car, for instance, is an instrument of freedom, yet there is a discipline of the street and of the open road.

Citizen service at European level could supply a common discipline, just as compulsory military service has done for France. The young, on reaching a certain age, would go abroad, in pluri-national groups, to do such jobs as repairing great monuments or working as volunteer nurses (citizen service would apply to girls as well as boys) or carry out map surveys in under-developed countries. And let no one raise the language difficulty as an objection: solving that will be part of youth's own task in building the future.

Contemporary family problems are interlocked with contemporary youth problems. They are arising in every part of Europe. This being so, are we not forced to devote some thought to the present slide of our family-based European civilization towards a civilization in which youth demands autonomy? Despite our having been brought up, for centuries past, on Roman history and having been taught to anatomize the causes of Rome's decadence, we still seem not to have realized that when progress has become such that it saps the foundations of a given society by rendering them meaningless, and no one comes up with a new set of foundations, the society collapses. No real provision has been made for giving young people a sense of the values required for our society's continuation and development. Religion, which used to provide a rigid morality and thus put a frame round social existence, has been transformed into the vision of ecumenicism: which is satisfying enough to the middle-aged but gives nothing for the growing young to hang on to. There must be something to replace religion, and the only answer is a training in the spirit of citizenship, a spirit springing from the socialization of society and from a morality of effort.

From his mother, as she went to and fro from the cowshed to the kitchen, and from his father working the ground on the family property, the child learnt that nothing is got without toil and that even great toil might bring in very little money. Today, when the child – who at any rate in most cases is destined to become a student – sees his father setting off to work in the car, which in a child's eye is a plaything, he gets the idea that work is some kind of pastime. When he sees his mother pushing buttons or turning switches he senses nothing of the modern species of fatigue, nervous fatigue. If he is asked to make an effort at school the teacher falls over backwards trying to keep the demand as small as possible and make the work pleasant. His amusements are more or less passive: if he likes skiing he goes up by ski-lift instead of using skis, and if he likes music he buys records instead of learning the violin.

Much must be done to enable parents and teachers to make up for some of the deficiencies of present-day education. The relevant steps can be thought out and put forward only at a level which is high and therefore in fact European, not national, and the proponents will have to be universalists with a European-wide educational TV service at their disposal.

This version will doubtless look summary and over-simple to some people, the kind of people who like to wrap everything up in an abstruseness which they confuse with brilliance; and who fail to notice that, by not getting down to hard tacks and coming out with straightforward political proposals which everyone can understand, they are responsible for the disintegration of European society.

The family of the child-as-king, where the parents want the children to have more and better than they themselves had, must give way to that of the child-as-citizen, in which the child is better brought up without being any the worse looked after. This change of front cannot be fairly entrusted to the child's teachers; we must fight the present tendency of parents to unload their responsibilities and difficulties onto the school.

Plenty of Americans have realized that the problem is funda-mental, and that the advanced countries may find themselves sapped at their very foundations, in other words their young people. It would be well, in this field as in many others, if Europe took the measure of the problem before she gets as advanced as the United States – of whose experience, we say once more, we must nevertheless make use.

TOWARDS AN EDUCATIONAL POLICY FOR EUROPE

Teaching, closely connected with the problem of youth – being, indeed, one of its leading aspects and arguably the most impor-tant of all –, needs to be altered throughout Europe, not only in its methods, in order to take advantage of new technical possibilities, but also in its syllabi. Teaching machines on the one hand, and the massive quantity of knowledge on the other, have made continuous education possible just when it has also become indispensable.

We have here a typical problem of the sort which demands shared study. There is no question of its being settled just by a few meetings between ministers for education. How are we to get to the bottom of it? Only a committee rising superior to national contingencies will be capable of producing overall reforms and making them converge in such a way that, in their turn, mentalities too will progressively become convergent.

By bringing together European-level ideas concerning the main directions to be taken by educational reform, this committee will strengthen the hand of reformers in the individual countries.

Europe must aim at a huge effort to adapt in the educational field. The planetary collectivity which is most successful in carrying out this operation will also make the biggest mark on the third millennium.

Thinking at committee level will not in any way exclude government initiative or the work of the social re-structuring organizations. But the latter must work in liaison with the committees. One way of ensuring this is to transpose to the general European plane the competitive spirit by which American universities are animated; they not only keep in touch with business activities but are also kept progressive by competition with one another.

The educational tasks ahead are enormous, and they include either the creation of universities-in-common or the Europeanization of the existing universities.

The first method should be used for new disciplines, the second for the established ones. If intellectual life is to be properly and normally articulated, Europe's universities must be conceived accordingly.

This orientation is particularly necessary in France, where there has long ceased to be any competition between universities and where, as a result of centralization, a ministerial administration holds undivided sway and imposes all the rigidity and anti-progressive restraints that one might expect.

Given the planetary character of educational problems, there would be much to be recommended in some kind of link-up between the Higher Institute, or European Committee, of Education and American organizations pursuing the same objectives.

It is highly regrettable that so much time has been lost without studying these problems. The Euratom Treaty provided for the creation of a European Institute at university level. We are in a position to state positively that this proposal was accepted without hesitation by the parties concerned. Yet nothing has been done about it. When a unanimously accepted idea remains a dead letter the diagnosis must be one of political spinelessness. Those in authority, instead of taking thought for major future needs, allow themselves to be overwhelmed and crushed by everyday obstacles, unimportant difficulties and petty debate.

As for choosing the working programme for the committee responsible for the universities, the only trouble is that the tasks are too many, not too few. The industry/university tie-up has been found to be essential everywhere – in Britain, Germany, Italy, France – and what has been achieved already is far less than what remains to be achieved. The examination system is itself under examination in all countries: how much do examinations matter, and what form should they take? Selection of candidates for higher education is another question which is under discussion everywhere. And so on.

Since Europe's best ideas find no outlet in practice, those actually applied, in the field of education as elsewhere, are usually imitations of American ones. Business schools are one example; with this difference, that in America a corps of genuine professors exists to teach in them – in the United States, management is a professorial subject just like, say, geography. In Europe we have hardly any such people.

When are we going to decide to do something in Europe other than devise mocked-up versions of organizations and methods imported from America, while the Americans themselves go on inventing new ones and are increasing their lead over the rest of the world? To get ourselves out of this situation we need a change on a big scale, in the European dimension.

Action is urgently called for. The burden of American patents, and the brain-drain, are two very serious signs of a disequilibrium under which Europe is labouring in relation to America, and which will go on worsening unless Europe mounts an operation to overcome it. Incidentally, can those who regard European action as merely marginal to national action produce any refutation of this statement?

MEDICAL PROBLEMS COMMITTEE

Here is another field in which European association is conspicuous by its absence, and yet to whose very nature the existence of national frontiers is irrelevant: the field of medicine.

In a country like France, the expectation of life (the average recorded or estimated life-span of children born in the years specified) rose from 33·5 years in 1805 to 65·5 in 1940 and 70·5 in 1960. The approach to health problems has been radically altered. Most men and women in the advanced countries are under medical attention most of the time, and illness has been put into a different perspective in consequence. New drugs have enormously increased the chance of cure in certain diseases.

Diseases themselves have changed: the commonest now are those associated with an ageing population and those produced by modern social conditions, the neuroses. Europeans must get together to combat the environmental ills which cause these human maladies. This is crucial.

The need for combined effort becomes even clearer if one looks at the prospects created by electronics for the study of the brain. Cybernetics is helping us to a better knowledge of cerebral rhythms and functioning, telling us more about the needs of the rhythm-life of the brain, its relationships with that of other individuals, and more, too, about the major laws of social psychology. It will also enable us to seek out the conditions for fuller, healthier individual development in the midst of present-day society, which is a primary aim.

The first duty of a large society, such as Europe's, should be to combine in a study of the problems of medicine, the science which, more cogently than any other, stands in everybody's eyes as symbolic of the unity of mankind.

The new sort of Medical Committee which ought therefore to

be brought into being would obviously have to be in touch with the scientific committees and the committees for the human and political sciences. Medicine has indeed a very direct bearing on prospective sociology, that is to say on the study of the revolutions in our lives to which sociologists are already devoting their attention, and of the effects of those revolutions on mentalities and structures (beginning with the structures of sociology itself).

A particularly powerful impact on people's minds is that made by birth control; a subject which really deserves a book to itself, but our role here is confined to making a panorama of the many problems affecting the future of all societies. The societies of Europe, heirs to a family tradition which is the resultant at once of legislation descended from remote antiquity and of our religious traditions, have suddenly found one of the securest elements in their foundations being sapped away.

How many people foresaw this and thought about it?

If there is any field in which we are advancing back-to-front, this is it. The United States was the country which produced the largest number of devices; everybody knew they existed; in religious quarters, recognition that they would cause considerable problems was reluctant and tardy; many scientists pretended to believe that the use of the new contraceptive possibilities would be confined to a minority; and in the end, everywhere, including the Latin and Catholic countries, the devices were widely used, illegally at first, legally later.

We may as well face the fact that they are going to be more and more widespread as they become more convenient to use, and this will happen despite recent interdicts from the church. The contest between 'efficiency' and morality will be like that between gunpowder and the breastplate. The pill is already being referred to as 'conventional'; there is talk of an 'after' pill, a monthly preventative and even a quarterly jab.

This is a problem of a kind which demands to be studied as a whole, together with its consequences, the impact of which ranges from education to family allowances, taxation and the armed forces.

Britain has already traversed a supplementary threshold by accepting abortion in somewhat the same way as France accepted the pill: rather bored, and slightly surprised. It is true that a doctor is still required in order to make the practice legal but he is given a wide choice of reasons to justify abortion, including the happiness of other parties. At this rate we shall soon be hearing that the birth of a child would be disturbing to the other children, or the parents, or the grandparents; or even the people in the flat below.

So abortion is about to make its official entry into our *mores*.

Clearly, the psychological problems directly or indirectly occasioned by medical progress are left to be regulated by chance more than anything else.

Our laws, not being based on the facts imposed by technical progress, are in danger either of becoming inoperative or of missing the point. For example, a campaign for divorce is going on in Italy. But is anyone looking at the fundamental part of the problem, namely the effects on the children of the divorced couple? There is a big difference between divorce in childless marriages and in those with children, and there is a definite correlation here with the neuroses of childhood, juvenile delinquency and even progress at school. The problem demands careful thought and also joint study from experts in different disciplines.

As technology is going to go on developing and, through certain of its branches, will bring new advances in the human sciences, ought we not match its development by trying to foresee and appreciate its psychological effects? It makes obvious sense to try and draw conclusions relevant to structures, particularly the structures of different social security systems.

Today, more and more diseases are becoming amenable to treatment; and many can be detected early which previously went unchecked. But research is costing more and more, and treatment charges are often high. While the cost of living has doubled in the United States in ten years, medical expenditure has increased more than four-fold in the same period. The same thing has happened in Europe and is still going on. In the States, having a baby used to cost 225 dollars ten years ago. It now costs 360 dollars. And what of the fees for some of the more ambitious operations now rendered possible by modern surgery?

To whom is society going to award prolongation of life, and from whom withhold it? Is money to be the deciding factor? These may be unpleasant questions to ask, but they are going to start asking themselves very soon and the answer will have to be found.

Organ transplants have already necessitated a change in the legal definition of death (and the new definition in France, incidentally, draws on electronic criteria: 'Clinical evidence of death shall be constituted by the cessation of cerebral activity as indicated by the electro-encephalogram remaining flat for a sufficient length of time.') Transplants are going to become more common, but sooner or later they will have to be brought within limits and these will have to be laid down. We cannot go on indefinitely treating everybody free of charge, using an increasing number of increasingly advanced techniques. Partly for personnel reasons: if we are to go on doctoring and nursing on the same scale as hitherto, everyone will have to be a doctor or a nurse, just as if we are to go on teaching with the same methods as hitherto everyone will have to be a teacher. And then there is finance: a heart transplant costs about 90,000 dollars.

In order to forestall the proliferation of optimistic fantasies (such as have surrounded the subject of cancer at all too frequent intervals), it will be essential for universalists to supply the information media with facts and intelligent guidance. But an even more important task for them will be to prepare public opinion for future changes in social security.

The whole system of public insurance is in a dubious state. The idea of a social security network covering every kind of health problem will have to make way for another, in which a distinction will be drawn between protection against the worst blows of fate and protection demanded against lesser risks as a result of living standards having risen.

Over and above the minimum safeguards, everyone should be allowed to insure himself in a particular grade (against ordinary risks but not exceptionally big ones, or against big ones but not little ones like 'flu, etc.), provided he can afford it. This switch to a liberal course is bound to come sooner or later; the providential bounty of the state is not in fact unlimited, and it is unfortunately possible that our contemporary principle of equality in illness will become a casualty of the tremendous expansion of scientific possibilities.

The big problems of socialized medicine and how to make it

work have come up in all the European countries. The data being similar in different countries, it is imperative to pool experience and spot the points at which the axes of experience in social security questions converge. Hence we need to set up, where medicine is concerned: committees for medical sociology, with a specific brief to reconnoitre the future; ginger-groups to keep an eye on regulations and standardize them as far as possible (in order to forestall the creation of the new frontiers which will soon be a block to the free circulation of workers of all kinds); and transnational commissions for research and intercommunication. These, as the reader will recognize, are illustrations of the three families of institution we suggested (p. 166) at the end of the first section of this chapter.

CHAPTER SIX

THE POLITICAL IMPERATIVE

THE EUROPEAN CHAMBER
OF POLITICAL THOUGHT

Modern society cannot be conceived in terms of economic laws alone. The policy our time demands is one of adapting structures, or creating new ones, wherever and whenever those of the past have been rendered obsolete by progress in equipment. At present there is a strong temptation to restrict European agreements to the economic field. This is a form of surrender. Societies with something original to contribute, and the wish to take part in the conduct of world affairs, need energy and impetus, and this can be elicited and sustained only by political action.

Europe's concentration on internal expansion and 'You've never had it so good' has allowed a void to develop, the extent of which can be gauged by the attitude of youth. In our societies, not only youth but the whole population needs worthwhile things to aim at. Without ideals, Europe is in danger of becoming a nonentity or being lured into some dubious adventure or other: the black banners of anarchy floating over the streets of Paris in May 1968, which some people are in rather a hurry to forget, should be remembered: they were a serious warning.

Changing equipment is demanding political mutations, and these will be meaningful only if they happen on the European scale. The radical transformations must be carried out at a good brisk pace, the tempo of the century; they may be a bit messy and they may hurt a bit, but that will be a small price compared with the upheavals now threatening us. The people whom the prospect of change upsets are the ostriches, the oysters, the closed minds – some of whom are the more dangerous for being cloaked in sham modernity. Their meddling is apt to inspire wistful thoughts of someone else who looked back: Lot's wife, who was turned to a pillar of salt. Now, if only . . . !

ECONOMICS IS NOT ENOUGH

The way the Common Market has developed shows clearly that while smooth economic functioning and good economic progress are essential, they are not enough in themselves. Who invented the Common Market, a community based on expansion through competition; and who shaped its characteristic features? A handful of moving spirits, fired by the American example; and the Americans themselves, anxious to block communist advance in Europe by creating a huge zone of prosperity. Both parties were concerned to erect new structures by means of a major act of politics. Things have been slipping since then: the original grand design gets overlooked in favour of arguments about the duty on cauliflowers. Are we really expected to believe that by passing the time in such deliberations we are working at the real centre of the political field?

We must get on with our structure-building. In other periods the time for this was after a war, round the treaty table, or after a revolution. From now on we must try to do it in peaceful circumstances, without war or bloody revolution.

The influence of statesmen is weak, and Europe is lagging behind the fulfilment of her destiny, because of the present weakness of political thought itself. Activity of high political stature is always preceded by a period of philosophical reflection. The events of 1789 would not have followed their historic course had they not been influenced by the *Encyclopédie*; and there would have been no Lenin without Marx. But, on the present-day European plane, there has been a vacuum where there should have been an original philosophy or at least, more simply, concepts intended to provide Europe with genuinely new structures: something more than mere imitation of America or the creation of a third power-bloc. There was certainly a sense of drive at the time when the Europe of the Six was getting under way, but this was powerfully dominated by emotional urges, a form of motivation too often confused with political purpose, which should always lead to the construction of something positive and should arouse and enlist feelings only as an aid to that end. The immediate aims, after all, were to reconcile neighbouring peoples who, from time immemorial and against their own interests, had made war on one another, and to inspire some sort of crusade against communism. No one had thought out, still less crystallized into a programme, the organization of a truly contemporary federalism. The participants simply moved forward together in a generous spirit from one milestone to the next, hoping indeed to travel far but without ever having clearly defined their objective. And, when all is said, they thought of Europe far more as a continent than as the potential mother of a federation and a force making for coherence and cohesion in the world as a whole.

The first European project possessed a foundation of historical importance, namely coal and steel. Those substances would have been a sound choice in 1914, since they were then the nucleus of Europe's great industrial problems. But it was soon to become clear that, far from being a basis for huge new organizational endeavours, they posed such formidable modernization problems as to make them a source of difficulties.

We have to be capable, on occasion, of cutting loose from historical precedent. Building the future involves mobilizing the public imagination. Europe ought to be a symbol of progress and the future, not of the more or less successful piecing-together of yesterday's left-overs. The Europe policy means nothing unless it sets organizations in motion which fit the demands of our epoch, and unless it works at the highest level of synthesis of which human collectivities are susceptible. We need escalation – towards a European federalism whose final implications are not European but planetary.

The new European institutions and achievements will, in their diversity, create the climate which encourages agreement and cohesion. We shall be able to pass progressively from the simplest fields to the subtlest. Federal structures should be thought of as the natural culmination of an existing *ensemble*, not as something imposed *a priori*. To try to draw up a constitution for European association without having well-built entities to build upon would be to put the cart before the horse; it might, indeed, amount to an arrangement in the style of a conventional international agreement under the familiar routine of foreign policy, which so often provides only an empty frame. And in any case a constitution so formulated would probably end its days in somebody's filing-cabinet.

Although essentially progressive and pragmatic, and impossible to define except in terms of its axes of development, the movement towards Europe cannot take on firm outlines without the support of a certain number of the political parties in various countries.

Is it merely wishful to imagine that all those who, in such parties, are concerned to build up the armature, the inner framework, of a new Europe, and to bring divergent viewpoints together into a coherent pattern, could hold a congress and issue a manifesto? Such a document could be based on ideas similar to those expressed in this essay; though ours, to be sure, far from claiming to be complete or pre-emptive, are intended only to stimulate other people's thinking.

This move should aim at contributing to:

(*a*) transforming the political setting, the political framework; and

(*b*) working out the content of a policy whose general direction will be planetary.

THE INEXORABLE MUTATION OF POLITICAL STRUCTURES

It is impossible that political systems arrived at at a time when there was not only no broadcasting but when most people were illiterate should not be due to change now that education reaches everybody. There is always a correlation between education and information on the one hand, and political structures on the other. The appearance of printing delivered such a shock to European thought in the sixteenth century that the power of the Church, connected as it was with political power, began to be questioned. The stream of information put out by the Encyclopaedists and all the partisans of development in the eighteenth century, when printing was the only medium available, transformed the monarchies. So it would be unrealistic to expect that the present revolutions in the techniques of education and information, and in the diffusion of both, will fail to cause considerable changes in political organization. The citizen, better informed than before and, as the human animal has always been, inquisitive, will infallibly be led to question, to a degree undreamed of by any sociologist, the system under which he lives and moves and has his evolution.

Had it been possible to foresee the emergence of broadcasting, television, films and tourism, would most of the constitutions now in force have been built in the way they were? These new facts of life – for such they incontrovertibly are – will push their way into the very functioning of democracy and become integrated there.

We invite any who doubt the inexorable quality of political change to join us in pondering on what was let loose in 1968 by the reform of French education. That reform had been urged for at least two decades by many forward-looking people; was executed rather badly and watered down into mini-reforms; and was then made the target for violent and aggressive student agitation on the streets, a totally unforeseen outcome. The same thing will happen to the other component structures of conventional democracy, and for the same reasons. Through contenting ourselves with largely outmoded structures we shall see the whole lot blown to pieces, in an explosion whose detonator will be some unpredictable crisis sparked off by blind chance.

But political regimes find it hard to change from the inside. It is federalism which, so pertinently, offers an exceptional opportunity for achieving, without shocks too violent to contemplate, the *aggiornamento* of institutions and of democratic functioning.

These observations lead to the conclusion that, though we must not wait for the corresponding political changes before beginning to get Europeans working practically together, politics must not merely drift passively in the wake of the changes being carried out in various fields. The design of politics must be boldly ambitious.

A EUROPEAN THOUGHT CHAMBER FOR
POLITICAL PROGRESS

To encourage the birth and promote the advance of the great project for Europe there can be no better means than to create a thought chamber for political progress; such progress to be attained by the diffusion of information and by seeking to foster a positive dialogue between authority and the citizen. Each of the different committees whose establishment we have urged would include a 'section for prospective political thought', associated with the chamber which would be the general body, and which would bring its powers of imagination and suggestion to bear on the main lines of federalism and federalist growth.

In the political sphere even more than in others, all we are aiming to do is to indicate directions in which studies might be made. The following considerations should therefore be regarded as suggestive pointers and no more.

What form will federalism take; or, in other words, how shall the re-allocation of functions be carried out between those sectors which must be thrown open to common action by the different countries, and those whose scope will remain national? Most of the problems to be treated being entirely new, it is difficult to find precedents in the existing federations and confederations. When the proposal to lay Switzerland's first oil pipeline came up, there were no legal precedents to refer to in that country's federal history, it never having been imagined that pipes would, could, or should cross the borders between the Cantons; canalized watercourses were the nearest approach to such a thing.

In order to fix the boundaries between what is, or is capable of becoming, federal, and what ought to remain national, it will probably prove advisable to set up, with all speed, an embryonic federal council and machinery for political representation. Delegates to the council could, if it were so desired, be chosen by the national parliaments, as under the present procedure for the European Parliament.

But there is another way, and a decidedly preferable one: to give the members of the European thought chamber, as constituting in effect the federal council, the power to make representations direct to governments. Its members could, in fact, be elected. It would be perfectly feasible to get the population at large interested enough to choose the men who were to serve on the committees in general and in the thought chamber in particular. The candidates for election would have been selected solely on grounds of their specific competence, not their national origins or political affiliations.

This would be an opportunity for getting out of the rut of our habitual notion of universal suffrage. This latter system, as applied on all sides, goes back, as we have said, to a time when most electors could not read. Really all it consists of is asking the voters to entrust a few men with the conduct of affairs, in the interests of all. More educated and better informed as they are the people are now in a position of greater competence and should be able to take part in electing the men whose job it will be to define the philosophy of politics.

Pushing the proposal further, we may observe that it is all the more necessary to install a tool for political thinking, in that the classical parliament no longer suffices to the modern political task. Is any member of parliament capable of being qualified simultaneously in law, strategy, technology, business and sociology? Of course not, and so these things are looked after by other men, over whom the citizen has no hold. By widening the field to which elections apply, we shall be enlarging the field of application of democracy as well.

The great schools of modern thought which have contributed to the development of social organization – whether it be Taylorization, or management, or, as will be the case soon, of cybernetic prevision and provision in the conduct of affairs – have exerted their influence everywhere except in politics. This cannot go on, and we must hope to see the world of politics organizing itself round dialogue, the determining element of democracy.

FEDERALISM IS DIALOGUE

The federal mentality which it has become so expedient to cultivate is, of its nature, a mentality of dialogue: dialogue between countries, between regions, between parliament and executive, citizen and administration. It is an element of the set of dialogue in general: men/women, parents/children, students/professors, trade union members/trade union leaders, employers/workers, customers/suppliers, doctors/patients; and so on.

Dialogue is the self-regulation factor of development.

Decentralization and liberalism inside a country, and federalism in the country's external relations, form a single whole and will advance together. This approach to political relations is of higher quality than that which holds fast to rigid principles and ideologies. The difference observable between the two is similar to that between altruists and egoists, or between the ecumenical movement and the upholders of the church indivisible.

All of which underlines how much better democracy will progress if its development takes place in a federal direction and setting.

Dialogue, if it is to be fruitful, cannot be immediately extended to the citizenry at large – a thought which invites reflection on the validity of universal suffrage. Since education and information are always progressing, it can no longer be said that only those with money are initiates in the mysteries. Equal, or on the way to becoming so, as regards political education, the citizens are divided into those who are interested in public life as a whole, those who keep in touch only with certain problems, and those who pay no attention to any. The replacement of the property qualification by universal suffrage in the nineteenth century was an advance; but the bad old days were no more unreasonable than the present situation. It is unreasonable and wrong that those who take the trouble to become informed should have no more voice in shaping the future of the society in which they live than those who are not interested in playing their part as citizens. When political education has been given firmer roots – in schools, and through radio and television – the rational course would be to ascertain whether citizens knew anything about the issues at stake when about to cast their votes. Extremely simple tests could be applied, and the mere fact of agreeing to undergo them would indicate at least some degree of political maturity. Without going back on the principle of universal suffrage for the election of some public representatives, there are others, including for example the members of our committees and of the thought chamber, in the election of whom it would be reasonable to allow only those citizens who could show they knew something about it all to get as far as the ballot box.

In the federal assemblies there ought to be arrangements whereby some questions would be decided on the principle of 'one country, one vote', and certain others would depend on a balanced system of voting power.

Some people will be startled by these proposals, but one must have the courage to formulate them. It is the same with democracy as it used to be with the Church or royalty: too many of its declared supporters regard it as unthinkable to change either its institutions or the professional machinery required to keep it ticking over. And yet the precedents mentioned here point the opposite way: there is no reason for regarding our idea of universal suffrage, our methods of representation and our political assemblies as sacred and inviolable.

In the next few pages we shall bring evidence to show that they are, on the contrary, certain to change. Our handful of illustrations could have been multiplied several times over.

DEMOCRACY IN QUESTION

The democracies, it will surely be agreed, are at present continuing their existence in a manner at variance with the principles which brought them to birth, and the time has come for them to break new ground. We should not forget the process by which governments made the transition from absolute monarchy to the constitutional systems now in force in most of the Western countries. It was motivated by a desire on the part of men of wealth and knowledge to be in dialogue with the king. The logical terminus of such a development is democracy-as-dialogue. What we see in practice, however, is that many European governments are becoming more and more personalized. Even the British system puts the leader of the government in a position of considerable importance. The only difference between democratic and despotic régimes is that in the former the people have, at intervals, an opportunity of reviewing the state of affairs. For the rest, in democracy as in other things, every period in history has the name of a man tied to it like a label. Democracy can continue only by calling in exceptional personalities to hold it together. The continuity of political thought has disappeared.

But American democracy is still different, and better. We have already mentioned its many defects; we have pointed out that some of its practices are obsolete and we have underlined its failure to bring political organization into line with that of business and industry. Despite these observations, one cannot but be struck by the fact that American society still provides conditions favourable to the functioning of democracy, the mechanism of which has the characteristic property of inviting or compelling the men who reach high station to surpass themselves. Was not this notably the case with President Truman? Institutions are good when they incite those serving them to give the best of themselves. But when, in order to survive, institutions require the services of exceptional characters, it is a sign that they are sick.

It is no solution to go on tottering from crisis to crisis, hopefully looking about for providential men who will enable the country to keep hobbling along somehow, like an invalid on his crutches. Like an army, a nation should never use tactics without strategy. And be it noted also that recourse to artifice or makeshift destroys faith in the value of the mechanisms of politics, when in many cases all that is needed to restore their effectiveness is to re-think them, re-adapting them to our epoch. In accomplishing this task, exceptional men will be useful, even necessary: they are better employed in building than in plastering; and public opinion, if duly informed, would soon come to appreciate them and back them up. It is undoubtedly possible to turn the position inside out like this; the arguments in favour of doing so are so strong that people's minds are ready for it and the ideological void is impelling us all towards it.

POLITICAL LEADERS HAVE FALLEN BEHIND THE ADVANCE OF KNOWLEDGE

The human sciences have made considerable progress but the politicians capable of reaping the benefit from them are few and far between; they are too busy with local day-to-day problems. And have they any real intention of bothering about the human sciences anyway? There are still too many politicians who think that the exercise of power merely entails a supple obedience to certain legal rules and economic principles, with the help of collaborators who are also in a sense their customers. They know nothing of sociological laws, or at the most exploit them superficially to ensure success at the polls and in the event of public hostility, to rock it to sleep. In other words they insist on licence to rule in spite of facts or to one side of them, and meanwhile – curiously, not to say disingenuously – proclaim themselves realists. So it is hardly surprising that politics should apparently be powerless to dominate the development of a society of ever-growing complexity; and that, for example, a transport bill recently introduced in the House of Commons by the government should have been the object of over 2,000 amendments.

What is happening in the field of the human sciences is what we may call the 'scientification' of knowledge, a phenomenon equally apparent in other disciplines. The development both of societies and of minds and attitudes follows laws of a biological character, human society being a biological extension of the development of man.

An era has opened in which the sciences of man are making it possible to enunciate the major principles which our rulers must, for their own sakes, learn to respect if they mean to create anything permanent and irreversible, just as architects are now designing with their eyes on laws of mounting complexity, laws derived from a knowledge of their materials, knowledge derived from the calculations of engineers. To make the best application of the laws laid down by the human sciences, to get them understood and accepted, is an exacting job, the action of a strategist organizing the battle for the future by drawing on whatever is best in the present.

We are not arguing that a knowledge of ballistics would determine the value of an army and its commander, but no one will deny that if the latter neglects the advice of his gunnery experts the army will be in for a very sticky time.

Something we urgently need to put far behind us is the classical contest of politicians in closed lists, and the tired old procedure which decided between winners and losers. The requisite qualities for attaining power in that setting are no longer suited to a world in which politics has become an 'architecture of the human sciences', a strategy whose ends must include making sure that productivity does not express itself only as the servant of immediate consumption.

In a firm – the paradigm we should hold always before us – ability to comprehend natural laws is beginning increasingly to count more than the personal temperament of the man in command, though not displacing it altogether as a decisive factor. Similarly, in a modern country and, *a fortiori*, in a well-led Europe, political teams should remember that attentiveness to the human sciences has now become their primary qualification. The power of modern information should be used to block intellectual speculation, sociological word-battles and legalistic recriminations and, in the positive direction, to make it possible for citizens to get at the facts which will enable them to exercise their power of choice as political adults.

This change, which it would be so desirable to see in the political world, will be very close to that effected in the eighteenth and nineteenth centuries, when the great scientific principles made their way into the most varied of fields, when the transition was made from alchemy to chemistry, and when Pasteur and Claude Bernard introduced experimental science into biology and medicine.

The spirit of the *Encyclopédie* brought forth enlightened despotism. Today, what it must promote is a democracy enlightened by the social sciences which, from economics to psychology, have themselves undergone during the twentieth century the beneficent influence of the exact sciences.

The prospective sociology sections of the various committees, together with the chamber of political thought, will have an essential role in this making-over operation: the role of the general staff in Europe's renewal. This latter should be the polar opposite of technocracy, which is the result of an abdication from major political functioning and leaves the field open to men who are capable only of perfecting obsolete methods and of finding out *how* to do this or that or the other; whereas the foreground problem at the present time is to find out *why* it should be done, if at all. A very different question.

WHAT KIND OF POLITICAL CREATIVITY
IS REQUIRED?

Political men tend to concern themselves with equipment rather than structures. They are doing the wrong job. It is the technicians' role to build factories, communications networks, laboratories. Of course politicians should give technicians the necessary support, but they should not persuade themselves that they have justified their existence merely by inaugurating technical feats which in most cases were not thought of, and in many cases not even authorized, by them.

They must make their own inventions and achieve their own realizations, in their own field. The new things they should be starting all come under the category of structures such as those of the Treaty of Rome.

By using the vast means of information to which we have referred, public feeling must now be alerted in favour of the new structuring which Europe needs. All too often, all people hear about in connection with Europe are her squabbles, stabs in the back and other diplomatic-technocratic forms of dirty work at the crossroads; and then one is surprised to find how little enthusiasm there is for ideas for a new, united Europe. It may not be generally known, for example, that nearly half the French citizens who were sounded in a recent opinion poll expressed the opinion that the Common Market was no concern of theirs.

Those politicians who really want to work for Europe and federalism should enlist the help of the general staff, as it were, of sociological strategy, and make it their cherished purpose to exercise their creative imagination as authors do in their books, engineers in their designs, and scientists in their discoveries.

Among many examples of indispensable renewals, let us pause for a moment to look at that of taxation.

What are we to think of income tax – which, after all, is a tax on work and is therefore directly opposed to the original purpose, that of taxing the rich on their rents? Its rampant and incessant growth, though presented as a social triumph, is unjust and dangerous because it discourages effort. It is only natural for qualified people to feel sour about a system which rewards them for responsibility and its accompaniment of risks by clapping on super-tax. Let no one be astonished when its baneful consequences come home to roost, as already in Britain, in the form of diminished productivity.

It is an easy guess that this is a field in which information science can produce sweeping innovations. Taxation needs to be re-thought with new ideas, from new premises, because things previously impossible are now possible.

The science of information can also transform the preparation, presentation and subsequent control of budgets, which have become so complicated that parliamentary intervention is rendered ridiculous while the administrative technocracy strengthens its grip.

The great need of Europe and the world, at the dawn of the planetary age, can be expressed in two words: political creation.

Generally speaking, great reputations have been made by statesmen such as Churchill, Tito, Franco and de Gaulle, who guarded and guided their countries' destinies through times of danger. It is natural to give them the gratitude they deserve; but those who, after such rescue operations had been completed, made a constructive contribution deserve even more. An Adenauer is a laureate under both headings, that of the man who saves his country and that of the man who plans and founds the future: he stands out as one of Europe's makers through having understood that the problems he had inherited were not to be solved by retreating into national introversion.

We must concentrate increasingly on making sure that men of outstanding ability are encouraged to devote their gifts to fostering development. Those with a deeply felt desire for such work are undoubtedly commoner than is generally suspected, but they are held prisoner by ingrained political habits. Thinkers and information specialists have a big responsibility in this respect. Part of their job is to point the way and show up the misuse being made of politicians, the ablest of whom are permanently tied to multifarious and largely trivial tasks, so that they spend less time on real reforms than on routine work and the celebration of past glories. As we have already said, the electoral tradition which forces them into positions of multiple responsibility is bad both for them and for society.

Having too little time in which to ponder necessary changes, they expend themselves on make-do-and-mend. The young, who dismiss politics as repulsive or boring, are not far wrong.

THE LOW PRODUCTIVITY OF POLITICAL INSTITUTIONS

The efficiency of industrial management, and the importance of making the best use of the best people, must be made to permeate our political institutions. Great progress can certainly be made in this direction. There are business leaders and leading sociologists who would have no difficulty in charting the problem: the names of François Bloch-Lainé and Raymond Aron, in France, and Baron Snoy, in Belgium, come at once to mind. But it would also be necessary to ensure that politicians listened to these expert voices, as any good managing director does to that of an organization specialist.

For the future good of democracy, we must hope that it will not be much longer before the relevant methods of working together are accepted in political assemblies. This would be one of the best ways of warding off the dangers of nationalistic technocracy and of giving politicians the chance of actually, and not just apparently, getting things done in the fields demanding their attention.

Seeking productivity at federal level would be one of the first tasks of the chamber for political thought. On the European scale, federal politicians and the members of the committees should be kept informed by an information set-up enabling all those responsible for seeing that statutory requirements were fulfilled to predict results and to make sure they were the best results possible. There is no doubt at all that if the designers of tomorrow's structures had the same facilities as the designers of tomorrow's aircraft, our political systems would become much more efficient, achieving greater control over the complex problems of modern society.

THE GAP BETWEEN THE HUMAN SCIENCES
AND POLITICAL ACTION

The studies of which we have spoken in connection with the committees for European studies, the creation of the chamber for political thought and of the various political councils or other organizations which might be set up in such a context, form a single whole. What they constitute is a necessary combination, like that achieved in military thinking by marrying the technical aspects of armaments to strategic planning. The comparison is a valid one: the task to be accomplished in the European political field at the dawn of the planetary age is strategic in essence; it consists of exploiting all the potential offered by new knowledge and technical achievements, both of which are centred about one of the great disciplines of our time, organization. This task is all the more indispensable in that the explosion of scientific and technical discovery is bound to be followed by a wave of new ideas about society, to the premonitory ripples of which we have already drawn attention. It follows that, if we are not to be caught unprepared, we must use programming methods.

Cybernetics is the equipment which, by vastly increasing our mental tool-kit, will enable us to hoist organization up to the level demanded by the amplitude of changes to be effected. By resorting to it, we shall raise the effectiveness of our associated democracies to a new order of magnitude.

Technology is unjustly saddled with responsibility for the imbalances disfiguring our epoch. Their origin lies not in technology but in the inadequate development of the structures required for controlling its use. Neither the inventors nor the manufacturers of the motor car can be blamed for congestion in our cities; the fault is with those who failed to foresee that the car would proliferate in accordance with a certain foreseeable number of laws, and who did not gauge in time the consequences of its use in cities. The result is the ruinous situation now confronting us.

Maurice Grimaud, a prefect of police, has justly said: 'Compared with that of our predecessors, our area of choice is singularly narrow. Whereas in 1900 it would have been relatively easy to extend Haussmann's work by progressively altering the street-plan of Paris, today's population density and land values dismay both town planners and financiers.' Which is yet another stimulus to make us look ahead. We already know that in less than twenty years' time the population of Paris will have increased by thirty-six per cent, and that it will be even harder to act in 1985 than in 1968.

As a rule, politicians get to grips with a problem at the point when it is turning into a crisis. It is typical that they should be worrying about the technological gap between Europe and the United States at least ten years later than it would have been really useful to attack a problem which people had been pointing out for a long time.

At present, politicians ought to be getting it into their heads that the worst gap of all, where Europe is concerned, is that between the human sciences and political activity.

THE CONTENT OF A EUROPEAN POLICY
WITH PLANETARY AIMS

One of the main objectives of this policy, and one of those most capable of creating solidarity between individuals in different countries, can be, and must be, wide, deliberate participation in building permanent peace.

The adult generations, with minds and attitudes influenced by the thinking of military men, would by this means deliver to the world a message that would exorcize its haunted past, and would endow it with sureties against a recurrence of those familiar and dreadful catastrophes. But time is short; almost too short. The rising generations have a tendency to see those events through the wrong end of the telescope – 'battles long ago'. Forgetting is easy and happens so quickly; in France, one out of every two individuals is unaware that the Low Countries were occupied by the Germans in the Second World War!

There are three planes on which Europe can take action, and whose priority is of the highest.

I. SUPPORTING INTERNATIONAL ORGANIZATIONS

If the Europeans do not concern themselves with promoting good faith in international relations, who else is likely to do so?

They should do everything in their power to recommend reasonableness in politics; which obviously implies, for a start, that reason and good faith should assert their supremacy in Europe; reasonableness begins at home. This is surely the only consistent attitude to take in that quarter of the world which gave birth to reason.

Europe, once united, would be in a strong position to encourage the activities of international organizations. She has experience on her side, and she can show credible proof of having totally and finally renounced any warlike intentions. She has considerable voting-power in world organizations; if the European votes were unanimous they would influence many more.

Support for international organizations in no way implies that they do not require re-thinking and improving. UNO is an advance on the League of Nations but can be improved further. The European nations acting as a single whole would be better placed than anyone else to effect the improvement, since the great military states (the USSR and USA) frequently exploit UNO for their own ends, as an alibi or a pretext. Besides, their very power diminishes the sympathy with which they are heard. Hence Manhattan is not the natural seat of UNO, which should transfer to Europe as soon as Europe goes federal.

In May 1968 (before the student explosion) the choice of Paris for the Vietnam talks was regarded as cause for congratulation, and rightly so. But we should not forget that Paris was chosen not as an arbiter but simply as neutral territory: which shows clearly enough that Europe, or at any rate France, among the countries of Europe, has accepted the role of a Switzerland in relation to the world. At one time she would have felt, wrongly, that being considered as neutral as Geneva implied a diminution of stature. We must continue in this path, keeping in view the development of that international morality which ought to be part of the programme of any great political creation. Just as, in our time, technical advance has outstripped the development of the social sciences, so individual morality has outstripped international morality. The standard of trustworthiness is much higher between individuals or firms than between nations, simply because it is still believed that reasons of state, like certain religious imperatives of which they are the heir, justify everything. But, while it may be right to retain this principle for use in certain rare cases, to use it right, left and centre, in an age when everything is bound to come out publicly in the end, can only brand the user as dishonest.

In the Middle Ages there was no difference between the

dishonesty of the merchants in the market-place and that of the barons, the King of France's vassals; the merchants cheated on their weights and measures, the barons fiddled the coinage. Nowhere was there any standard control of quality. Since then, weights, measures, coinage and qualities have been regularized, but, in too many ways, international relations have remained at the moral level of the Middle Ages. National interest is used as a cover for aggressions against peace which, in an inter-dependent world, quickly recoil on those who fomented them. Contrary to what might be thought, relations between firms have more to teach from a moral point of view, as regards any real improvement in international harmony, than relations between countries.

2. STARTING A SYSTEM OF INTERNATIONAL POLICING

Europe, in the widest sense, can afford to provide for her own defence with nuclear explosives and inter-continental ballistic missiles, in addition to conventional forces. She will not thereby cut an aggressive figure, a federation, like a coalition, being essentially defensive. The European Defence Community came to nothing because it was conceived as the nucleus of a super-nation. But an EDC in a federated Europe would have no such built-in cause for failure. Implicit in the EDC period, moreover, was the idea of a choice between the two great powers, Russia and the United States. Today the horizon would be different, because of the integration of federal European defence in a planetary context and the potential liberalism of Europe.

In this connection, the study committees would have to bring the notion of '*défense tous azimuts*' into sharper focus. It was adopted not long ago into French terminology but could in fact be only of European application, because no unit smaller than Europe, in whatever combination it pooled its military and industrial potential, could realize it in practice. It should be remembered that, in view of the speed of aircraft or missiles carrying nuclear weapons, defence requires a radar network on a certain scale, that of Europe, without which no *force de frappe*, however powerful, carries conviction as a deterrent.

The 'all round' formula ('*tous azimuts*') is a transposition, in planetary terms, of the attitude of the Switzerland of yesterday to the Europe of today: that is, a determination to defend one-self against aggression from any quarter, north, south, east or west. '*Tous azimuts*' is a departure from the traditional patriotic mystique: the French Army in 1914 was directed against a single enemy, Germany, and conversely. Classical patriotism is binary. The abandonment of a binary strategy automatically includes abandoning a certain notion of one's country, the kind of patriotism which is charged with aggressiveness.

An army conceived in this new way is much closer to a police force than to the traditional military spearhead. It reflects a more rational mentality, one which can be useful to the rest of the world as well. By adopting the principle of such an army, Europe would have a chance of bringing about in the field of armaments and defence the mutation for which mankind is waiting, and which would lead to the establishment of a substantial force for use by the world organizations, and tending to encourage disarmament by nations everywhere.

Moreover, this mutation would awaken the interest of the young, many of whom, including some of the very best, no longer see any sense in the conventional compulsory term of military service. Indifference would be succeeded by militant transnationalism.

Federalism is the only political formula capable of bringing together territories with a similar way of life without prior military conquest. It corresponds to the idea of contract and conscious engagement. We must satisfy by new means, we must 'civilize', man's deep longing for conquest, an animal instinct which is inherent in the notion of territory and which has caused so many offensive wars.

To this effect, Europeans must first promote and adopt the formula and then become its missionaries.

3. SUPPORTING GREAT WORLD CAUSES

Just as the military spirit must evolve into a new form, so must the colonial spirit undergo a metamorphosis.

It is essential to seek and find a common policy with regard to the extraordinarily difficult problems of the third world, which, together with youth problems, are those most urgently requiring to be solved. The new European attitudes are beginning to take shape and form. The European communities have already carried out searching inquiries and reflected on the types of relationship which should arise between Europe and the newly developing countries. But, by federating Europe, we would associate more closely in the tasks before us all the peoples of whose life for the last hundred years the evolution of the third world, step by step, has formed part. No other group of countries has such an accumulation of experience to draw upon, not even the USA and the USSR.

Instead of launching into simple, bilateral operations of an administrative, financial or commercial kind, Europe must aim higher. To seek bilateral agreements only means exposing oneself to more and more claims on one's energies, and to continually rising costs, without the money spent making any contribution to the cause of development. For the latter pre-supposes not just money and technicians, but new structures.

Thus conceived, Europe's influence inside the 'poor' countries would be profound. Ideological reactions against Europe would be less violent than those against America. Europe will therefore have to convince the latter that, in the matter of relations between the whites and the third world, a federation can successfully achieve what a unitary power cannot. And America would have every reason for her own sake to put her faith in world federation, since she is in danger of sticking hopelessly in the mire if she continues to go it alone.

This is yet another example of what Europe can be in relation to America: not greater, but different.

The authoritative voices whose task it would be to expound to the public the thoughts arising from this development, and to put across their practical implications, would have at their disposal a tribunal on the world scale, in the form of the European committees we have proposed.

Thus we see, once more, the necessity of setting up study organizations for problems of common pertinence. Association between the countries faced by the difficulties of the third world must not cause us to overlook the necessity for associations between enterprises, and the establishment throughout the world of industrial action organs whose members would be firms in Europe, America and the newly developing countries.

The quest for peace on the international level is sometimes

regarded with amusement; it is 'Utopian' and thus one of the favourite butts of the 'realists', those 'realists' who are to be feared whenever they are the carriers of excessive pessimism. The optimists have no need to feel shy of their own desire to change the face of things. Ecumenicism, and the changes taking place in the bosom, if not the heart, of the Church, illustrate how possible it is to dissociate oneself from the ideas of other days, from particularisms, even from superstitions as these are in some cases, in order to create or follow new directions. The priests have not only hung up their soutanes and changed into civilian clothes; they are also, in two senses, changing their minds. For many of them this is no easy task; the Church, too, is having to review its structures. But these fundamental changes were needed to fill the chasm of emptiness which had begun to appear in religious life.

It seems fair to say that European politics is awaiting its John XXIII.

METHODS AND ACTION

Europe is faced by the threefold necessity of mobilizing creative imagination on behalf of federalism, getting governments committed irrevocably to a course of action, and passing from the planning to the executive stage in an era of fluidity, leaving countries which did not join the various European communities at the start the opportunity of doing so when they feel ready.

There is no lack of ideas. Hardly a week passes without a conference being organized somewhere – by a professional group, a trade union or a university, and the accounts of the proceedings are full of proposals worth remembering. But however good these ideas are, however useful the studies, they remain dispersed. To collect and above all to ensure their being translated into action, the organizations envisaged by us as needed are: initiative centres, creative commissions, thought chambers.

This circuit of establishments must come as the result of an inter-governmental decision, which will not take place without a weighty push from public opinion and a real determination to transcend the limitations of the nation as a form of organized existence.

Any country accepting the inception of a federal Europe, and the creation of the necessary federal organizations, would be committed to making regular contributions to its, and their, finances; which could be done, for example, by levying a percentage on the annual budget or, better still, as a proportion geared to the number of inhabitants or the size of the gross national product. The country would also be committed – an even more essential matter – to establishing, as an integral component of its governmental structure, machinery for getting federal proposals actually carried out within a stated length of time.

AMBASSADORS ACCREDITED FROM EUROPE TO NATIONAL GOVERNMENTS, AND NOT ONLY FROM GOVERNMENTS TO EUROPE

The set-up of a federal Europe, pragmatically and in its main lines, is not very difficult to sketch. It would be sufficient that there be a minister with a high grade of responsibility, and provided with real powers, in every government, as permanent spokesman for Europe; that he should have facilities for subjecting projects for federal action to detailed study; and that he should be able to submit them to his country's parliament for acceptance or rejection, failure to implement them within the prescribed period (which would vary according to the nature of the matter in hand) being automatically taken as a sign of abstention.

The bodies formulating proposals at federal level – the committees and the chamber of political thought – would, as we said, be composed of people chosen for their abilities and qualifications, but not equipped with a mandate to represent their respective national administrations. They would be appointed for a limited period, it being taken as a fundamental postulate that all projects studied were intended for execution in accordance with a strict time-table.

The commissions would be composed of members of whom, say, one-third would relinquish their jobs after every two years, every member being appointed to work on a single mandate only. Appointment could be by vote. We have said this already, but we think it necessary to clarify it in greater detail. The selection of men for the different roles to be distributed in the study of Europe's problems would require new methods, designed to catch and hold the interest of the citizens of the various countries. In particular, the selection of those we have called 'universalists' could be carried out by consultations which, if not popular in the broad sense of the term, would at any rate be widely understood in the countries concerned. Public opinion would be aroused by the press and the other information channels. The Eurovision Song Contest holds the viewers' interest; why should not the selection of the universalists, on a different level and by different methods, do as much? Contemporary means for the diffusion of information would thus produce a new kind of star, the intellectual star or star thinker.

The federal organizations to be created would not necessarily all have their headquarters in the same city. In Switzerland, for example, the Polytechnicum is in Zürich, the High Court sits in Berne, and a number of international organizations are based on Geneva. A similar spread could be applied to Europe. The federal capital, whatever city was chosen to play that part, would be the crown and complement of this deliberate dispersion. This is rendered perfectly practical by telecommunication and information-handling which enable data to be transmitted almost instantaneously over long distances; 'cool lines', in fact.

FROM PROPOSITIONS TO PRACTICAL APPLICATION

The Parliament of Europe, both as it now is and as it ought to develop, would have a definite function to perform, that of a consultant to whom the various bodies would turn in order to test the substance of their proposals. Until such time as a federal political framework has been set up, the Parliament's role should remain consultative only, decision being still, at this stage, the prerogative of the individual states belonging to it.

The size of the tasks ahead must not intimidate those who will have to tackle them. If the problems are many, difficult and complicated, there are (we have said this more than once before but we must say it again) – there are computers; and provided these are used properly there is a very good chance that the problems will prove soluble. In contemplating what we have to achieve, we must remember the mechanical possibilities.

It would be impossible to build a living federal structure which met the needs of the age of advanced techniques without mobilizing those techniques on behalf of the optimum organization of society.

As for the role of governments and states, they would be required, once they had decided to put their money on the federal method, to pronounce themselves for or against the projects placed before them. To decline one or another of them would not mean opting out of Europe. But it would be absolutely necessary, where essential projects involving the structure and growth of the whole were concerned, for such Europeans as had put their hand to the plough not to look back. There would be some projects which could receive the support of countries not officially ranking as European: we are thinking of some East European countries, Mediterranean countries like Israel, or distant ones like New Zealand or Canada, which might be attracted by federal European action.

Practical application of proposals would depend, we repeat, on bodies designed to meet specific needs. In many cases, however, the job to be done would be to make 'moulds', such as company law relating to transnational firms, or a patents law; the functioning of such 'moulds' would be supervised by a sort of permanent council with better instrumentation, and more effective in operation, than the present Court of Justice of the Six. This Council or Commission for the Surveillance of European Development, which could be geared-up with the Chamber of Universalists, would be responsible for averting the growth of new 'frontiers' between countries. The spirit running through it should be creative, not juridical; the legal mind is too prone to compose, or to try to compose, laws which will stand for centuries, with the result that interpretation, so enjoyable and indeed profitable to its specialists, has time to grow into an exceeding great tree.

In order to draw up a programme for launching the movement towards European association, the immediate task will be to organize preparatory meetings like those which preceded the negotiation of the Treaty of Rome. This would depend on the advance adhesion in principle of a certain number of countries in which the climate of opinion was already favourable.

Federalism *à la carte*, with its apparatus of committees, offices, commissions for methodological research, and its chamber of political thought, would be a highly complex organism. Probably, therefore, this completely new-style Europe would begin its life in a certain amount of disorder. But creation amid disorder is preferable to sclerosis within order: it has the power of attracting more men of good will and arousing more enthusiasm and resolution without, over a period of time, creating more difficulties.

Care will be needed, even in federal operations of secondary importance, to secure higher output – greater efficiency – from our new European organizations than that yielded by the existing international bodies and those of the Common Market and the E E C. The reasons are the ones we gave in discussing how to make better use of politicians.

There are three levels of output: that of firms; that of the administration; and the weakest of all, that of international organizations. This is a particularly grave matter when the organizations in question are seeking to safeguard peace. For generation upon generation there have been men in the Western world whose mission in life was to preach 'Love one another'. Someone once calculated that if the output from this noble undertaking had been only one per cent per generation there would be no more wars today. The harsh contrast between the actual facts and this conservative estimate must not – cannot – reduce our confidence in ultimate success. The more difficult a task may be, the more important it is that humanity's best minds and hearts should devote themselves to it.

NECESSARY TRANSITION: FROM THE SPIRIT OF CONTRACT TO THE SPIRIT OF CO-OPERATION

For years, international work has been carried out in a spirit of contract, not co-operation. This observation is aimed at many supposedly co-operative institutions which are so only in name, the reason being that they are dominated by the 'foreign affairs' attitude. Nevertheless, there are a good many diplomatists who, despite having served so far in their country's foreign ministry or its embassies abroad, are capable of converting their mental habits to those required by federalism. It is indeed no rare thing to meet professional foreign servants who are deeply distressed by the certainty of being excluded from the work that really matters, and who would love to switch their energies into circuits other than those imposed on them. Their special training, and their good will, must be utilized; we must get them interested in the functioning of the commissions and committees. This functioning, incidentally, ought to take group psychology and the techniques of working as a group into account.

Current ideas on the delegation of powers likewise stand in need of revision. Those without experience of international official gatherings – which were practically unheard of in earlier days – have no idea just how loaded are the intricacies of the arguments which go on there. The mentality of a conventional negotiator reflects his anxiety to be able to tell his superiors, on getting back from an international conference at which he has been representing his sovereign or his country, 'I've defended your interests to the best of my ability – and I did manage to fool some of the other fellers.'

At the Congress of Vienna, Talleyrand and the representative of Berne, who was trying to enlarge the frontiers of the Swiss Federation, but who was incomparably less brilliant than the Prince of Benevento, happened to sit side by side with him. Talleyrand said one day to his neighbour on the other side, 'I would give a large sum of money if it would make this man from Berne less stupid,' and the man from Berne, overhearing him, answered, 'It would be well worth it!' This is said to have been the germ of Geneva's entry into the Federation.

That is a typical case of what used to be possible by secret negotiation, influenced as it was by society machinations, tattle at balls and the intrigues of the ladies. All very attractive, doubtless, but it had to go and it did so, completely, because we have learnt since those days that if everyone gets together everyone can finish better off than when they started, without any of the chicanery that used to be the rule.

Another way in which the present movement to converge towards working together on a common task differs from the old diplomacy is this: under the old system, plenipotentiaries usually leave their capitals with imperative instructions from their governments; each has his brief and none has any escape. In a sense this makes their job simpler but it also decelerates international work, sometimes indeed makes it seize up; production per diplomat-hour is reduced. Supporters of the old system answer this objection by saying that if a plenipotentiary was dispatched with highly flexible instructions and was tired after his journey or a banquet, he might be at less than his best and liable to error; he might for example be taken in by eloquence, whose purpose is to achieve just that.

Though a cut-and-dried mandate may have something to be said for it in negotiations of the old type, instructions to representatives have to be quite differently conceived when plans for a common constructive task are the subject for discussion.

In this as in many other matters, the most important thing is to give knowledge and competence their head, trust them, leave with a reasonably generous margin for manoeuvre, – provided that those, chosen for their possession of these qualities, should not themselves fall victims to the diplomatic spirit, for in that case they would simply be continuing the notorious tradition of those 'committees of experts' who are accused of having strangled so many tender young projects at birth. In professional quarters, where the spirit of efficiency reigns, as in industry, discussions hardly ever fail to reach the best solution because the instructions received beforehand by both sides have been so flexible. This is an example to be imitated, though it must be recognized at the same time that the change is bound to come slowly. For what must be changed in fact are not only the attitudes of those conferring but the structure of the negotiations themselves, a prospect which becomes more delicate as the problems treated become more complex.

In order to serve the federal organizations with minds directed always to productivity, European public servants must be chosen by the appropriate criteria. Language problems, formerly considered fundamentally important, are rapidly fading into the background. Competence is what counts.

Every effort must be made to use television and *'télégestion'* (direction and management from a distance) to obtain a higher speed of working, to keep the individuals concerned fully informed of the latest developments in the problems they are concerned with and to cut out unnecessary travelling by recourse to conferences by video telephone, and thus to spare officials that artificial life they are so often compelled to live, far from their natural, professional and familial environment.

INVENTING WAYS OF WORKING IN COMMON

A big contribution to the efficiency of the component bodies of the federal organism would be the creation of a permanent training-school for federal officials, similar to those for trans-national engineers and managers. It is indeed curious that such a school does not already exist, even at administrative level.

In addition, it would be necessary to look into the coaching desirable for the chairmen, secretaries-general and staff of international commissions and meetings, too often appointed by mere chance of circumstance. The Russians have already made a start in this direction: they train a certain number of people who thereafter represent their country at international meetings. It would be a good idea to do something on the same lines.

Efficiency, instead of precedence and the 'Who's next for chairman?' permutation, should be the keynote of the situation: all too often there is a wasteful conflict, protocol *versus* productivity.

Many other leading principles need sharply reviewing. Hitherto, authority in international matters has been *sui generis*, different from familial, employers', professorial or governmental authority. Today, when all is dialogue and dialogue is all, authority in international affairs is changing like everything else.

In many cases, the hunt for the right collective decision will impose the necessity for a college (on the analogy of the College of Cardinals or a College of Electors) to hold the reins of decision-making, and this procedure will become general as a matter of consistency.

Although the 'one country, one vote' principle can be satis-factorily maintained in some fields, there are many others in which a subtler, more fruitful variant is required.

One of the possibilities is variable vote-value; already used in some places, but susceptible of further improvement. There is the 'tempo' method, for instance; it could be used in the political thought committees. The system is for each participant

himself to suggest the number of units his vote should be worth
– its weight, as it were; and, as he has to do the suggesting in
the presence of the other participants, he finds himself in some
sense evaluating his own valuation.

These rapid observations have been made in order to show
that, in the realization of that progression which we call
European federalism *à la carte*, innovations of method are not
only necessary but possible. Once achieved, they could be
extended to other transnational bodies.

Of course we shall have doubting Thomases of two kinds
raising objections to the creation of federal bodies: the pessimists and the limpets – the men who hate all change. They will
talk about unnecessary apparatus, parasitical entities and so on.
This is one of the reasons why it would be necessary from the
start, from the moment the formation of these bodies was
announced, to make sure they did the job. About this, however,
there can be no doubt: there simply is no common measure
between the increased wealth which would result from pooling
the resources and efforts of the European countries and the
cost of federal organization. We can be sure of staying at our
present low general level of output if we go on in our traditional
compartmental way; and it is to just the extent that we are sure
of this that we are entitled to hope for an enormous change in
our productivity, a rise from one order of magnitude to another
if we step up our arrangements and our lives to continental
scale.

The difference between American and European wealth is a
gauge to what may be expected from federal organization.
Only a minute increase in European productivity would be
needed to pay for the installation and maintenance of Europe's
organizational set-up – provided, of course, that the setting up
was undertaken in a business spirit, in the broadest and best
sense of the term: the spirit of enterprise.

Many economies in personnel would be found possible if it
was decided to abolish all jobs which have become superfluous
at the national level. To list activities which could be discarded
in the most diverse fields, the dead weight which could be
eliminated so as to release staff for re-employment in the new
structures – new because working on the European scale –
would make a good subject for debate in national parliaments.

Creating these new European bodies would also supply the one for remoulding traditional administrative machinery, which certainly needs it and is ripe for reconstruction in any case.

Many are the young Europeans who will certainly be attracted by service in federal European positions, especially if the new organizations have modern equipment, rather than in national positions which they feel, rightly in many cases, to be both cramped and cramping. Think for a moment what an impression would be projected by a Europe which put the whole battery of modern information methods at the disposal of those whose job it was to think in new terms, erect new structures and assign their creative tasks. What a contrast to our national administrations, which, as the heirs to the past, are too often content with premises lavish rather than rational, with poor equipment and with antiquated methods.

Our first joint European institutions, despite their imperfections, have yielded benefits which we owe not only to the great men who have served them but also to the buildings in which they are housed. We are thinking especially of the EEC premises in Brussels. Buildings are frequently symbols, and symbols are necessary: the Capitol in Washington impressed, and impresses, Americans eager to believe in the Union. It is vital that Europeans should find themselves gauging the stature of their continent from the advanced nature of the offices from which Europe's affairs are conducted. What we want is not the old monumental stuff; we need cybernetic architecture.

Under federal organization, people should be encouraged to move from the private into the public sector. This will be all the easier the more closely the methods of each resemble those of the other.

One of the characteristics of Switzerland, as of America, is that men pass with equal ease from responsible positions in industry to the administration, and from the administration to industry. This two-way traffic also goes on in the socialist countries, where all industries are state-run.

Europe is very rich in cadres. The public services have a long and impressive tradition in some European countries, notably France. Too often, however, their work is ineffective and their energy frittered away in well-worn grooves, wearing them even smoother than before, because the system is out of date. In a federal environment, on the contrary, they would become highly effective. It is not men who need criticizing, but institutions which should be radically re-thought. Here again, Europe's accumulated experience is one of the treasures of an under-administered world. Those who know how difficult it can be to find top administrators in Africa, say, or South America, are in a position to appreciate Europe's extravagance in squandering a valuable asset by squashing her public servants into their national pigeonholes or forcing them to dance the archaic quadrille of formal international relations now superseded by time.

There are many useful men to whose abilities a federal setting will give the opportunity to expand, whereas now, by restricting their scope and activities, they expend their energies perforce on routine tasks, extravagant perfectionism or departmental and inter-departmental rivalries. The real waste of vigour and intelligence occurs not where new administrative organs are being set up but where good men are held prisoner, year after year, in worm-eaten structures. And like certain diseases, this waste, though producing no surface signs, quietly and malignly destroys the organism from within.

Instead of accusing federal creations of bringing about extra expense, and opposing them on grounds of economy, it would be far more desirable to endeavour to abolish archaisms. Here we put a finger on one of the catch questions in all creative change-overs, namely the fallacy that you can expect to finance the future on the savings made by selling off the scrap metal of the past. On the contrary: it is necessary to have faith in an evolution which cannot be avoided.

Finally it may be remarked, on the question of the productivity of federal bodies, that by ascending to the international plane and changing your techniques of work accordingly, using telex for example, you also provide a powerful stimulus to the reform of regional administrations (does the reader know that some of the documents in the 'Chunnel' negotiations have to be signed on paper with a little streamer of red tape, as used by the British Foreign Office?). Innovation on the international level will produce repercussions at home.

What has to be created, therefore, is not only a federal system but a whole organization, a whole political and administrative society of a certain type, with officials who should be able to feel proud of being 'federals' (just as expatriate employees of multinational companies should be proud of being transnationals, rather than irked by the label 'foreigners').

THE CRUCIAL ROLE OF THE TRANSNATIONAL OFFICIAL

Often enough – too often – there is a difference between the European official and his national counterpart; and this could well figure among the impediments to the building of a broadened, federal European structure as envisaged by the present writers.

The public servant under a national administration is securely anchored in the habits and the hierarchy of the service to which be belongs. He knows – unless things start happening on the streets – what to do and how to do it. As a rule he goes uneventfully up the professional ladder, and if he is ambitious (and why should he not be?) he knows the right doors to knock on and the right appointments to angle for; the only pivotal decision he has to make is whether he will get faster promotion by serving the government of the day or by ingratiating himself with his colleagues. But in either case he is zealous in defending not only his own position but the prerogatives of his employer, the administration. Official recognition sometimes comes sooner than high material rewards, though the latter are larger and commoner than government servants like to admit. The successful functionary is decorated amid flags in the courtyard of the Invalides or its equivalent elsewhere, but no such honour awaits his 'stateless' counterpart, virtually anonymous, lost somewhere in the depths of one of the international organizations.[1] Yet the second has no slighter claim to his country's gratitude than the first.

Any official who decides to leave the safety of service at home and work for Europe is taking on a much bigger risk. If the move merely amounts to a tour of foreign duty as one of the laps in his *cursus honorum*, he can go back to the home administration and pursue a career all the more brilliant for his having

---

[1] '*Les machins*', in the original. When General de Gaulle was President of France he was fond of referring, at least on unofficial occasions, to the United Nations Organization as '*le machin*', 'the contraption' or 'the what's-its-name'. (*Tr.*)

acquired merit by special service abroad. But if he goes into Europe in a pioneer spirit, eager to get beyond nationalism and serve federalism, create the future rather than perpetuate the past, he is playing pitch and toss with his own personal future.

He must expect to be attacked; by some for betraying his country's interests, by others as a dreamer. Since he is just as likely as anyone else to have a wife and children, and needs and ambitions, he will be permanently divided between his determination to devote himself to the task he believes in and his anxiety lest he find himself on the scrap-heap one day, a cast-off from the struggle for society's future.

It is therefore essential to put into operation a system taking account both of nations and structures as they are, and of the need to give Europe the impetus and 'heart' without which she will never be more than a satellite of America, a useless and more or less resigned creature living on her investments while the world about her is alive with problems.

It is of cardinal importance that anyone should be able to pride himself on working on the transnational, federal side. Already some of those who have taken the plunge are finding themselves rewarded by a much deeper sense of satisfaction than if they had stayed at home, serving under national auspices.

To attempt the establishment in Europe of organizational methods adapted to the problems of our time; to dare to hope that Europe will stand as an exemplar in the eyes of the world; to launch ideas which are forces and forces which are ideas, and which are in harmony with the planetary age – all this, surely, is one of the most beneficent forms that human thought can take, and represents a transposition into twentieth-century terms of the fire and energy which carried the eighteenth century forward from the age of monarchy.

FEDERALISM, FRATERNITY, LIBERTY

Any good all-round scholar will say that the great slogans of other times, such as *liberty, equality, fraternity*, have impinged deeply on social development, despite their candidly Utopian ring. They are not to be rejected for their Utopianism, far from it, but they must be expressed nowadays in terms suitable to an age which has seen the birth of data-processing and information science.

The political parties in the various countries are at the cross-roads: the test of their capacity to build the future will show a positive result if they decide to put the organization of society on a federal basis at the top of their list of objectives. It would be in their own interest to do so, for if they insist on continuing to restrict their discussions exclusively to policy at home they will end in a quagmire of unreal disputes: most of their problems are economic and the solution at any given moment is not a selection from a thousand possibilities or even, usually, two; which makes nonsense of any pretension, when in power, of being in sole possession of the answers, or, when out of it, of being so much cleverer and wiser than the government.

On the other hand, there are highly fruitful openings for serious debate on the construction of society in the contemporary context.

EUROPE'S ROLE

Europe can play the decisive part. Her past is long, her experience great, she has known and discarded many ideologies, and will consequently be all the more justified in steering a pilot course for others to follow, affirming her awareness of the fluidity now typical of human development, and pursuing a consistent policy in spite of that fluidity. Whatever weight she can command should be thrown into the struggle for new structures everywhere, structures that are in line with social and technical development and that allow humans to feel human in the twentieth century.

Politics is still dominated by the short view and is half blind to the great possibilities lying ahead for Europe. In 1968 there were parliamentary elections in three European countries, Italy, Belgium and France; not one of the innumerable electoral placards said 'Vote European'. But would that have been any less attractive than 'Vote Communist'?

If shut minds are the rule, as they seem to be, the fault lies where we have said and shall continue to say that it lies: namely in the lack of adequate structures. A young person is not at first bewildered by the world about him; but put him through an archaic education and you will see molehills turning into mountains, non-problems into problems; we are manufacturing social and political misfits. A child is not born a nationalist or a racist or an anarchist, he becomes one. If federal organization came into being the case would be altered: we should see that the young are just as quick to adopt new structures as they are to pick up the use of new tools.

The crucial problem is to pass, without intolerable difficulty, over the threshold between the past and a future which differs from it fundamentally, especially in politics.

Man as a political animal, even if he happens to be American, is compelled to inhabit the world as he finds it. If he wants success on easy terms he has only to put up with the existing structures; and this applies to the public servant as much as to anyone else. But in that case success will be a poor thing, empty of all historical meaning.

So it is vital to help those in authority to get rid of their preconceptions and climb out of the tangle of old apparatus. We must somehow put some ambition into them – of which, contrary to appearances, they possess remarkably little. They will latch on to the new idea more easily if it is expressed in the open, discussed in the European forum, and backed by an enlightened public opinion.

This act of political adaptation will require, at the start, a 'night of the Fourth of August' on the part of governments. Is that beyond imagination? And why should there not be a night of the Fourth of August for nations too?

That of 1789 took place and entered history only because the necessary cohesion, an underlying consistency, was already present in French life. Because today, whatever anyone may think, a similar cohesion is already present in Europe, we believe it is no mere Utopianism that urges us to express this hope.

CONCLUSION: THE PASCALIAN WAGER

'You can't see the wood for the trees' was never so true as in our own time. There is an imminent danger, as successive waves of technical invention come crashing in on our mental shoreline, that the size and complication of immediate problems, the chaotic ups and downs of twentieth-century life, and

the way the individual is confronted by more and more problems, each more insistent than the last, will afflict mankind
with a myopia more deadly than any known before. We mean
there is a grave risk of losing sight of distant objectives, the only
ones capable of stimulating the liveliest minds, irrespective of
age, and of firing the enthusiasm of the young. Luckily there
are still plenty of young people whose openhearted idealism
abhors a vacuum.

This danger is aggravated by another cause of dislocation,
one not commonly recognized, namely the glaring discrepancy
between progress in the handling and interpretation of computer 'languages' and the paucity of advance in sociology; a
paucity specially regrettable in view of the degree to which,
both in running the economy and in the life of the individual
citizen, sociology could and should stimulate our effective
participation in collective living. Form is being allowed to
obscure content; words and arguments are a cloudy mask
covering the real significance of things and events. 'They all
talk like it was in a book,' was the comment of a woman voter
recently, explaining why she found it so hard to make her pick
between the various candidates. There is a mute conspiracy of
circumstance to encourage oratorical and stylistic effect, to
divert attention from the real visage of problems, to cause real
competence to be confused with spurious and *vice versa*. Our
educational system makes no provision for the initiation of the
young into the fundamental data of our century, though care is
lavished on applying the glossiest intellectual varnishes. Many
writers – notably Raymond Aron, with his usual vigour – have
pointed out the negative effects of certain intellectual approaches
which, since those to whom they are taught are still young and
immature, encourage superficiality at the expense of hard
thinking; a vice to which all of us are prone at that time of our
lives when artificiality holds a peculiar and deadly attraction.
And what holds true of youth holds equally true for trade
associations and their endless windy arguments, and for those
young, virulent nations which, having risen from the ruins of
the colonial empires, are inheriting the ethos which has been
accurately described as a 'civilization of expression'.

This tree which hides the wood, this form which veils the
content, and the 'tribalization' which impedes communication

between groups, in a period when the need for the harmony of human development makes it essential to set up an increasingly intensive and planetary information-field, form sources of imbalance which put social structures under strain and sometimes in jeopardy; they give rise to tensions and dissensions which show themselves in the most varied forms, especially among the students, and among the peoples of most of the new countries, and among the victims of technological segregation.

On top of all this, we are compelled to observe that tactics has been allowed to take first place over strategy, the drawback being that the qualities useful for winning battles are not necessarily accompanied by the type of foresight and vision demanded for thinking about tomorrow and organizing for it.

At this moment in history, when technology has supplied the tools for the instantaneous diffusion of messages and images throughout the world, creating thus a real 'noösphere', it is essential that the structures of our understanding as well as those of our education should be modified, so that our minds should be attuned to these forerunners of the coming universality.

To effect this, what is needed is simplification. We must make more room in people's minds, so that they can absorb in outline some of the things they used to have to learn in full. No one learns what a forest is by memorizing the particulars of every individual tree.

We are well aware that this simplification will be subjective, and to that extent arbitrary, until information science has developed to the point of imposing uniform criteria. For a while there will be the danger which, in the linguistic domain, is implied by the formula '*Traduttore traditore*'.

We hope not to have laid ourselves too wide open to this charge ourselves by trying to plot, as on a road map, the routes Europe should follow in advancing towards the destiny allotted to her by the planetary age.

Throughout this study we have tried to stress the main thing: the fundamental transformation which manifold technical innovation has rendered imperative in the organization of human societies. It is much to be hoped that those in charge of political strategy will do the same.

The great changes going on have been produced as much by

the development of radio and TV, which are altering at once the volume and the nature of information, as by the car, which has become a need in modern society to the point of giving a shake-up to Marxist ideology, or by progress in medicine, which is going to upset a good many inherited ideas. We are already involved, experiencing those changes and beginning to feel their effects. The cracks appearing in political structures everywhere are among their consequences.

Cybernetics and information techniques are going to procure a complete change in the ways man lives with his fellows. The cybernetization of human society will forcibly involve a metamorphosis in some degree, of mentalities and structures, because the possibilities available to man will differ profoundly from those of which he has availed himself till now. The changes will touch every single field there is. Education is where they will thrust hardest, and the result will be the biggest mutation achieved by mankind since the invention of writing and, much later, of printing; a mutation, moreover, bringing with it the necessity of permanent education, i.e. keeping oneself always up to date. This will entail a thorough revision in our ways of teaching, of moulding human nature for social existence. But, since part of this education (using the word in its broadest sense) will come from beyond the frontiers of one's own country and yet be absorbed in the living-room at home, it can be anticipated that with such means at our disposal many projects which were Utopian only yesterday will become solid fact tomorrow.

We are being offered a chance of teaching men much more than hitherto and getting them to communicate much more, over any distance. The possibility held out to us is that of developing the ancient principles inherited from the earliest civilized times, in particular those of the Talmud, which says the wise man is he who learns something from every man, and which bids us love our neighbour as ourselves. We have entered an epoch in which our means of communication, by bringing people closer together, will eventually enable man to regard all mankind as his neighbour.

This cybernetic revolution, already under way, is a highly significant feature of the present period of fluidity in which, under the influence of a crescendo of technical discovery in every field, all our structures and all our mental attitudes both can and should be radically re-examined.

But the question is decidedly not one of conceiving new structures as rigid as the old. Until now, the value of a structure varied directly with its age and continuity. Laws and rules were conceived for eternity: Solon's laws were carved in stone; Hitler thought he was building something to last a thousand years; the CECA was set up for a hundred years and has proved obsolescent in six. We have got to change our ideas: we need supple, adaptable structures which can be modified as new potentialities emerge, especially in the material realm, which is the necessary substratum enabling thought to rise to new heights and its immaterial achievements to radiate further than the parish pump. So, what we need to question is the stability of structures in so far as it conduces to their degenerating into paralysis. Otherwise they will put the brakes on human happiness by reducing the chance of optimizing new discoveries.

We have already said, but must say again, that the role of statesmen and politicians in this period of fluidity is to modify laws and regulations and adapt them to new situations, and to act so that minds can change and evolve and a harmony can be established between technical development, the development of social structures and psychological and intellectual development. In our society, which is now in a state of permanent gestation because of the speed-up of technical innovation, politicians and statesmen must be, above all else, builders. They must accept the inexorable consequences of fluidity.

The initial postulates that modern politics has to reckon with are characterized in time by fluidity, and in space by the emergence of the planetary dimension. The logical outcome can only be a change in the nature of authority, of the various authorities which regulate social functioning. Authority used to be associated directly with function: the paterfamilias really was the head of the family and wielded an authority neither his wife nor his children dared question; the landowner was, within his boundaries, monarch of all he surveyed; and the boss of a factory or a business had a divine right like that of the head of the reigning dynasty. All of which lies far behind us now: social dialogue is the rule, monarchies have become constitutional, woman is man's equal, and 'the boss', thank heaven, has become a manager.

This does not mean the old reflexes have dissolved and, with them, the temptation to snatch at absolute power. Absolutism is being challenged everywhere by dialogue and contestation, but it should be remembered that their corollary is the entry of collective discipline into our lives.

Everywhere, in fact, a certain socialization, a pooling of interests, is taking place. To render possible the effective functioning of a society in which every individual is an integrated particle of the whole, what now needs to be intransigently maintained is no longer the classical ideal of individual freedom, necessary though that was at one time as a force with which to oppose absolute authority. On the contrary, what is needed is the gradual advance towards a collective discipline which will apply in every field of modern society. Man-in-car is free to drive from Paris to Rome or Madrid or wherever, but once on the road he has to conform to the highway code of every country he drives into or through.

Everyone is strictly dependent on society for his education, health, security, retirement and more beside. His happiness and prospects depend on his society functioning well, and it is in his own interest to submit to the rules its functioning and maintenance demand. Data-processing should bring great advances in this direction through its potential for initiating dialogue on a big scale. The fact that we now have means for putting people in touch, creating an informed public, will also create agreement in what are now areas of disagreement and venomous opposition because of under-information, diversity of sources and unreliable statistics. These considerations on collective discipline, freedom through collective consent, are overwhelmingly important: if this discipline does not come about naturally it will be imposed, and then goodbye to freedom. Cybernetics makes it possible to orientate human society in one or other of two very different directions: *either* the computer will serve a Moloch State, in which the life of the individual will be run to a plan devised by groups of technocrats or by political minorities on absolute power; *or* the computer will be used to enlarge the area of individual choice while also protecting and promoting the public interest.

This great option is emerging simultaneously with a number of others, and such a cluster of sudden options means that the moment has come to think of the whole group of structural changes which the society of today must undertake. If it omits to undertake them the result will be frustrations and disorder, leading inevitably to conflict – either terrible conflict between nations or violent local clashes between small groups.

It follows from these observations that a new strategy must be applied to politics. For, now that politics has entered the epoch of fluidity, it is subject to the same adaptive needs as military strategy in passing from warfare of position to warfare of movement. Starting from the present and its inertia of various kinds, we have to make ready for a very different future. A strategy of the future is what the political leaders of the various countries must apply themselves to defining and executing. To this end they must be in possession of the fundamental data concerning our about-to-be-planetary world, and deduce from them the appropriate goals for modern collectivities. Instead of entering the future backwards – which was fair enough when development was still slow but becomes dangerous when evolutionary speeds are changing – we must throw a beam of light on the road ahead. A knowledge of law was sufficient for running a country when it was still thought that the main thing was to apply a set of laws which were almost like abstract entities (hence the large numbers of lawyers in politics), but the case is altered now. The development-prospects in science, technology, medicine, the human sciences – all this is now needed, and the ability to use it to determine limits, to foresee what is both possible and desirable. Politics and the part it plays in society must be governed by this choice; any statesman is like an architect reconciling the requirements of the engineer, the demands of art and the financial resources at his disposal.

What we have tried to present in the chapters of this book is a moving panorama of these data for the construction of a new political strategy. We know we have only scratched the surface of the problems; have, indeed, not even listed them completely. But our aim is to draw attention to the main possibilities offered by the present epoch for transforming human societies and attitudes, not to draw an inventory.

We have been particularly concerned to show that all the conditions are present for enabling these great changes to be made efficiently. We have also tried to show that this would not be so if those responsible for the nations' destinies were to turn their backs on their political duty as men of the twentieth century.

Finally, we have tried to point out the major commandments whose observance, especially in Europe, is indispensable if we want technical progress to be paralleled by progress in structures, attitudes and ultimately in man himself. These commandments we shall now recapitulate.

COMMON PROBLEMS DEMAND COMMON SOLUTIONS

The nations of Europe – the world's oldest nations – are those for which the imperatives of renewal and adaptation appear to be the most urgent. They have what we may call an ardent obligation to realize a higher degree of cohesion between peoples who are now all confronted by the big changes characteristic of our century, and therefore all find themselves in much the same position. They must bring out the resemblances which are the result of their sharing the same civilization; liquidate the antipathies which have marred their history; and face the fact that the challenges inherent in our epoch amount above all to a single challenge to unify their efforts by forming an association open both in space and in time. And while we earnestly hope that such an association will aim at better conditions of life for Europeans, and that it will promote such progress of the mind and spirit as will embody in active form some of the highest aspirations typical of the European tradition throughout its history, we must also hope that it will serve as an exemplar to the rest of the world and that Europe should once more be the leader in the matter of human organization, the world's pilot, steering the course which will lead to the establishment of new relations between human beings. Europe's emotional phase – the period of postwar reconciliation – is over and done with and must now be followed not only by an economically successful Europe (a necessity too obvious to require emphasis) but, above all, by the Europe of culture.

Raising the standard of living of our continent's inhabitants, for which economic cohesion and integration provide the pre-condition, is the necessary condition for raising our intellectual and spiritual standards. Along with rising material standards must come the defining of goals and ideals above and beyond bare material considerations. Europe has the luck to be able to attempt this; she is, even, alone in being able to set an example to the rest of the world in this respect. These possibilities impose a considerable duty on Europe's political leaders, for it is not only in the interests of Europeans that it is timely to act, and act quickly; the way must also be pointed and demonstrated to humanity, to help it find a new form of organization inhabited by a new and living spirit. This spirit is defined by the word federalism, but a federalism with a content that can be much richer than ever before because all the technical means are now coming together to make joint achievement possible to an extent not hitherto dreamed of. It can be said without exaggeration that the tools humanity now possesses are the best that could possibly have been conceived for reinvigorating and developing the federal idea. If we decline to do this we shall brand our epoch as one of those which turned a deaf ear to destiny.

Our technical array, in very fact, makes it possible to think in terms of new constructions, transnational associations, submerging and obliterating the old frameworks. We must have the know-how to seize this chance of demolishing the limitations inherited from the past; we must progressively change the face of the world. Bringing national collectivities closer together, and enabling them to develop each in its own way within a federal framework, corresponds in some degree to the free development of the individual in society for the collective benefit as well as his own. These two kinds of associations are complementary, and they can be generalized; that is, realized on the world scale.

A Europe emerging in this form would have shaped a differing model from those now exemplified by the most powerful countries in the world, the United States and the Soviet Union (and which China will soon be exemplifying too, perhaps): for those countries are at present, and in spite of certain appearances to the contrary, developing in accordance with unitary ideas which were still prevalent during the last century, the result of which in world organization is a ruler-subject relationship.

Only Europe can become an example of a power of the same order as the present great powers but with a different organizational anatomy, a structure which supersedes, though it will not have forgotten the possibility of, hegemonies of the military kind and relations based on force.

An organization of the federalist type would canalize any residue of the spirit of domination still remaining in Europe, and would give it a chance to spend itself on tasks of greater quality. Active Europeans would also get the chance of furthering certain spiritual values on a world scale, and active citizens that of campaigning for structures which make room for the individual. Cybernetics must not reinforce hegemonies and strict planning, it must be on the side of federalism and the person, the free development of individual gifts.

An associated Europe, by its very existence and its manner of handling the major problems of the contemporary world, would undoubtedly temper the tendency of the other powers to pursue hegemony, without being compelled to take sides with any of them.

Those who launch themselves on this European adventure will of course run up against problems. But they should convince themselves that it is easier and better to share the future than the past, and that if we decide to work creatively and in common the outlook for Europe will be much better than if we reinforce national structures.

The stake is worth playing for, and working for. Statesmen who opt for this road will be able to build up for themselves a totally new kind of authority. The important thing is that some of them, supported and inspired by the most authoritative intellects of our time, should make up their minds to commit themselves wholeheartedly to the aim of a federal Europe.

Supported by public opinion, which must be told clearly what are the real issues at stake (whence this book, which we hope will ignite a train of effective action), the statesmen in question will win a clear superiority, the superiority of the innovator and pioneer, over their conventional colleagues, increasingly bedevilled by the vicissitudes of the petty political in-fighting bequeathed to them by the past.

Everybody is aware the task is difficult, particularly those who have taken part in various types of European creation in the last few years. But to face difficulties immediately evokes courage; and courage pays, courage confers authority. Hitherto military courage has been the most highly prized species, but we are now in a position to value civilian courage equally highly. It is, after all, one of the elements of the general mutation whose imminence can be felt in the air.

The purpose of our last two chapters was to plant beacons along the line of conduct we think apposite for statesmen.

EUROPE'S FUTURE LIES IN A PASCALIAN WAGER

Those who decide to alter course in this direction will feel as if they were making a wager, the European wager. And in effect, like all great battles, the battle of Europe and the future *is* a wager.

But, in our conviction, it is a wager like Pascal's: one in which you have everything to gain and nothing to lose.[1]

Either Europe draws back in fear from step-by-step federalism and jibs at the prospect of innovating, of standing before the world as a model designed to meet the demands of the dawn of the planetary age, in which case she is done with as a collective entity with a mind and individuality of its own; or else she chooses to venture forward on this road and faces, at worst, the danger of not benefiting from her wager as much as she had hoped. The choice being put in these terms, it seems

---

[1] 'There is unbelief and there is religion, and we have to choose; for to make no choice is of itself a choice and the more dangerous of the two, involving the risk of everlasting punishment. How then do we resolve the problem? Every argument of a speculative kind is excluded by hypothesis: neither contention is truer than the other; so there is nothing left but to estimate practically which is the better course. Now, by staking on religion I lose the right to live as I please, since I must accept the intellectual and, above all, the moral discipline of the Church; and I win the chance of eternal beatitude; I risk the finite in order to possess the infinite. How can I hesitate? Reason is disqualified, at least temporarily; passion resists but only by dint of its own blindness, for but a moment's reflection is enough to show up its vanity and tenacity. In reality, to any man conducting his mind in good faith and enjoying full liberty of judgment, the finite vanishes in the face of the infinite; this present life, if one has a true and accurate knowledge of oneself, is nothing, so that even were one's hope deceived one would have nothing to regret, and this it is that crowns the triumphant cogency of the wager.' – Blaise Pascal (1623–62), *Pensées*.

inconceivable that Europe should decline to try her luck and seize the only chance left to her of cutting a figure of any consequence in the world.

A Europe operating at this level, even if only partially successful in attaining her objectives, would still get far better results than those to be had by letting her structures stay as they are now.

Is this Utopian? If we were to gauge, one by one, all the resistances to be overcome, all the obstacles to be surmounted in all the sectors concerned, before the necessary tasks can be accomplished, we might well, on totting them up, sink back discouraged and conclude that the goal lay beyond the reach of human capabilities.

But this is the wrong way to look at it, because there is no question of attacking the component tasks one by one, and without a sense of teamwork and 'belonging' on the part of the attackers. We must create at the highest level, the political level, a united movement and launch a big operation bearing on all fields at once, large and small, so that success in one brings success in another and starts chain-reactions, with structures vitalizing mentalities and *vice versa*. Or to put it another way, the tactical plan must be the exact opposite of that used by Horatius to keep the bridge.

The size and scope of this plan have the potential for kindling imagination, but not the ideologies. These are in fact only the prolongations of the religions they sought to combat or replace, and they are declining into paralysis and rigidity and impeding development. What we in turn have to do is to show that modern technical achievements now make it possible, if one knows how to use them properly, to make social idealism a more practical proposition than before. We can now realize more and more effectively the things which have always been the objects of men's dreams and ambitions, but in forms differing very widely at different times: though the urge towards justice and charity belongs to no one period in particular, the arrangements and achievements in its satisfaction have been shaped by each period respectively. The very formulation, the conception of the urge has had to take them into account. The long process of transition from the alms-house to social security is a measure of the progress made, but does not exempt us from the necessity of perceiving clearly the changes in social and human relations which have accompanied it.

Nothing venture, nothing win; Europe must venture, or else sink into obscurity. The fundamental values of the nineteenth century have been eroded. The cohesive forces of the national state are dwindling. Patriotism is not what it used to be; which is understandable, its foundation having been antagonism between neighbours. Changes of attitude towards monarchy have caused it in some cases to disappear, in others to be safely caged and to serve as cover for bold social changes. As for the pride of colonialism, it has been transmogrified into complexes.

Again, the tides now swirling through the Church are shaking its basic connections with patriotism, connections which had lasted down to the epoch when the counterblast to *Gott mit uns* was masses sung for the victory of France, and *God Save the King*.

In short, our time-honoured myths have just about worn out. Wherever there is a residual pocket of nationalism it takes on a terribly narrow form which is no substitute for the fiery zeal of the past.

But the design for a supple and adaptable federalism whose outlines we have attempted to draw contains possibilities for a new European perspective, a promise of new growth.

To get together and study the great basic problems which will necessarily arise in every contemporary industrial country, to sustain every form of association which lifts us towards the characteristic level of the century, to think in common, prepare and construct in common all the means to a shared future and a community enlarged to planetary dimensions, is incontrovertibly the sound way of making the most of our industrial capital and of the moral virtues handed down by our forefathers. It is also the only way of ensuring an opportunity for Europeans to shine as brilliantly in the future as some of them did in the past. It is only through a European Union that Europe can have a future worthy of her past, and we hope we have amply demonstrated that this is so.

HOW EUROPE CAN BE HERSELF

Europe will remain Europe only if she retains her civilizing mission. These are big words but we must not shrink from using

them; the meaning is real; every European has had an uneasy
conscience since the internal wars of his continent and the
decolonization which followed them. He must therefore recover
the self-confidence which has sustained him over so many
centuries in the fulfilment of his vocation. When the Europeans
are convinced that they once more have a great road to travel
they will also have the courage to set about all the difficult
reforms necessary in order to meet technological and political
challenges now and in the years to come.

To withold assent and to reject federal Europe would amount
to condemning ourselves and consenting to merge Europe into
America. The intervention of American economic power in the
affairs of the various European countries will be all the weightier
if Europe fails to associate. The more one fears American domination – and fears it even if there is no conscious intention to
dominate – the harder one must try to get Europeans to get
together and stop going it alone in a futile 'resistance'. The
influence of American power is, indeed, one of the elements of
Europe's potential cohesion, as witness the success of *Le
Défi américain* That notorious phenomenon, the brain-drain,
so symptomatic of European decline, can be checked only
by European creativeness. There is no question of taking up
a hostile position towards America but of giving to her, as an
interlocutor, a Europe valid in her own right, who can contribute ideas and tools (in the widest sense) and take responsibility
for solving a proportion of the problems of organizing the
world.

In her relations with America, Europe will stand a better
chance of earning respect and getting her proposals listened to
if she can present herself as a single force instead of recriminating
in a state of dispersion. European structure is needed in order
to curb the excesses that representatives of American firms in
Europe are sometimes capable of committing, like invaders in
a country conquered or to be conquered.

Nothing is more characteristic, in this connection, than the
way the more enlightened American firms take into consideration the necessity of encouraging European cohesion by giving
a separate individuality to the net of branch companies, or
associated companies, or associated companies under licence,
which they have established in Europe. This is a much more

adult procedure than having men who do not know the country in which they have planted a factory or a store, as the case may be, run the show dictatorially from a distance, like those Europeans who, in the bad old days, set up their warehouses in Africa, their godowns in Asia.

By endowing their whole outfit of branches with the European touch, a soul of their own, the parent American firm partially Europeanizes its own representatives (especially if Europeans are admitted to the board of directors); whereas if they remain isolated in the countries to which they have come they remain one hundred per cent American. We must encourage this transformation.

Another factor underlining the importance of the choice before us is the argument that Europe will be doomed to a remorseless dissolution of her influence, or called upon to play a new part, according to whether she presents herself as a united entity or a ragged, dispersed one. If each European country seeks to exploit its former links with the new, emergent countries – links whose origins in colonialism render them in any case highly ambiguous – we shall quickly see the new countries doing all they can to exploit dissensions between Europeans (playing off one country against another). This approach will only sharpen the existing antagonisms. If, on the other hand, negotiations, dialogues, are set going between Europe and Ultra-Europe, both the progress of Ultra-Europe and the cohesion of Europe will be the better for it.

So, both in the case of the third world and that of America, the alternatives are the same: preservation of the past will bring decline, an accelerating decline at that; the federal innovation will be a fulcrum, providing the opportunity of playing a real part in the life of the world.

Add to this the fact that the dangers of technocracy would be less in a European framework than in that of the present condition of separateness. The ideological void, which is at the root of many of the disturbances now shaking the countries of Europe, would be more easily filled up by active federalism than by national programmes which are inevitably too narrow and which do not ring true.

What we have to succeed in doing is to divert the vigour wasted on international rivalry into association and restructuring, a task where the planetary overtones give an uplifting resonance.

Historians will raise the objection that the axial changes usually take place after a war or a bloody revolution, the most typical example being obviously that of the Russian revolution in 1917. They will also point out that the clearsightedness of a few is powerless to illuminate the darkness of the many, and that the eighteenth-century Enlightenment was followed none the less by the collapse of monarchy.

But are the technical instruments the same as they were then? History does *not* repeat itself, for the reason that the fibres which form its warp and weft are continually changing in character. It can be seen, for example, that social upheavals are taking new forms nowadays. The workers' revolt which followed the mechanization of muscle has been succeeded by the cultural revolt, that of the students and intellectuals, with the arrival of cybernetization. The resulting climate is capable of cradling huge changes and crucial advances, such as have been heralded by social movements in the past.

Reference to the past shows that human minds must be given high and difficult targets, higher than mere everyday acquisitiveness. The great movements of tomorrow must be ecumenical in their character and drive.

In most of the white countries, in both Eastern and Western Europe, there is a crisis of conscience placing the established order under inquisition. This will lead only to anarchy or some brand of reactionary oppression if the frame of the essentially egoistic nation is the instrument employed to contain them.

We should remember, in our dawdling and dithering, that the present favourable circumstances for vigorous European advance are not eternal; they will last only just so long.

The Europe we want and need could have been born from the emotional climate, the mood of shared suffering, which followed World War II. Today, the imperatives in Europe are technical. But the generation now growing up is determined to assert its rejection of a society which it regards as mediocre, not having been through the experiences which attended its birth and also not realizing the importance of material prosperity. This generation has not known the trials and sufferings of its predecessors and cannot and will not admit them as an excuse for refusing to innovate. Consequently there is a danger of its running off into a violent political wild goose chase of some sort, for want of having been given any constructive objective

There are still a few years left for the generations which have known war, and for those of their members who have glimpsed the size of the challenge of the technological era, to build a Europe different from that designed twenty years ago, which has given us much but is unequal to the demands of the planetary age.

Should we let time run out it may well be that the mental climate will take some unforeseeable turn. We may find ourselves psychologically encircled by the repressed, the chronic rebels and the under-developed. There are, in certain of the reactions of today's youth, advance symptoms of the big problems we shall be faced with if we do not embark on the structural redesigning rendered imperative by technological conditions.

Some of the young are already vehemently attacking their elders for not having built the new Europe directly after the war. Others simply question everything. We have, at the moment, a second chance to canalize the forces of youth. We may not get a third.

These ideas had already been put forward in *Simples propos*, (published by Fayard in February 1968); we would not have wished them to be so painfully confirmed by the events in May and June of the same year. Confirmation of that sort underlines the need for publication. The public is far too little aware of the nature of the present-day world, the contemporary facts of life.

It would be wrong to try to anaesthetize public opinion. It must be told what big issues are at stake. When well informed it often reacts affirmatively, and in spite of pockets of rejection or hesitation here and there, prefers movement and change to the old order of things.

There is a special need to ensure that the crucial decisions affecting us all shall be widely known and thoroughly debated.

That is why we should be pleased to see the initiation, on the basis of the observations presented in this book, of a broad campaign of information both in various European countries and outside Europe, aimed at showing that association is

Europe's only chance; and that this re-organization of our continent would prove not only indispensable to the Europeans but helpful to other countries struggling to adapt themselves to the exigencies of our century.

For if there is one thing of which we may be sure, it is that the thrust of technical progress makes structural adaptation essential. If the adaptation is not made the very future of our civilization will be in the balance. This possibility must be averted by means of the wager we have proposed. A risk? Yes; but a far smaller one than that which would be incurred by refusing to take it.

INDEX

LOUIS ARMAND

Louis Armand was educated at the Ecole Polytechnique and the Ecole Supérieure des Mines. His wide interests in problems of the application of science and technology led to his negotiating the preliminary agreements with Eisenhower and Dulles for EURATOM, and for a year he was Chairman of that Community. A member of the French Academy, he has been Secretary-General of the International Union of Railways since 1961.

MICHEL DRANCOURT

Michel Drancourt is Editor-in-Chief of *Enterprise* and head of the economics and political science division of *Réalités*. He is especially interested in the growth of industrialization in France, and has lectured on political affairs and economic development throughout Europe and North America.